PENIS ENVY
AND OTHER
BAD FEELINGS

PENIS ENVY AND OTHER BAD FEELINGS

THE EMOTIONAL COSTS OF EVERYDAY LIFE

MARI RUTI

Columbia University Press   *New York*

Columbia University Press
Publishers Since 1893
New York   Chichester, West Sussex
cup.columbia.edu
Copyright © 2018 Columbia University Press
Paperback edition, 2021

Library of Congress Cataloging-in-Publication Data
Names: Ruti, Mari, author.
Title: Penis envy and other bad feelings : the emotional
costs of everyday life / Mari Ruti.
Description: New York : Columbia University Press, [2018] |
Includes bibliographical references and index.
Identifiers: LCCN 2017049985 | ISBN 9780231186681 (cloth) |
ISBN 9780231186698 (pbk.) | ISBN 9780231546768 (e-book)
Subjects: LCSH: Critical theory. | Negativity (Philosophy) |
Emotions—Social aspects. | Neoliberalism. | Feminist theory.
Classification: LCC HM480 .R88 2018 | DDC 128/.37—dc23
LC record available at https://lccn.loc.gov/2017049985

Cover design by Julia Kushnirsky
Cover photo by Geoff Spear

This book is dedicated to those who threw the lifeline:

Sean Carroll
Doreen Drury
Jess Gauchel
Steph Gauchel
Alice Jardine
Marjorie McClung
Jean Russo
Josh Viertel

CONTENTS

INTRODUCTION

For a long time, Sigmund Freud has been accused of being a misogynist because he claimed that women suffer from penis envy. I remember that when I first came across this idea in college, I threw Freud's book across my dorm room and declared him "a fucking idiot." I don't blame anyone for having the same reaction: surely there's something outrageous about claiming that when a little girl sees her brother's penis, she instantly starts to covet it because she recognizes her own inferiority.[1]

But after studying feminist theory and related fields for three decades, I've come to see that it's possible to spin Freud's claim differently: in a society that rewards the possessor of the penis with obvious political, economic, and cultural benefits, women would have to be a little obtuse not to envy it; they would have to be a little obtuse not to want the social advantages that automatically accrue to the possessor of the penis, particularly if he happens to be white.

Because Freud (who was otherwise a pioneering thinker) wasn't always able to transcend the blatant sexism of his nineteenth-century cultural context, his wording at times implies that it's the penis itself—rather than the social privilege it signifies—that's the object of envy. Nevertheless, it's possible to read his argument about penis envy as an indication that women in his Viennese culture, who didn't have many public outlets for their frustration or rage, were aware that femaleness carries less social currency than maleness. In other words, what many have taken as a mortifying insult to women—Freud's notion of penis envy—can be reinterpreted as an embryonic sign of female dissatisfaction; it can be reinterpreted as a precursor to feminist political consciousness.[2]

Given the historically subservient status of women in Western societies—as in most other societies—we might wonder less about the existence of penis envy than about why it's not more pronounced. To this day, our society implicitly (and sometimes explicitly) codes the possessor of the penis (the man) as "having" something while coding the one who doesn't have a penis (the woman) as "lacking" something. This in turn suggests that a man is an active subject whereas a woman—the one who "lacks"—is a passive object: a nonsubject who requires completion by the subject (the man). Why, then, aren't women screaming bloody hell? Why isn't every woman an ardent feminist?

Later in this book I'll examine some reasons for this state of affairs, including the possibility that women have been taught to eroticize—and therefore find pleasure in—their subordination. But first I want to assure my male readers that this book is aimed at them as much as it's aimed at women. In part this is because it touches on other bad feelings besides penis envy, such as depression and anxiety. But in part it's because I believe that many men suffer from penis envy just as much as women do.

This claim is less counterintuitive than it may at first appear, for if the penis functions as a socially valorized emblem of phallic—heteropatriarchal—authority, then even those who possess the organ may feel like they aren't able to exercise its authority; they may feel like there's a discrepancy between this icon of robust confidence and the insecure realities of their lives. In this sense, if the cultural mythology surrounding the penis can make women feel deficient, it can make men feel like frauds.

But if phallic authority is a mere fantasy-infused cultural mythology, why would anyone be stupid enough to feel bad about not having it? In response to this question, I want to suggest that the mythological status of the phallus may actually increase its appeal. After all, many people routinely desire things that they imagine others to have, such as the good life, happiness, peace of mind, perfect relationships, mansions with no heating problems, and so on. That these things may not in reality exist—that the lives of those who are envied may in reality be less enjoyable than they appear from the outside—in no way prevents them from being objects of envy. In the same manner, phallic power doesn't need to be empirically "real" to function as an object of envy; the fact that the ("masculine") social prestige of the phallus is illusory—more on this topic shortly—doesn't change the reality that we still live in a heteropatriarchal society that conditions us to want this prestige.

The penis as a signifier of phallic power is a collective fetish, a magical totem pole that's meant to protect us from danger, including any and all "enemies of the state." This is why the pissing contest between the American government and its opponents is unlikely to end any time soon. Yet this contest also highlights the purely fantasmatic nature of phallic authority that I've just called attention to because it reveals that this authority frequently can't deliver what it promises: no matter how many missiles the government accumulates, it can't keep the other guy from pissing in its backyard (or hacking into its computer systems).

This is also the personal predicament of those men—by no means all men—who make the mistake of thinking that their penises automatically make them powerful: there will always be times when their power falters, when they're forced to reckon with the inherent fragility, precarity, and vulnerability of human life. This is why those of us who recognize the imaginary nature of phallic authority mock their red convertibles, flashy belt buckles, enormous cowboy hats, ostentatious hairdos, gilded high-rise residences, bombastic gestures, and exaggerated finger jabbing; we know that they're caught up in a delusion of power, that their posturing hides a shakier reality.

In stressing the imaginary (mythological, fantasmatic, illusory) foundations of heteropatriarchy, I don't mean to suggest that its impact on women isn't real. Much of the time, it feels all too real, whether one is walking down the street, working in an office, or trying to have a romantic relationship. This is why this book has more to say about the persistence of heteropatriarchy than is considered polite in our (allegedly) postfeminist world, a world that has supposedly reached gender equality.

In entitling this book *Penis Envy and Other Bad Feelings*, I wanted to signal that I mean it to function as a biting feminist critique of heteropatriarchal society, the kind of society where "penis envy" still persists as a bad feeling among others, although admittedly—partly because of its Freudian baggage—it's often not called that; instead it often gets coded as female (or feminist) exasperation, irritation, or anger. But let's not forget that when women get genuinely enraged, they (rhetorically if not in reality) frequently resort to the trope of castration, of wanting to cut off the willy of this or that guy. In this sense, the penis as a signifier of a thoroughly annoying phallic privilege haunts the lives of many women, even if they only acknowledge it during moments of extreme wrath.

This is why my title elicits a chuckle from many women (and men) who identify as feminists, who intuitively make a connection between penis envy and other socially generated bad feelings that disproportionately burden women. Comparable bad feelings may also burden non-phallic men, including many racialized men, as well as those who resist the gender binary altogether, trying to forge lives that counter the hetero-patriarchal demand that everyone fall in line with normative masculinity and femininity. Many queer, genderqueer, and trans individuals inhabit this space of rebellion, frequently at a great psychological, emotional, and practical cost. So, on the one hand, no matter how illusory the power of the phallus may be, it remains fundamental to socially dominant masculinity. On the other hand, it's useful to recognize that no one—not even the guy with the biggest dick—can ever fully live up to ideals of phallic power. That's exactly why men can experience penis envy just as easily as women.

The French psychoanalyst Jacques Lacan—whose ideas will appear in this book from time to time—can be credited for being among the first to emphatically draw a distinction between the phallus as a signifier of social power and the penis as a bodily organ.[3] Lacan deliberately "deliteralizes" Freud's notion of penis envy by illustrating that the mythological glory of the phallus isn't supported by anything in the empirical world, and least of all by the shriveled reality of the penis; he illustrates that it's the social prestige of the penis rather than the organ itself that's the target of envy.[4] This is why he speculates that the penis only carries power when it remains veiled, covered over: staring at its fleshy pathos without the mediation of clothing or other attention-grabbing props instantly dispels any illusory power it might have.

This may be why the northernmost region of Europe—where I reached adulthood—is among the most gender-egalitarian places in the world: because people in Finland, Sweden, and

Norway routinely engage in the bizarre ritual of getting naked in order to sweat things out in a blisteringly hot room (the sauna), it's hard for them to maintain the fantasy that the penis is anything but a dangly part of the male body—a part whose dignity remains an open question. Even seeing the Washington Monument on television on a regular basis can't quite dispel the impression left by the steady parade of flaccid penises seen in the sauna.

THE GENDER OBSESSION DISORDER

Perhaps my most memorable encounter with a flaccid penis was when I asked my father—in the sauna when I was seven—if he was going to die. Startled, he said, "Why do you ask that?" "That tumor between your legs looks pretty bad," I responded. So much for penis envy. Since then I've seen enough erect penises to know that things don't always look quite so desperate. But there's something about the visuals of my childhood that makes it difficult for me to take the organ too seriously. I learned very early that it means nothing in particular, that it's just something that (most) men have in the same way that (most) women have other bulging things.

Bodily organs themselves have no meaning; it's the collective mythologies that cultures impose on them that do. That American culture chooses to valorize what men have and devalue what women have is obvious from casual statements such as "Don't be a pussy" and "Grow a pair" (and, no, this doesn't mean a "pair of breasts"). Such dichotomous thinking centered on the genitals has consequences. One has to wonder what it does to a woman's psyche to hear "Don't be a pussy" used repeatedly as an insult.

Or take another common female-disparaging statement: "You throw like a girl." When I hear this taunt, however playfully uttered, I think of the chilling effect it will have on girls, on the next generation of women, on the ability of men and women to view themselves as equals, because *clearly* the implication is that there's something defective about being a girl; there's no other way to interpret this statement, often made—in real life as well as on television—by fathers to their sons (and perhaps even in the presence of their daughters).

In this context, I also think of the fact that when I was a girl, I played baseball—not softball—and that when people say "You throw like a girl," they're describing a style of throwing that none of the girls on my team used. According to the reasoning of gendered thinking, these girls threw "like a boy." That's not because they were genetic mutants but because they played baseball, "a boy's sport." This illustrates that how American girls and boys throw has nothing to do with their biological makeup, but rather reflects the fact that in the United States they're made to play two different sports that require different styles of throwing a ball. It's the social insistence that girls and boys need to play different sports rather than female and male physiology that determines how they throw. And even if physiology were the reason, I'm not sure why a girl's way of throwing should be deemed inferior.

When I moved to the United States from Finland at the age of twenty, I instantly fell in love with the country; it felt like "home" very quickly, in large part because Americans turned out to be astonishingly generous and welcoming. Even though Homeland Security has given me hell for three decades—a theme I'll discuss in chapter 2—I've always felt that this country is where I'm meant to live. This feeling awakened immediately upon arrival. But there was one fly in the ointment: Americans seemed weirdly, even creepily, obsessed with gender differences.

Because I had grown up in a culture that doesn't make much of gender, that doesn't believe that gender is a determining factor in a person's character, I was startled to discover that many Americans think that a person's gender gives them instant insight into his or her motivations, behavior, and personality. I was shocked to hear statements such as "Well, he's a guy—so what do you expect?," "That's a guy thing," "Men think with their penises," "Men don't get emotions, so don't waste your time trying to explain it to him," "Of course you want to get married—you're woman, aren't you?," or "Ignore her—she's PMSing."

To me, such statements were as ludicrous as saying that someone acts the way he does because he's white, Catholic, working class, from Ohio, or works as an auto mechanic. Of course people did say such things as well. But when they did, they seemed to be aware that they were trading in stereotypes—that what they were saying might not be altogether accurate (or fair). In contrast, the notion that men are one way and women an entirely other way seemed completely taken for granted: people talked as if gender stereotypes reflected some sort of unquestionable truth about men and women.

These days, there's a lot of talk about gender dysphoria, about the (supposed) confusion that some people, such as those who are transgendered or ambiguously gendered, (supposedly) experience about their gender identity. But it seems to me that it's not those who fail to conform to our society's starkly dichotomous system of gender who are pathological, but rather those who can't stomach the fraying of this system. If anything, I think that we should worry about the *gender obsession disorder*—which is what I, prompted by my friend Steph Gauchel, propose to call it—that rigidifies so many American minds: the fact that many

Americans remain positively fanatical (the word *fundamentalist* comes to mind) about gender differences, about making sure that men and women remain recognizably male and female. That homophobia lurks behind this fanaticism is certain, for a clear gender distinction has traditionally been the foundation of heterosexuality.

Anything that meddles with the binary of (male) haves and (female) have-nots threatens the defenders of heteropatriarchy because this binary is (along with racism and economic inequality) one of the cornerstones of our current social order. For instance, a friend of mine whose gender isn't easily readable complains about strangers constantly trying to force a clear-cut gender identity on them, as—to mention just one recurring scenario—waiters do when they emphatically (if somewhat nervously) pin a "*Ma'am*, can I get you anything else?" on them even though they look just about as far from a ma'am as your average Patriots player (and, really, is there *any* thirty-something person in this country who thinks of themselves as a ma'am?). The problem here is not on my friend's side but on the side of those who are so disturbed by gender variance that their first impulse is to fix it, to push the person whose gender is ambiguous back into a box plainly marked as either "male" or "female."

Unfortunately, it's not those who are infected by our culture's gender obsession disorder—arguably the majority of Americans—who suffer the consequences of this pathology, but rather those who become the targets of the discomfort (and sometimes wrath) it generates. The reason transgenderism has recently become a political lightning rod, among other things giving religious bigotry a renewed life and bizarre legitimacy in a nominally secular political system, is that many people in our society simply can't tolerate the possibility of the traditional heteropatriarchal gender order—which, let's face it, is premised on the idealization of maleness and the devaluation of femaleness—collapsing. They fight this collapse with all the ammunition they've got because nothing disturbs them more than the idea that the distinction between men and women is a cultural construct rather than a biologically determined reality (and that it could therefore be reconfigured over time).

This is why so many state officials and ordinary Americans resented President Obama's 2016 directive about public schools needing to allow transgendered individuals to use the bathroom that matches their choice of gender identity. If the idea that some of the haves might want to give up what they possess by transitioning to femaleness (or some other form of embodiment/identity that doesn't privilege the penis) is bewildering to the defenders of a penis-centered society, the idea that some of the have-nots might be able to acquire a penis is just plain horrifying. And even more horrifying is the idea that some of the have-nots might—at the height of love making, when the fleshy penis, alas, often falters (more on this in chapter 6)—wield a factory-manufactured penis that never goes soft. This really has the defenders of heteropatriarchy shaking in their boots.

Back in the 1980s, when I first encountered the insistent gender binarism of American culture, I didn't have the intellectual tools to understand its insidiousness, so I tried my best to get used to it. But every time someone said, "You're a woman, so . . . ," I felt belittled, not because I dislike being a woman but because I felt that the person making the statement was resorting to a cultural cliché because they were too lazy to do the work of getting to know me as a person; I felt reduced to a walking caricature.

For example, someone once said to me, "Of course you struggled with math in high school more than with foreign languages—you're a woman." In fact I struggled with math because our math teacher taught it to us in a piecemeal fashion, one detail at a time, whereas my brain (a theorist's brain, a philosopher's mind, though I didn't know this then) works better with the big picture, with abstraction (if one is going to follow stereotypical reasoning, it works like a "man's brain," the kind of brain that reasons in a conceptual manner).

When learning a new language, I could read the relevant grammar book from cover to cover well before I knew enough vocabulary to speak the language. Once I grasped the basic structure of this language, I could learn it effortlessly. One summer I used this method to learn enough French in the span of six weeks to gain admittance to the University of Paris. Another summer, I used it to learn enough ancient Greek in the span of six weeks to read Aeschylus (though don't ask me to read him now). There was no such summary for the basic structure of math when I was in high school, at least not in my remote neck of the woods, and this was the reason I found math challenging. Being a woman had nothing to do with it.

THE PORTABLE PHALLUS

What we all know but often try to ignore is that for many people, and for women and the ambiguously gendered in particular, dichotomous thinking about gender is a considerable source of bad feelings such as lack of confidence, anxiety, and anger. Such thinking makes me want to scream *Why is this so important to you? Who cares what the equipment between your legs looks like?* People are people. I care about whether they're interesting, thoughtful, empathetic, amusing, damaged, or whatever else they happen to be. Whether they are male, female, or anything in between (or beyond) seems entirely beside the point.

The world clearly doesn't agree with me, for it continues to allow social power to accrue to the possessor of the penis. As much as things have improved for Western women since Freud's time, there's no denying that our society still equates power with the penis. This is why it's easier for men to assert authority than for women. There are of course many women who do, but the process can get complicated. As a female professor, I've learned to approach the matter with a degree of irony. For example, I'm aware that I never lecture without holding a pen. If I forget my pen in my office, I borrow one from a student. It doesn't matter whose mini-penis I'm wielding. And it also doesn't matter if the pen actually works: for all I care, it could be jammed or out of ink. I just need it to complete my outfit, like an accessory.

I think of the pen as a portable phallus: one that I can pick up when the situation calls for it. There have been times during the last three decades when I've had to grip it fairly tightly in order to project authority, not just when I walk in front of students but also when I walk in front of colleagues to give a talk. Earlier in my career, when I had no "credentials," I often felt that I had to hold it so tightly that my knuckles went white. Mercifully now, at this relatively late stage in my career, things are more relaxed: when I accidentally drop my pen, I can say, "Gosh, I just dropped my phallus," without fear that this will instantly undermine my right to deliver a lecture. Best of all, I've learned that most students and colleagues "get" it, rewarding the situation with appreciative laughter. I wish I had known this earlier; I wish I had realized that they know just as well as I do that my so-called authority is a masquerade.

One of the many things I appreciate about Lacan—and this is what some of my fellow feminists misunderstand about him (because he's not always easy to understand)—is that he illustrated that phallic authority is *always* a masquerade, regardless of who displays it. Men can pretend to possess this authority because they have a penis, but in actuality they don't have it any more securely than women do; in actuality, they're just as "lacking," as fundamentally woundable—"existentially," psychologically, emotionally, and physically vulnerable—as women are. To emphasize this point, he even used the term *castration* as a synonym for this woundability, suggesting that castration, metaphorically speaking, is the human condition. Although Lacan was far from a feminist, he gave feminist theorists a lot to work with when he declared that men are just as "castrated"—lacking—as women are.

Like his contemporary Jean-Paul Sartre, Lacan was interested in the lack—the encroaching nothingness—that gnaws at the foundations of human life;[5] he was interested in the feeling of emptiness that often permeates our being even when things are in principle going fine. His explanation for why we feel this way was developmental. He hypothesized that the void at the heart of human subjectivity is an inevitable byproduct of the process of socialization that molds an infant—who is initially a creature of unorganized bodily functions—into a culturally viable being, into a child who understands the basic codes of behavior that she's expected to adhere to. This process is necessary because it allows the child to become a member of her society. But it comes at a price: it forces the child to encounter a symbolic world of meanings that she has had no part in devising; it throws her into a vast universe of complex (and often enigmatic or inscrutable) signifiers, including language, in relation to which she's asked to find her bearings. This experience, according to Lacan, is intrinsically humbling, bound to make the child feel inadequate to the task.

Because children can't always fully process the signifiers that surround them, including what adults are saying to them (or around them)—because they can't always figure out what adults want from them or why adults want certain things done in a certain way—they're never able to feel completely in control of the universe they inhabit. This feeling of failure lingers into adulthood, making each newly minted human being feel like it has lost something precious, like a piece of its being is missing. This is the "castration" that Lacan is talking about when he talks about the subject's (ontological) lack-in-being.

With lack comes the longing to fill it, which is how desire comes into being. I'll return to this idea in the first chapter. For now, what's important is that Lacan recognized that we tend to resort to reassuring illusions of wholeness in order to conceal our lack, that we tend to devise fantasies of grandeur and stability to fend off the specter of weakness and instability. Arguably, heteropatriarchy is an elaborate collective fantasy of this kind: by allowing (some) men to imagine themselves as more powerful than women, it makes it possible for them to keep ignoring their lack, their profoundly vulnerable status.

Heteropatriarchy doesn't offer women the same coping mechanism, which makes penis envy a logical sentiment: if the penis symbolizes wholeness, then hell, of course I'm going to want it (or more precisely, I'm going to want what it symbolizes). Indeed, as I noted above, even many men want the figurative penis (the phallus as a signifier of omnipotence), which is why penis envy—envying the other guy's imaginary dick—is a common predicament among them. Only those who manage to fully enter into the heteropatriarchal fantasy of seamless masculine omnipotence may be inoculated against this envy. But even the Donald Trumps of the world may one day—the day when they have to face their mortality—realize that their omnipotence is an illusion.

Another name for penis envy might be resentment. Nietzsche thought that resentment was the sentiment of the weak.[6] So be it: measured against the heteropatriarchal fantasy of phallic power that I've outlined, most of us, including most men, are weak, and many of us have excellent reasons to feel resentful. We also have a wide array of other bad feelings to choose from: depression and anxiety are perhaps the most obvious ones, but there are numerous others to fall back on, such as bitterness, loneliness, frustration, annoyance, irritation, and utter disillusionment.

The cultural fetishization of the penis may be one reason—though certainly not the only reason—that women have historically been especially prone to bad feelings such as depression and anxiety: it's harder to feel good when you can't hide behind a fantasy of omnipotence. Many creative, artistic, spiritual, and intellectual men have found themselves in the same predicament, for such "effeminate" men have never been convincing as pillars of phallic power. Nor have they necessarily been keen to emulate this power. Quite the contrary, many of them have chosen to stare right into the abyss of existence: instead of aspiring to phallic power and its illusory veils of protection, they have chosen to confront the intrinsic insecurities of human life head-on, with the result that they have produced works of unfathomable beauty while often feeling unfathomably awful.

While phallic men (and some women) fought wars, built castles, and forged empires, less phallic men—and the rare women who were given the opportunity to participate in public life—created the kinds of legacies of the mind that demand a courageous encounter with the nothingness (lack) at the core of human existence. Note that the divide here is not between men and women but rather between those who adhere to fantasies of phallic power and those who are either forced or prefer to contemplate the precariousness of life beyond such fantasies. Though the former are often portrayed as the heroes of history, the latter seem more heroic to me, and this is the case even though they have carried a greater burden of bad feelings, including penis envy.

TOO BUSY TO COMPLAIN

You might assume that from the perspective of the dominant social order—the cultural status quo—it's good that those who feel disempowered also feel bad: so focused on their misery that they don't have the strength to rebel. But the trouble is that bad feelings such as depression can make us so sluggish that we're unable to keep up with the demands of daily life—and this is *not* good for our (hugely pragmatic) social order, which values productivity above all else. What's more, bad feelings such as anger, frustration, and disillusionment can make people disobedient. Some of us might become feminists or trans advocates. Some of us might start to say that Black Lives Matter (even as we understand that having to state this fact is in itself a ridiculous state of affairs—*of course* they matter; we shouldn't need to say so). These outcomes aren't what the powers that be want, which is why they offer those who can't hide behind the fantasy of phallic omnipotence an array of alternative coping mechanisms.

Perhaps the most effective of these is an extensive entertainment system that allows us to push our bad feelings aside. There are few things that numb our malaise as successfully as tuning into our Netflix account and watching our favorite fictional character tackle problems of such enormity that our own seem insignificant in comparison: if Alicia Florrick (*The Good Wife*) can get around her husband's dick, then surely I should be able to navigate the sea of dicks that surrounds me! Even better, a couple of hours of staring at the spellbinding screen will recharge me so that by the next morning I'm once again ready to tackle the challenges of everyday life. This is why social critics have long thought that mass entertainment is essential for the smooth functioning of capitalism.[7]

Another effective coping mechanism is a commercial culture that produces a profusion of enticing objects that we can use to plug the gaping hole within our being: a trip to a well-stocked department store or even a shiny grocery store bursting with abundance—look at all those cheeses, cookies, and potato chips!—can serve as an antidote to any incipient sense of dissatisfaction that we might be grappling with. But this antidote only works if we have money to spend, if we have been relatively successful at participating in the final coping mechanism I'll mention, namely an individualistic and positivity-centered social ethos that valorizes good performance, high productivity, constant self-improvement, and relentless cheerfulness.

This ethos, which I'll discuss at length in this book, tries to keep the more irrational aspects of human life—such as bad feelings—in check so as to enable us to participate in the life of the economy, so as to ensure that we have some money to spend when we start to feel depressed, anxious, disenchanted, or otherwise appalling. This ethos is hardly benevolent. It's not out of compassion that it strives to suppress bad feelings; rather, our society shuns bad feelings because it wants us to work harder, faster, longer, and better. Essentially, it makes us too busy to complain about our bad feelings, including penis envy.

When male colleagues less accomplished than I am tell me that I'm not ready for a promotion, I may think, "Now might be the time for a little penis envy." When I find out that I'm being underpaid in comparison to male colleagues who haven't published nearly as much as I have, or taught as many students as I have, or supervised as many dissertations as I have—that is, who haven't worked nearly as hard as I have—I may think, "Now might be the time for some grumbling." When the building manager gives my office to a new male hire fifteen years my junior—specifying (I kid you not) that the office is "too nice" for me—I may think, "Now might be the time to talk to the Dean." But what squashes these thoughts is the realization that *I'm too busy for this sexist shit.* "Fuck 'em—I need to meet my deadline," I mutter to myself, thereby allowing the system to proceed as it always has.

This system of performance, productivity, self-improvement, and enforced cheerfulness, which scholars in my field (posthumanist theory, or critical theory broadly understood—an explanation to follow) call *neoliberalism,* is impressive at dexterously suppressing the bad feelings that heteropatriarchy generates.[8] Equally impressive is its ability to sideline the bad feelings, such as chronic overagitation and anxiety, that its own stressfully hectic pace of life produces: it keeps us so breathlessly focused on our goals that we feel like we can't afford to stop to think about why we're feeling bad. It in fact tells us that we shouldn't be feeling bad in the first place because bad feelings, like insomnia, are a waste of time; its utilitarian pragmatism makes us feel so bad—embarrassed—about feeling bad that we quickly muffle any budding negative feelings.

THE SEDUCTIVENESS OF THE AMERICAN DREAM

It's because I suspect that many people are tired of muffling their bad feelings that I want to give these feelings a hearing in this book. Don't get me wrong. I'm just as complicit with the achievement-centered, fake-positive ethos of neoliberalism as the next person: I've performed to the point of exhaustion, stayed productive, tried to improve myself, and done my best to stay optimistic. I smile easily. I say *it's okay* even when it's not. And I'm also just as glued to my television screen as the rest of the work-weary, and moreover addicted to the kinds of lowbrow thrillers, action movies, and teen shows that no professor in the critical humanities should in principle admit to liking (as I write this in 2017, I'm watching *Pretty Little Liars, Orphan Black, Elementary, Gotham, Scorpion,* and *Arrow*).

Nor have I been immune to the American dream, which, in the U.S. context, is in many ways synonymous with neoliberalism, as I'll demonstrate in the first chapter. This dream is seductive because it tells us that we're in charge of our own destinies, that no matter how dreadful the cards that life has dealt us, we can eventually end up with a winning hand. It tells us that hard work and a positive attitude are the key to a successful life, that it's our personal responsibility to make "something" of ourselves, and that even when things get tough, we have the power to forge a better future; the American dream, in short, tells us that our efforts will in the long run be rewarded however bleak things might at first seem. Indeed, in many ways, the bleaker the beginnings, the more triumphant the ending is supposed to be.

My beginnings were bleak enough, in some ways perfectly designed to recruit me into the fantasy of salvation that the American dream offers to those who might otherwise feel hopeless. I grew up in poverty, in a tiny isolated village next to the Russian (then Soviet) border, in a house with no running water, indoor plumbing, or central heating. A shortcut to imagining what life was like is to envision using an outhouse in subzero temperatures that freeze your wet hair into icicles in twenty seconds (which was the length of time it took me to get from the sauna back to the house in the winter, sprinting as fast as I could). I watched my mother wilt away tending a conveyor belt at a factory and my father work harder—and sleep less and worry more—than anyone should ever be expected to. I spent about five hours a day commuting to school, waking up before 5 A.M. to bathe in a bucketful of glacial water before heading out, and returning in the evening to the task of getting firewood from the shed in order to heat my room—the window of which had during the day developed a sheet of ice even on the inside-facing pane—before tackling a mountain of homework.

It might have been a bit like *Little House on the Prairie* if I had had a kind father and a warm mother who loved to cook. Alas, this was not the case: I lived primarily on bread and cheese (and under constant disparagement from my father). But I can't blame either my mother or my father, for it was my mother's willing-ness to commute to a far-flung job that ensured that we—usually—had bread and cheese to begin with, and it was the brutality of my father's life that (I think, after several years of talking to a shrink) made him as forbidding as he was.

That I made it to Brown from this background, thrived in graduate school at Harvard, became a professor, published ten books, and amassed many of the insignia of cultural capital that my parents lacked, is undoubtedly in large part due to my dili-gent (*desperate* might be the most accurate term here) allegiance to the pillars of the American dream: hard work, perseverance, and emotional resilience. If I was willing to work like mad, it's because I hoped that my efforts would eventually yank me out of the life I was leading.

They did. As a consequence, even though I see through the ruse of the American dream—a ruse that places an emphasis on the individual's ability to withstand hardship in order to distract us from social inequalities that make it impossible for many people to succeed—I'm not going to claim that there's *no* value to suppleness in the face of trying life experiences. Likewise, although I believe that the suppression of bad feelings in the name of phony positivity is psychologically coercive, basic honesty demands that I admit that I would mourn the loss of the hospitable American smiles I've grown to appreciate. And even though I would not mourn the collapse of heteropatriarchy, I would definitely mourn the collapse of my DVD player. This makes it difficult for me to rail against all aspects of neoliberalism with the same venom as some of my colleagues in posthumanist theory do.

Posthumanist theory (or critical theory) in the sense that I study, teach, and write about it—and here comes the explanation I promised above—consists of an interdisciplinary blend of continental philosophy, psychoanalytic theory, cultural studies, politico-economic commentary, ethnic studies, affect theory,[9] and feminist and queer theory. This blend tends to produce vehement critiques of contemporary (capitalist, neoliberal) culture. Parts of this book produce precisely such critiques. Yet my complicity in the very system that I examine somewhat tempers my critique; there are times when it causes me to hesitate.

Frankly, I don't know how to interpret this hesitation. I don't think that it arises from a politically conservative impulse. It's just that it feels hypocritical to utter a wholesale denouncement of a system that I've (at first guilelessly, but over the last decade with a degree of self-awareness) participated in—and the benefits of which sustain my life as it is currently configured. If I were willing to forgo the benefits, relinquish the life that I've fashioned, that would be one thing. But as long as I'm not, it feels like I need to remain vigilant about how I approach the matter: critically, to be sure, but also with some skepticism about how easily, even routinely, the critique rolls off the tongue. This is a tension that in all likelihood haunts many progressive critics. It's just that we don't often talk about it, perhaps because there's no good solution to it.

Participation in an unequal social order doesn't—and shouldn't—neutralize one's ability to condemn it. But complicity feels more complicated. I have no qualms about slamming heteropatriarchy because even though I've by necessity participated in it (in the sense that no one in our society—not even gays, lesbians, and queers—can entirely escape its ideological reach), I don't feel complicit with it; it hasn't brought me any benefits. But neoliberal striving (or the American dream, if you prefer) has brought me the kind of material comfort that I never knew as a child. This makes it hard for me to attack neoliberalism with the same uncompromising forcefulness as much of posthumanist theory does even though I understand that it has both precipitated the crumbling of Western welfare states and solidified the West's political, economic, and military dominance across the globe.

BITS OF MEMOIR

The complexities of my personal relationship to the neoliberal ethos that I dissect in this book may be the reason that I failed—as I initially tried—to write it in an impersonal voice: the personal kept seeping in, with the result that the chapters that follow mix theoretical reflection, cultural critique, and political commentary with personal anecdotes; they contain bits of memoir. In some ways, this isn't unusual in my field: not only does feminist theory have a long history of drawing on the personal—of making the personal political and the political personal—but recent critical texts such as *Testo Junkie* by Paul Preciado, *The*

Argonauts by Maggie Nelson, and *Love in the Dark* by Diane Enns have followed the tradition of Walter Benjamin, Roland Barthes, and Chris Kraus in combining the theoretical with the autobiographical.[10]

Preciado labels this genre *autotheory*.[11] Nelson describes it as *wild theory*, the kind of theoretical writing that crosses genres and disciplinary boundaries.[12] Conceptually speaking, it makes perfect sense that I'm drawn to this type of writing, not only because my work routinely crosses disciplinary boundaries but also because there's an obvious parallel between breaking the patterns of straight (heteropatriarchal) culture and breaking the mold of "straight" academic writing.

I've long thought that much of the best theoretical writing arises from a personal place. Nelson quotes Eileen Myles on this: "My dirty secret has always been that it's of course about me."[13] As Philip Sayers points out in the context of analyzing Nelson's approach to authorship, this stance goes against the grain of the last few decades of posthumanist scholarship that has insisted that the process of writing erases the identity of the person who writes, that the author is "dead," replaced by the text (or discourse), as Barthes and Michel Foucault—the latter of whom will play a significant role in this book—famously argued.[14]

I've always thought it bizarre that Barthes, who wrote many intensely personal—and spectacularly beautiful—books,[15] advanced this idea. But it made sense in the context of the critiques of the humanist, Enlightenment subject of consciousness, autonomy, and agency that reigned during the height of poststructuralism and Derridean deconstruction, that elevated the text—the play of signifiers, the process of signification—over the mind and body of the author. Although some feminist scholars, like some scholars in race and ethnicity studies, continued to turn to personal, anecdotal writing,[16] in posthumanist theory the autobiographical was shunned as a pathetically naïve modality of meaning production; personal experience was not considered a valid foundation for saying anything in the register of "high theory," as this type of theory is sometimes called. However, as Sayers argues, this attitude has recently started to shift: the personal has increasingly been resurfacing as a legitimate component of theoretical writing.

This doesn't mean that the person who writes and the "I" of the text are identical. Sayers quotes Luce Irigaray on this insight: "Who I am for you and who I am for me is not the same, and such a gap cannot be overcome."[17] I concur. We have no direct, unmediated access to our experiences, particularly when they're umpired by writing (language). No memory of the past, no account of what has happened to us, is straightforwardly accurate; there's an element of fantasy, of the imagination, that enters into the telling of every personal story. In addition, although this book contains autobiographical elements, I wouldn't characterize it as a memoir per se, for to write a memoir, I'd have to remember the details of my past—which I for the most part don't.

I have only disconnected memories of my formative experiences: I recall the daily terror I felt in relation to my father but not (most of) his wounding words; I recall my mother's depressed indifference but not its specific manifestations; I recall the gentleness of my first kiss but not where it took place; I recall the thrill of getting into Brown but not what I said in my application (or even how I managed to take the SATs behind my parents' backs); I recall disliking my housemate in graduate school but not her name; I recall the mortification of getting a scathing peer review on my first book but not the substance of the review; I recall the fatigue generated by too many years of teaching but not the particulars of my lectures. I suppose that the most accurate thing to say is that I have access to an emotional history without having access to all the tangible details that produced that history.[18]

When I visit my mother—who is now a cherished friend (things can change, yes?)—she reassures me that this is because my brain is cluttered from too many years of thinking: "You're pushing out the memories to make space for new thoughts," she says. But I know that this isn't true. I know that I've actively sought to forget so as to live on. I'll return to this theme at the end of this book. At this juncture, I simply want to say that the gaps in my memory mean that I can't write a memoir, that I only have bits of memoir to work with. I also don't want to write a traditional memoir because I think that it would be insufferably boring. As you can probably already tell, what I have is yet another rags-to-riches story but without the riches—that is, a *dull* story. But I hope that I can make something interesting out of it by blending it with theoretical rumination.

WHAT IF YOU CAN'T MAKE IT?

So I proceed with bits of memoir—anecdotes and fragments of personal history—dispersed within an otherwise diagnostic text. In this context, I want to emphasize that even though there's no way around the fact that my personal story in some ways follows the outlines of the American dream, the point of telling it is not to celebrate "having made it" but rather to foreground the bad feelings that have accompanied the draining process of trying (and often failing) to make it. Most important, I want to emphasize that I don't wish to suggest that the American dream possesses some sort of intrinsic validity or that it's available to everyone.

Quite the contrary! I know that this dream harms, even breaks, those who are most seduced by it while at the same time making them feel terrible about, and responsible for, their damaged lives. This is because, as I've already mentioned, an essential part of its ideology is to conceal the social factors—such as systemic racism, poverty, and the lack of basic educational opportunities—that keep many people at an insurmountable distance from it; it makes people feel personally accountable for impediments that are socially generated.

I may have grown up poor, but I haven't experienced racism, except indirectly by being cognizant of the ways in which I, as a white person, am implicated in it on a structural level even if I don't subscribe to it on a personal level. In addition, I've had an abundance of educational opportunities, starting with a decent high school; due to Finland's strong public education system, my father's inability to make a living didn't keep me from getting the same schooling as the daughters of doctors and lawyers. My unstable immigration status poisons my American life, barring my access to any sense of safety, permanence, or legitimate belonging. Still, I recognize that this barrier pales in comparison to the obstacles faced by, say, those whose lives have been scarred by systemic racism.

Much of what I've said about phallic power arguably (though maybe not invariably) only applies to white men, and even among them, perhaps only to those who have managed to attain positions of political, economic, and social power. It's not only women of all colors who have been denied access to this power (and some more than others based on hierarchies of wealth, race, citizenship, and sexual orientation, among other vectors of discrimination). Poor white men can also feel socially impotent, metaphorically castrated. Black men, in turn, have historically been castrated not only metaphorically but also literally: recall that during Jim Crow, castration, in addition to lynching, was the punishment that black men suffered at the hands of white men when they were suspected of sexual relationships with white women. That castration was the penalty for a (sometimes merely imagined) sexual transgression of the color line is surely not a coincidence; it's a particularly brutal indication of our culture's obsession with the penis (and phallic power) as well as with the question of who gets to have it and who doesn't.

Against this cultural backdrop, it's not insignificant that some black male rap artists grab their crotches in a bold gesture of defiance. This is a symbolic way to assert agency in a society that continues to "castrate" them through poverty, unemployment, police brutality, and incarceration. Here I'm not talking about castration in the ontological sense that Lacan does when he analyzes the lack within our being, the lack that transforms an infant into a socially intelligible individual. Instead, I'm calling attention to context-specific—in this case racially motivated—forms of violence, forms that systematically negate (render lacking) some individuals so that others can thrive.

I'll return to this distinction between ontological and context-specific modalities of lack momentarily. Here I merely wish to state the following: the United States may no longer officially condone segregation, but given the large number of black men in prison, and the large number of black men and women in low-paying jobs (or with no jobs at all), it has found a way to uphold a de facto separation of blacks from the rest of society. Other racialized individuals of all genders also experience discrimination and disempowerment ("castration") in countless ways that weave bad feelings into the texture of their everyday lives. Many writers both inside and outside the academy have explored this topic.[19] As a result, although I do not focus on racial discrimination in this book, an awareness of how fundamentally

XXXVI   INTRODUCTION

it shapes American society is necessarily a part of my conceptual apparatus.

THE ELUSIVENESS OF THE GOOD LIFE

What, then, is my conceptual apparatus? What are my main goals? Foremost among these is to describe some of the major trends of our neoliberal cultural moment and to grapple with the emotional impact of these trends, which, as I've stressed, valorize a seemingly benign—but perhaps psychologically eroding—combination of good performance, high productivity, constant self-improvement, and relentless cheerfulness. Besides the violence of gendered thinking, I'm particularly interested in the fantasies of the good life that motivate our actions and that often problematically keep us faithful to scenarios of living that falsely promise a better future, a future that endlessly recedes, never actually materializing. Lauren Berlant has dubbed this phenomenon *cruel optimism*, explaining that we're caught in the claws of cruel optimism when we believe that forms of life that hurt us will eventually pay off and make us happy.[20]

Berlant's well-coined concept succinctly names the gist of the American dream: the hope that hard work—effort, striving, diligence, and doggedness—will be rewarded. This is why the critique of cruel optimism—of false hope—is among the main theoretical threads that run through this book. I'm willing to guess that the bad feelings generated by this hope, by this treacherous fantasy of a better future, among Americans are quite heightened these days in the sense that many of us, even those in relatively privileged professions, let alone those who are working several jobs to make ends meet, feel like we're working so hard that we don't have time to live. Alternatively, we're too exhausted to live when we actually get a chance.

Anecdotal evidence—talking to colleagues, students, and friends, and listening to collective chatter about what life feels like in today's America—indicates that the good life eludes many of us; it's slippery, constantly sliding from our grasp. We're often viscerally aware of our cruelly optimistic relationships to it even when we can't name the problem. And when we're given a chance to name it, it can leap forth with a degree of insistence.

In the spring of 2017, I taught a seminar on bad feelings at Harvard, admitting fourteen students out of the forty-eight who wanted to take it: the demand for the course was in itself a sign that there's something about the topic of bad feelings that resonates with the emotional tone of contemporary everyday life.[21] Of these fourteen students, half wrote final papers that talked about their personal experiences with depression, anxiety, anorexia, stints in mental hospitals, and suicide attempts. I even received a couple of papers that focused on the feelings of inadequacy, frustration, and "ugliness" generated by Grindr, the social media app popular with gay men, which advances impossible-to-live-up-to ideals of (white, muscular, normatively masculine) attractiveness. My students were obviously self-selected for their interest in bad feelings. Still, the acuteness of bad feelings, the power of bad feelings to lead to hospitalization and suicide attempts among these twenty-something students, was disheartening. And it's most likely not a coincidence that many of them—contrary to the usual stereotypes about overprivileged Ivy League students—came from backgrounds of poverty, racial discrimination, and familial hardship.

Along related lines, after a public lecture I recently delivered on some of the themes of this book, a man from the audience, visibly flustered, asked me for a written version of the talk. He said that it had startled him into realizing that his effort-filled life was making him despondent. During the last decade, I've regularly felt the same way: not a month has gone by when I haven't seriously considered quitting my frenzied job as a professor, a job where the demands crowding my inbox increasingly drown out the intellectual content that used to make me feel alive. Why don't I? Because, like so many others, I don't know how to survive—how to make enough money to live—outside the life that I've painstakingly patched together.

But I do know how to talk about the quandary that so many of us find ourselves in, so I'll try to describe it, to examine its contours. I'll talk about the psychological, emotional, and physical corrosion, the chronic vexation, the defeating fatigue, and the difficulty of changing one's course that characterize many Western lives. This is a somewhat delicate endeavor because I have no interest in suggesting that things are now grimmer than they were during earlier times, that we're now more oppressed than people were during the eras of slavery, segregation, colonization, or the Inquisition. Yet I also think that it's important to understand the manner in which our tendency to buy into dominant narratives of what the good life consists of can actually impede our flourishing, leading to a general attrition of the quality of our lives.

I'll also demonstrate that our culture's conviction that effort will be rewarded takes insidiously gendered forms in the lives of many women, not only because they're still having to work harder than men to make it in our achievement-oriented society, but also because they're bending over backward to sustain their relationships, remain attractive, and keep smiling even when they don't feel like it. The four pillars of our society I've foregrounded—performance, productivity, self-improvement, and positivity—demand that women push their bad feelings about disrespect and denigration aside. In other words, the ethos of achievement that surrounds us tells us that we're not going to succeed if we start grumbling about how we're being treated because, well, Americans don't grumble: like Jack Bauer of *24*, they get the job done even when they're limping, bleeding, and out of bullets.

TWO LEVELS OF BAD FEELINGS

This book doesn't deal with bad feelings that arise from chemical imbalances or other physical factors and that consequently require medical intervention. Rather, it considers bad feelings that could in principle be avoided by a less performance-driven, less pragmatic and utilitarian cultural environment. It also considers socially generated bad feelings that could be alleviated by more egalitarian collective structures; it focuses on bad feelings that result less from the complexities of the human psyche than from the unfair social (political, economic, and cultural) arrangements that surround this psyche.

I've started with Lacan's rewriting of the Freudian notion of penis envy in part because this gives us a concrete example of a bad feeling—in this case the envy of social prestige—that could easily be misread as a purely individual, psychological matter (as an idiosyncratic "female complaint") but that is in fact socially produced through an unequal distribution of power and agency. As I've pointed out, it's not the bit of extra flesh that boys have between their legs that little girls covet, but rather the privilege that this bit of flesh endows on boys as well as on the (sometimes, though thankfully not always, insufferably arrogant) men that these boys one day become.

The first four chapters of this book continue the analysis of these types of socially generated bad feelings, focusing particularly on ones that arise from gender inequality and from heteropatriarchy's uncanny ability to keep reinventing itself.

Romantic disillusionments resulting from unrealistic, sugarcoated expectations about the power of love to heal wounds will also receive some attention, as will the (often suppressed) bad feelings associated with the snowballing pornification of heterosexual culture. Along the way, I'll consider the emotional costs of traumatic familial histories, such as my own. One of my main aims is to illustrate the ways in which such histories—not merely mine but more generally speaking—can linger long after they have in principle been transcended. Like social inequalities, they are a source of the kinds of bad feelings that are produced by environmental factors, by strenuous, wounding, or abrasive circumstances, more than by (or at least in conjunction with) purely psychological processes.

That said—and here comes the distinction between ontological and context-specific modalities of lack (negation, deprivation, dispossession, wounding) I alluded to above—I want to acknowledge that there are some bad feelings that may be intrinsic to the human condition (ontological): "existential" in the sense of being unavoidable. As a matter of fact, although I find Lacan helpful for explaining socially generated bad feelings, I find him perhaps even more helpful for addressing bad feelings for which there is no cure. This is why the last two chapters of this book draw on Lacanian insights to discuss bad feelings such as melancholia and anxiety.

I don't mean to imply that melancholia and anxiety can't be socially (or intersubjectively) produced, for frequently they are, as I'll also demonstrate in the final chapters. Yet it may also be that an undertone of sadness and anxiety is an inescapable component of human life. Our cheerfulness-promoting society tries to deny this. But this only intensifies the difficulty of coping with moments of existential malaise. This is why, toward the end of this book, I'll propose that even though many of our bad feelings could be avoided by conjuring away the environmental factors that cause them, there are some bad feelings that we may just need to learn to live with. As Lacan explains, there's no "Sovereign Good,"[22] meaning that there's no ultimate remedy for bad feelings that are existential (inseparable from what it means to be human).

My aim in making this argument is not to augment despair. Rather, I believe that understanding the reasons that some bad feelings are unavoidable can make it easier to bear such feelings. When we can't name what's ailing us, we also can't address the problem; looking the other way, dodging the issue, rarely works as an effective coping mechanism for feeling bad. In contrast, admitting that certain types of bad feelings at times emerge in the lives of most of us creates an awareness of our common human vulnerability, with the consequence that we may be less likely to blame ourselves when such feelings overtake us, not to mention making us potentially more sympathetic to others who may also be experiencing them.[23]

THINKING OUT LOUD

This insight is perhaps the only (tentatively) guidance-providing—rather than diagnostic, descriptive, or analytic—component of this book. My training in critical theory, in the critical humanities, makes me recoil from the very idea of giving advice on how to live, including on how to deal with bad feelings.

I'm of course used to calling for an eradication of collective wrongs. Doing so is common in my field: for critical theorists such as myself, the "givens" of our society are a source of suspicion; the predictable makes us wary. We tend to assume that whatever the collective social order presents to us as a "fact" is actually a fabrication, a cultural myth that has merely been remarkably successful in concealing its fictitious origins. This is why we dig deeper than the surface of taken-for-granted cultural ideals to determine how these ideals have become ideals in the first place; it's why we look for the ideological origins of what our society conditions us to take as the natural order of things. And we don't usually hesitate to ask for a more just social system. But we do hesitate to give advice on how people should go about their lives.

For this reason, I for the most part avoid prescriptive (*do this*) statements. My approach is broadly contemplative. I don't rely on empirical research, lab experiments, or statistical findings. Nor do I claim to possess the key to the good life. Rather—as is the way of philosophers—I think out loud on the written page. I strive to promote a greater level of self-reflexivity by bringing complex collective, existential, psychological, and emotional matters into relief in a manner that I hope will allow readers to reach their own conclusions about the best way to proceed. That is, I try to induce inquisitiveness among readers who are willing to follow a train of thought to conclusions that sometimes remain unresolved.

Some readers may be used to a more practical, "self-helpy" style. To some degree, this may be due to the very system that I criticize in this book: neoliberal pragmatism demands a "scientific" approach of hard facts that can (supposedly) then be applied to real-life dilemmas. All I can say is that if concrete, step-by-step advice on how to go about alleviating bad feelings is needed, then a book written by a self-help author, medical expert, or psychiatrist might be a better guide to consult than this book, for it is not my goal to give such advice.

That said, if this book is not a self-help guide, it's not an entirely academic text either. I've used the same "crossover" style that I've opted for in this book—a style that seeks to speak to both academic and nonacademic readers—a few times before, but this book, by focusing on the everyday, the quotidian, and by drawing on personal experience, leans more heavily toward the nonacademic than my previous books in the genre.[24] Some academic, particularly theory-loving readers may prefer the more opaque, allusive style of "autotheoretical" writers such as Barthes and Nelson, for there's something mesmerizing about this style for those of us who are theoretically motivated.

Truth be told, one day I would like to write like Barthes and Nelson, both of whom blend snippets of autobiography with snippets of theory that are usually left unexplained, that are only accessible to readers who are already "in the know" about certain theoretical trends; the writing of these authors is replete with pithy references to ideas that only those already snugly lodged within the folds of contemporary theory can fully process. I feel that if I ever manage to write a book like that, my intellectual mission will be accomplished; such a book feels like my destiny. But I'm not there yet. In the book that you're currently reading, I didn't (yet) want to only address those already "in the know" but rather those—and this includes not only many nonacademic readers but also many graduate students entering their doctoral programs and colleagues who aren't theoretically oriented—who do not yet know.

It may also be that by writing lucidly, I am—and this is probably nothing to be proud of—trying to preempt the theory phobia that runs rampant in today's academy. I have (some) colleagues who resent me for the simple reason that contemporary theory happens to be my field. I've never understood why. After all, I don't resent scholars whose approach is more literary, historical, or empirical. I believe that there's room within the academy for all kinds of interesting scholarship. And when a colleague does something—for instance, analyzes poetry—that

I'm not able to do, I admire rather than resent her. So I'm not sure why theory so often elicits such strong hatred.

Given that I opened this book with Freud's notion of penis envy, it seems important to raise the possibility that this hatred escalates when the theorist is female. It may be that because theory (philosophy) has traditionally been coded as "masculine," women who aspire to theorize are judged to wield illegitimate (and therefore infuriating) phallic power; they become the targets of envy. I'll return to this theme in chapter 4. Here let me simply state that this attitude is misdirected in the sense that being a theorist—at least the kind of theorist that I am—means giving up the fantasy of (phallic) mastery; it means that I can never be sure of anything, that everything is purely hypothetical, that the point is to question everything rather than to provide answers.

The problem may be exacerbated by the fact that many female theorists also happen to be *feminists*: because post-WWII (mostly French) theory, including deconstruction, arrived in the American academy during the 1970s and 1980s in large part through the work of feminist theorists,[25] contemporary "theory" is often intrinsically feminist, so that it's sometimes difficult to tell if the phobia, hatred, and envy I've referred to is directed against female theorists because we are theorists, female, or feminists (or a combination of these).

This antipathy is one reason that female theorists can find it harder to claim their voice than male theorists. We may be encouraged to use our own voice to discuss "feminine" topics such as love, intimacy, and relationships, as I did in *The Case for Falling in Love*.[26] But the minute we attempt to speculate (theoretically) about matters of general interest, such as the contours of the good life, we're asked to show our credentials, that is, our penises. Being a female theorist may give me illegitimate phallic power in the eyes of some nontheoretical colleagues, but it's an impediment—a castrating factor—in the world of publishing, at least in the world of mainstream publishing, the kind of publishing that reaches nonacademic readers.

I once even had a literary agent tell me that I should write a history of menstruation rather than the loosely philosophical book about the meaning of life I was proposing. This is what I wanted to say in response but didn't: "I'm not a historian. I don't have a clue as to how to write a history of anything. And why menstruation? What in my academic training and publication history makes you think that I'm an expert on the topic? Or is it that, as a woman, I'm supposed to just automatically know how to write about it? Like men automatically know how to write about the meaning of life by virtue of being men?" I didn't say any of this because I didn't want to insult this well-meaning man. I stayed polite, as women too often do in these situations.

But at some point, one gets tired of hearing that female theoretical voices carry no credibility. Last year I attended an academic meeting where a (female) colleague kept complaining about a prominent, hugely published feminist theorist who, in my colleague's opinion, illegitimately "gets away" with the kind of writing that doesn't footnote everything. "She should be forced to footnote her ideas just like everyone else," my colleague insisted. I kept looking at her and thinking "penis envy": in this case, the envy of a fellow female (and feminist) academic who has been able to break the code within the (American—the French are better on this) academy that tells us that only *really important thinkers*—that is, male thinkers—get to write books without footnotes.

In this book, I've rebelliously minimized notes. And I steer clear of academic debates that would render the text uninteresting for nonacademic readers. For this reason, the theoretical apparatus I draw on is for the most part invisibly plaited into the fabric of my argument. My objective is to showcase theory's applicability to the kinds of basic questions that many people— both inside and outside the academy—are asking about what it means to live well, what the obstacles to the so-called good life might be, and why these obstructions can be so taxing to deal with, why they can feel largely intractable. Expert readers will hopefully discern a number of new directions for thinking about the psychological, emotional, and physical costs of daily life under neoliberalism. Others will hopefully gain some under- standing of the extent to which dominant social ideologies per- meate their everyday lives.

Some of what I'm about to say I've said before in more aca- demic texts. There are some ideas that I repeatedly return to, that never feel quite "done." Sometimes this is because it feels like I can push these ideas further now than I might have been able to a couple of years ago. Other times it's because I'm not yet ready to let go of them. Certain ideas have a way of sticking; they demand a rearticulation in a new context, particularly when I shift to a different rhetorical register, as I do in this book by let- ting the personal slide into the mix. I suppose that I feel that some ideas are worth sharing with multiple audiences.[27]

The first chapter of this book explores the dominant happiness narratives of today's pragmatic neoliberal society, focusing on their cruelly optimistic tendencies. Mobilizing Foucault's theory of biopolitics, Lacan's theory of desire, and personal material, it scrutinizes the deceptive seductiveness of the American dream of beating the odds. It also contemplates the themes of positive thinking, the metabolization of suffering, quotidian microtrau- mas, and the intergenerational transmission of trauma, focusing on the attrition of life that can result from our attempts to pur- sue the good life in our achievement-oriented cultural moment.

Chapter 2 investigates the ways in which our society's pragmatism can overtake even our intimate lives, causing us to rationalize our relationships, to trade passion for utilitarian concerns. It also contains a critique of the social glorification of marriage as an institution that's supposed to usher us into the folds of the happily ever after, asking if this is what marriage usually accomplishes. I don't mean to suggest that no happy marriages exist, for clearly some do. Nor do I want to argue that love doesn't have the power to exalt us and even to alter our destinies. In some of my earlier books, I've written at length about this power.[28] Yet I have reservations about the sentimental ways in which our society celebrates love's institutionalization in marriage, for this institutionalization causes us to value stability and longevity over ardor and adventure. What could be more pragmatic than this? What's more, our society's overemphasis on romance as a route to happiness obscures other components of life that might be equally enriching, with the consequence that we may end up depressed and pining for love even when we have a multitude of other things that have the potential to contribute to a meaningful life.

Chapter 3 focuses on the damage done to women, as well as to (straight) romantic relationships, by our society's obsessiveness about gender differences and the stereotypical manner in which it categorizes individuals into a rigidly dichotomous system of gender. The chapter counters evolutionary psychological explanations of gendered behavior by a socially constructivist narrative of how gender becomes a lived reality. By showcasing the falsity of the quick fix that gendered thinking promises, it argues that such thinking is in the final analysis designed to let men off the hook for emotional incompetence, hurtful behavior, and relationship failures.

Chapter 4 proposes that what we call postfeminism is merely the latest edition of heteropatriarchy, that what looks like liberation is often merely a clandestine version of male dominance. It critiques the ways in which straight women are taught to eroticize their sexual objectification. In addition, it considers the dilemmas of pornification in the heterosexual context, including the fact that now that straight women are supposed to be sexually free, they have no political or cultural space to complain either about the misogynistic content of heteroporn or about the compulsive porn consumption of the men they love.

Chapter 5 examines the specificity of human desire: the fact that desire obstinately wants what it wants even when what it wants seems slightly insane (or at least inconvenient). This specificity renders desire partially resistant to social manipulation, giving rise to a stubborn, and potentially ethical, faithfulness to objects of desire that our social environment might deem inappropriate. Yet it also causes us to make irrational—and frequently painful—romantic choices, at times resulting in the kind of paralysis of desire (melancholia) that keeps us from finding a new object of desire even when the old one is no longer available. In this sense, it makes us enormously vulnerable to disappointment and other agonies of unrequited love, sometimes even asking us to replace the very thing that feels most irreplaceable to us.

Chapter 6 draws on Lacanian insights to investigate anxiety as a bad feeling that can arise in relation to other people. The goal of the chapter is to explain why so many of us feel like we are living in an age of anxiety by tracing anxiety to three causes: the fear of being wounded; the fear of being engulfed; and the fear of being overagitated by the enigmatic messages that emanate from others. The chapter also distinguishes between anxiety as an unavoidable component of human life on the one hand and anxiety as a context-specific, circumstantially generated bad feeling on the other.

The conclusion rounds up the discussion by highlighting the paradoxes of neoliberalism, including the fact that even those most critical of it might find it hard to discard some of its rewards. It also considers the advantages of forgetting as a way of life, drawing a connection between the ability to "declutter" the mind by acts of forgetting and the ability to "declutter" one's life by rejecting the lures of commercial culture. The book ends with personal reflections on loss, mortality, and writing.

Some readers may appreciate knowing ahead of time that, as my argument develops, I move from a predominantly Foucauldian register to a more Lacanian one. Even though Foucault works well for the critique of neoliberalism that I stage in the first two chapters, and even though he helps me explicate the impasses of (straight) female subjectivity that constitute the focus of the middle chapters, I've always been more Lacanian than Foucauldian. This isn't just because, for partly personal reasons, psychoanalytic theory—among other things a theory of how to handle suffering—compels me but also because Lacan leaves more space for agency and self-determination than Foucault does.

Readers who are used to the commonly held idea that both of these thinkers swim in the same soup of poststructuralist criticism may find this a surprising claim, but chapter 5 illustrates why I believe it to be true.[29] I also believe that, contrary to common (academic) wisdom, Lacanian theory offers a dexterous critique of heteropatriarchy. A full account of this aspect of Lacanian theory—which has to do with the universalization of lack and the mockery of phallic authority I've already referred to—resides beyond the purview of this book,[30] but I touch on it in chapter 6. However, the differences between Foucault and Lacan don't render these thinkers incompatible. In many ways, they complement each other, which is why chapter 1 begins with a combination of some of their most basic arguments.

PENIS ENVY
AND OTHER
BAD FEELINGS

1

THE CREED OF PRAGMATISM

We live in a hard-nosed society that strives for streamlined efficiency in all areas of life. As I've noted, this society valorizes good performance, high productivity, constant self-improvement, and relentless cheerfulness. It expects us to maximize the functioning of our minds and bodies alike so that we can lead happy, healthy, and well-adjusted lives. Foucault goes as far as to argue that in the Western capitalist world, we've come to view the individual as a miniature economic enterprise—a *homo economicus*—and human life as a process of perfecting the effectiveness of this enterprise through various projects of self-development. More specifically, he claims that the market mentality that governs capitalist economies has been applied to the individual, so that we've learned to think of our lives in terms of input and profit, of smart investments and optimum functioning.

Foucault calls the ideological apparatus that produces this way of life *biopolitics*: a nebulous politics of *bios*, of life, that shapes our experience without needing to resort to the overt repressiveness of nondemocratic societies. Biopolitics permeates every pore of our being; it insinuates itself into the fine weave of its texture. It shapes our basic goals—career goals, personal goals, relational goals, and existential goals—at the same time as it dictates our understanding of what the good life entails.

Biopolitics is even wily enough to include strategies to offset the alienating effects of envisioning the individual as an economic enterprise. It offers "warm" values such as solidarity, collaboration, friendship, and romance to counter the coldness of lives otherwise driven by profit-related motivations. And it offers close-knit families as a solution to the fragmentation of our social world. This is why we're constantly told to become members of communities and form loving families. Relationality is proposed as a solution to the fact that our society is built on stony principles of fierce competition; it's meant to compensate for the otherwise instrumentalist inflection of our culture.

Biopolitics consists of subtle control mechanisms that allow us to believe that we're free to choose how we live when in fact our choices have been largely predetermined by the political and economic needs of our society. Foucault explains that the biopolitical apparatus of liberal democracies produces freedom through heightened control. On the one hand, it tells us that its main objective is to ensure that we're "free to be free."[1] On the other, its attempts to generate freedom demand that it micromanage the conditions in which we can be free, with the result that it establishes a whole array of new constraints, often relying on the idea that without such constraints our security is threatened, that they exist solely for our own protection. Post-9/11 American society is an excellent example of this paradox in the sense that elevated levels of regulation have been installed—and are largely tolerated—in the name of freedom.

Unlike more overtly tyrannical systems, the biopolitical apparatus of neoliberal democracies relies on ideological manipulation that remains for the most part invisible. The brilliance of such clandestine manipulation is that it causes us to *want* to behave in ways that serve the system's needs; it grants enough benefits—such as an increased ease of everyday life—to induce us to embrace its ideals without hesitation. Foremost among such ideals is pragmatism, which dominates our society to such a degree that people tend to measure their worth primarily by their accomplishments. Even those who fail to live up to the expectations of this system are impacted by it in the sense that the sparkly version of the good life it paints becomes a goal that they reach for even when it repeatedly eludes them.

This is the emotional impasse that Berlant calls cruel optimism: reaching for what repeatedly eludes us. Berlant defines cruel optimism as the stubborn belief that ways of life, social arrangements, ideological attachments, and relational scenarios that injure us will someday reward us, specifying that we're trapped in cruel optimism when something we ardently desire is in reality an impediment to our flourishing; cruel optimism entails the hope that things will eventually get better even when they're extremely unlikely to do so. Berlant moreover suggests that there's something about our neoliberal (late capitalist) society that heightens such misguided optimism.

THE QUEST FOR SATISFACTION

I'll circle back to this idea that neoliberal society heightens cruel optimism at the end of this chapter. But I want to begin by proposing that on a basic level human beings may be constitutionally predisposed to forge a cruelly optimistic relationship to the world, that cruel optimism may be built into the very structure of our desire. If it's the case, as Lacan claims, that it's part of the human condition to feel lacking, then it's logical that desire arises as an (optimistic) pursuit of objects, people, ambitions, activities, and modes of life that we hope will compensate for that lack, granting us a sense of wholeness and belonging. But because the lack within our being is constitutive of our subjectivity (the price of being human), it can never be definitively cured. From this point of view, cruel optimism is simply the tangible manifestation of desire as a quest for the kind of satisfaction that is inherently unattainable. At the very least, it's possible to argue that the structure of desire—the fact that desire seeks a fulfillment that's intrinsically impossible—is the foundation upon which cruel optimism develops.

Let me state the matter slightly differently. Lacan argues that we can never accurately identify the piece that we feel is missing from our being for the simple reason that we haven't in reality lost anything; the x that we believe we have lost isn't a concrete entity but rather a fantasy object: an object we imagine would complete our being if we ever found it but that doesn't actually exist. In this sense, the objects, people, ambitions, activities, and modes of life that we reach for are always substitutes for an original lost object that we can't name; they're the (at least partly) nameable stand-ins for what remains unnameable.

Although such substitutes often manage to grant us partial satisfaction (more on this in chapter 5), they can't ever fully (or consistently) satisfy us. If anything, when our desire for x—which in the final analysis is always a desire for self-completion—meets the quotidian world of living, our fantasies of satisfaction can come crashing down. When they do, it's usually too difficult for us to focus on the (unnameable) lack that generates these fantasies, with the consequence that we try to replace the fantasy that has shattered with a new one; we try to replace the nameable object we have lost with a new nameable object. In other words, we repeatedly choose the promise of satisfaction over the stoic recognition that the void within our being can never be healed.

This is why most of us find it very difficult to live without objects of desire.

Consumer culture—neoliberal culture—capitalizes on this predicament, offering a multitude of products and services that promise satisfaction. As Todd McGowan argues, as subjects of consumer culture, we're constantly on the brink of having our desire realized but never quite reach the point of full realization.[2] In this manner, consumer culture guarantees its vitality by creating an endless loop of dissatisfaction: it keeps us in thrall by offering us the prospect of satisfaction—essentially, the fantasy of a better future—without ever entirely satisfying us, with the result that we keep going back to its offerings in the hope that we'll eventually find what we're looking for. Existentially, the consequence of this is that we're constantly oriented toward the future, living in a state of anticipation (in a state of cruel optimism) that keeps us from being fully present in the moment.

Advertising explicitly feeds the notion that if we feel unsatisfied, it's simply because we haven't yet found the right products and services: it tells us that the latest version of a Nike running shoe is better (more satisfying) than the version we already possess. In addition, it organizes our desire by signaling to us which products and services are most likely to allow us to thrive within the dominant social order. McGowan gives the example of a beer commercial that relies on the image of a male drinker surrounded by a group of beautiful women wearing skimpy bikinis. It's not that the (straight) men who watch this commercial are deluded into thinking that if they purchase the right beer they'll instantly find themselves besieged by attractive women. Rather, the commercial tells them that drinking the right beer will buy them social approval. The same is obviously true of commercials that market specific watches, shampoos, detergents, and vacation packages. In acquiring these products and services, we imagine we're acquiring a membership in our cultural order (which in a sense we actually are). This is one way to alleviate the lack within our being.

Because no commodity fully coincides with x, because no product or service fits seamlessly into the hole within our being, consumer culture prospers. It even finds ways to convert our attempts to resist it into opportunities for profit extraction. Let's say that we reject the social ideal of marriage—as some people did during the 1960s and many continue to do today—on the basis of the fact that the institution creates too many avid consumers of family-centered products and services. Let's say we advocate sexual promiscuity instead. Well, the economy finds it easy to translate this change in cultural attitudes into new products and services, this time designed to enhance our sex appeal so as to allow us to attract multiple partners.

Or let's say that we reject the fashion industry by shopping in vintage stores, only wearing secondhand clothing. Well, the next time we open a fashion magazine, we see ads for vintage clothes that look exactly like the ones that our rebellious stance motivated us to wear. Even social movements such as feminism can be turned into commercial opportunities so that female "empowerment"—say, images of women who showcase their professional success by wearing an elegant Donna Karan suit or by carrying a sleek Gucci briefcase—becomes an advertising trope. This doesn't mean that social movements such as feminism are useless, but it does mean that we need to retain a degree of skepticism with respect to how the principles of these movements can be appropriated by a system that is driven solely by profit-related considerations.

THE IDEOLOGY OF POSITIVE THINKING

This commercial fantasy of eventual fulfillment—which in many cases becomes synonymous with cruel optimism—is supported by an ideology of positive thinking that tells us that our success depends on our ability to cultivate a hopeful, confident go-getter attitude.[3] This quintessentially American creed conditions us to believe that a positive attitude will enable us to achieve our goals regardless of how many obstacles we encounter. Barbara Ehrenreich gives a chilling account of how this attitude permeates even our approach to illness in the sense that we're trained to think that remaining positive will help us overcome diseases such as cancer. She describes how the medical establishment as well as some of her family and friends met her diagnosis of breast cancer with the insistence that optimism would be the key to curing it.

While this attitude may at first glance seem benign enough, it has a harsh undertone in the sense that it suggests that our failure to attain the good life, including "lapses" such as cancer, is always ultimately our own doing, the consequence of our inability to maintain a sufficiently hopeful state of mind; as Ehrenreich explains, the ideology of positive thinking implies that "there is no excuse for failure."[4] It permeates large swaths of our culture, giving rise to the notion that success is attainable through ambition, striving, and calculated risks; that there's no hindrance that can't be overcome by perseverance; that effort will invariably be rewarded; and that dissatisfaction is always a temporary state, a mere stepping-stone to satisfaction.

This mentality of positive thinking exploits human resilience, our ability to survive repeated disillusionment; it implicitly chastises us for failing to be elastic enough to recover from hardship. Consider what happens after a catastrophe. We're encouraged to mourn our losses as quickly as possible, to get back on our feet, and to get back to work. How many times have you heard a character on a television show announce after the death of a colleague that the best way to honor his or her memory is "to do our jobs"? How many times has the president of the nation—or some other high-ranking official—told us to proceed with our lives as usual?

It's not a coincidence that a big part of American national(ist) mythology is the idea that Americans are an unusually resilient people, able to bounce back from any setback. This mythology deftly combines the ideal of working hard with the ideal of being tough. When someone sinks our ship, we resolve to build a better one. After a natural disaster such as a hurricane, we're told that we shouldn't let the tragedy derail us. After a terrorist attack we're told that we shouldn't allow ourselves to be intimidated, that the brave thing to do is to "defend our way of life" by "sticking to our routines." Such sentiments sound noble— and perhaps on some level they are—but they're also an attempt to keep us productive.

This mentality extends even to personal heartbreaks: when you lose a loved one, you're allowed to grieve for a while. But if your grieving becomes prolonged, if it starts to appear excessive, if it seems to hinder your good performance, you're urged to pull yourself together. In other words, our society approaches grief with the same uncompromising efficiency as it approaches most other aspects of life: you're supposed to deal with it as expediently as you can so that you can get back into the swing of things.

Short-term grief is a sign of your basic humanity, reassuring everyone that you're a compassionate person. But long-term grief—depression—is coded as a weakness of character, something you'll need to transcend (with medication, if necessary) so that you don't become a burden on society. In this sense, the pathologization of bad feelings—including the sadness that arises from the inerasable lack within our being—in our society is one of the side effects of its deep pragmatism; from the viewpoint of this society, the problem with bad feelings such as depression is that they cause the individual to retreat into her private world to such an extent that she fails to fulfill her social and economic responsibilities.

More broadly speaking, our society's levelheaded pragmatism generates a very specific vision of the good life: a vision centered on what Sara Ahmed calls dominant "happiness scripts."[5] Such scripts cause us to pursue certain types of aspirations more or less automatically without giving alternatives much consideration. Insofar as they dictate our basic life choices, they are one of the most powerful biopolitical influences in our lives. We probably have a fairly clear sense of the kind of happiness such scripts promise: financial affluence, professional acclaim, relaxing vacations, enriching friendships, harmonious marriages, well-behaved children, and so on. However, given how often these scripts fail to deliver what they promise—how often we don't attain either wealth or fame, our vacations end up being stressful, our friendships complicated, our marriages devastating, and our children rebellious—their persistence as cultural ideals is striking.

Like cruel optimism, dominant happiness scripts can make us overly patient with our plight by giving us the impression that our exertions will in due course bear fruit, that once we figure out how a given script works, we can make it work for us. Our investment in our favorite script can in fact be so strong that when it—say, the script that assures us that effort will be rewarded—disillusions us, we don't think of questioning the script itself but instead assume that we have failed to enact it correctly; our faith in a specific happiness script can make it hard for us to admit that this script has made us miserable. For this reason, the crisis moments of life—moments when we lose faith in the choices we've made—constitute important moments of reckoning, of having to admit that our trust in specific happiness scripts has misguided us, that what was supposed to make us happy hasn't done so.

In a society that values cheerfulness, it can be hard to acknowledge disappointment. If anything, people who complain about their disenchantment can be seen as social irritants, as troublemakers who intentionally seek to deplete the happiness of those who haven't yet lost their faith in the happiness scripts that govern their choices. The latter often want to avoid thinking about anything that might erode this faith, which is why they shun the disillusioned as a threat to their mode of life.

In this manner, those who fail to live up to dominant ideals of happiness end up carrying the burden of bad feelings whereas those who prosper push these feelings aside, sometimes even accusing those who try to express them of sabotaging social progress. Instead of admitting that access to the good life as it's defined by our society is unevenly distributed, and that bad feelings are therefore likely to accrue to those who—perhaps because they are victims of systematic marginalization—can't quite "make it," the proponents of dominant happiness scripts prefer to suppose that those who struggle are the architects of their own discontent.

The happiness of some, then, augments the suffering of others. Because our society values efficiency, bad feelings are seen as a waste of energy, as what keeps us stuck in the past. Good feelings, in contrast, promise to orient us toward the future. They are assumed to fuel performance, productivity, and the ability to let go of problems; good feelings, in short, are seen as a vehicle of social mobility. This link between good feelings and social mobility in turn obscures the inconsistency of our culture's message about how the good life is to be attained: the fact that, on the one hand, we're told that this life will result from tireless striving but, on the other, the creed of positive thinking assures us that if we just manage to visualize it in vivid Technicolor, it will be delivered to our doorstep in a gift-wrapped box topped with a pretty bow.

REFUNCTIONING SUFFERING

In the positive thinking scenario, it's of course a given that we have—or will someday have—an impressive doorstep to begin with, preferably in a high-end brownstone in Manhattan or a waterfront mansion outside of Malibu. As should be clear by now, the insidious underside of positive thinking is the assumption that if you can't attain such a doorstep, it's because you have fallen off the cheerfulness wagon. Maybe you just haven't made enough of an effort to imagine in enough detail what it would look like to succeed? Although the ethos of positive thinking—which tells us that success is a matter of envisioning it—blatantly contradicts the strict work ethic of the American dream, the two are also compatible in the sense that they both rely on the idea that every hardship can be transcended and even turned into an opportunity of some sort. If the ethos of positive thinking dictates that an optimistic attitude will be rewarded, the American dream dictates that anyone can make it in our society if they just try hard enough.

This mentality assures us that obstacles will strengthen us, make us more nimble, and in the long run enhance our performance: in a way, the American dream doesn't really even count unless our triumph is preceded by some degree of struggle. It takes an instrumentalist approach to life's difficulties, implying that it's worth going through arduous stretches in order to ensure a hard-earned success; it refunctions suffering by turning it into an eventual gain, thereby ignoring the structural impediments—such as racism—that make it impossible for some people to succeed no matter how hard they try.

I recently pulled an all-nighter in my office (thereby revealing my allegiance to the very performance-oriented system I'm criticizing here). At 10 P.M. the two-man cleaning crew arrived. It consisted of two friendly Latino guys. All night they cleaned diligently. I heard them move from classroom to classroom, office to office, bathroom to bathroom. By 7 A.M. everything gleamed. These guys were definitely doing their jobs—and then some. They were efficient. They were performing well. And they even had a positive attitude, flashing me a cheerful smile of camaraderie—can't believe you're still here!—whenever they passed my office. When they were leaving, one of them said, "I'm gonna take the T to my other job now."

He was going to clean some other building after having made mine perfect for the students who were about to stream into their classrooms at 9 A.M. I of course know that many people can't make a living from just one job; and it's not like my own job gives me a forty-hour work week (I was pulling an all-nighter, after all). But the incident was a concrete reminder that effort alone will *not* always lead to success; hard work isn't going to allow this custodian to beat the odds.

Nor will effort necessarily help my doctoral students land academic posts that match their qualifications: most of them will never become professors no matter how brilliant and industrious they are. In part because one of our society's most prominent happiness scripts tells them that the tremendous investment they have made in their education will one day pay off, many of them will spend years trying to get on the tenure track at a reputable university. Though some of them may succeed, most of them will end up with impossibly heavy teaching loads in temporary positions that pay less than entry-level clerical positions. Burdened by student loans, they will frequently work even harder, trying to write books—the golden ticket to the tenure track—while simultaneously attempting to manage their crushing teaching assignments. They will be unlikely to be living the good life as defined by our society: the life of enjoying the rewards of your hard work.

Some of these bright young scholars will eventually look for alternative employment, often after years of futile attempts to make it within the academy. But many will stay in the race because, as I argued above, it can be very difficult to abandon a happiness script that you have banked your future on. There are three hundred applicants for a professorship? Okay, so the odds are bad. But your determination will carry the day! Success is just around the corner, right?

This theme resonates with me personally because I spent my teenage years watching my parents strive without getting anywhere. My mother, as you already know, drove to a faraway factory to make a minimum wage. My father routinely worked several temporary jobs (also doing manual labor) at once. He worked particularly hard during the summers when he drove a tractor converting peat into fuel—I never quite understood the process—more or less around the clock, taking a break only when it rained very hard. Both of them were caught up in a cycle of effort that led absolutely nowhere. It made a bare existence possible by putting food on the table. But beyond this, there was no purpose, let alone joy, to their striving. Its only tangible result was the chronic pain of broken backs (and understandable grouchiness).

Now that my parents are retired, I see the brutal years of labor etched into their faces. They paid a price that nothing can redeem because there's now no going back to a time before numbing work schedules throttled their spirits; the pursuit of the good life did not make their lives good but rather made them prematurely worn out. Yet despite this obvious lack of results, I internalized the idea that hard work would be rewarded, which is why I worked and worked and worked, and not just at school. After I turned fifteen, I spent my summers working two jobs in Helsinki, starting at 7 A.M. and ending at 11 P.M. (the evening job also allowed me to work the weekends). It never occurred to me that this was an odd schedule for a teenage girl to have.

AMERICA WAS EASY

That I understand the treacherousness of the ideal of refunctioning suffering makes it doubly annoying that I remain emotionally attached to the story of rising from the ashes as my personal creation myth: the story of how I became who I am (those in the know will detect the Nietzschean undertones of this wording). To this day, I tear up at movies that depict people beating impossible odds. I love watching action heroes fight their way out of underground dungeons, slaying thirty bad guys in the process. And if there's one Finnish word I still feel attached to, it's *sisu*, which connotes a combination of robustness, resilience, perseverance, and sheer doggedness. I know that my personal mythology tells me that I made it out of my dungeon—or more precisely, the room with a slanted ceiling next to the attic that no one else in the family ever visited, not even when I was sick and vomiting into a bucket—because I had more *sisu* than the average person. It's not that I thought that I was born with it: I believed that obstacles had forced me to acquire it and that this then allowed me to deal with any new obstacles.

This reasoning is circular and insidious but it's also the reasoning of the American dream. And it's how action heroes are born. Your planet explodes, your parents die, and you're sent to Earth to be raised by the Kent family: the result is Superman. Your parents are murdered in front of you and you're deathly afraid of bats: the result is Batman. Your father kills himself in front of you, you're marooned on a tropical island and tortured for five years: the result is Green Arrow. A shipwreck strands you alone in Africa as a child and you're raised by apes: the result is Tarzan. It's striking that all of these stories begin with the death of a parent (or two). The Freudian in me suspects that this is one reason I've always been fascinated by them.

But what's important in the present context is that those in the know will understand why I mention Superman, Batman, Green Arrow, and Tarzan in the same breath as Nietzsche: the superman, after all, was Nietzsche's invention, though it's not really a concept that anyone cares to talk about these days. (Still, I thought that it was a nice touch that in the pilot episode of *Smallville*—one of the recent retellings of the Superman saga—the young Clark Kent drops a volume by Nietzsche when he's exposed to the green kryptonite necklace worn by his high school sweetheart, Lana Lang. Lana looks at the book and asks Clark, "So, are you a man or superman?") It's not that I wish to resurrect Nietzsche's *Übermensch*—the darling of Nazis and precocious teen boys alike—or that I buy into the idea that we can all triumph over obstacles if we just try hard enough. Just the opposite, for not only has my parents' fate made me skeptical of this idea but my academic training in progressive theory has also taught me to recognize the systemic social marginalization that keeps many people, including the poor, the *sans papiers*, some women, and many racialized, queer, or trans individuals, between the rock and the hard place. Yet I also know that traces of my ridiculous personal mythology regarding *sisu* linger. And I can understand how that mythology came into being.

Consider the weird setting of my story: a remote three-house village by a mysterious lake surrounded on three sides by the Iron Curtain; knowing that every house was filled with pathology, with aggression born of desperation; knowing that our house had been one of the last outposts of the Finnish-Soviet war, which is why half of "our" land (land that my father's family had owned for generations) was on the Soviet side—the side where all the good blueberries, lingonberries, and cloudberries always seemed to be, on the other side of the barb wire fence; knowing that if they had, after the war, decided to draw a straight line on the map instead of going around the lake, I'd have been born a communist.

Knowing that a nurse and two soldiers had died while trying to escape Soviet snipers by jumping out the kitchen window, that an uncle had been killed in the war, that another uncle had drowned in the lake, that yet another uncle—the village hermit who never went further than the first bend on the only road that led out to the world—was so sickly and wheezing because he had lost a lung in the war, that my aunt had died of tuberculosis during the war years, and that my other aunt, the one who worked in a clothing factory in Helsinki, had once run across the field outside my bedroom window to get to the wooded mountain on the far side as bombs exploded around her.

Playing in the damp and eerie cave where I knew that people like my aunt had hid during the war; hearing (faint) Soviet war practice on the other side of the border and pondering when they might decide that the berries on our side looked juicier; wondering if Soviet soldiers (or nearby trolls) were watching through their binoculars when I hung up the laundry in the yard; believing that I shared the upstairs of our house with the ghost of a very unhappy woman who had killed her baby with a broomstick and who haunted the hallway whenever the moon was full (this part of the story is probably not true but I still think of this woman when I visit my parents and the floorboards in the attic space next to my room inexplicably creak at night); and—during idle summer hours when my father wasn't home—watching my positively brilliant but schizophrenic uncle Paavo (different from the hermit I mentioned above) pace up and down the kitchen while he talked nonstop about Freud, UFOs, and telepathy (he had equal faith in all three, which some might say makes him pretty sane after all). This uncle also never left the village, except when he went off his meds: then someone from miles away would call to tell my father to *tule hakemaan tämä hullu* ("come get the crazy").

Then there are the specific memories I associate with *sisu*: getting up at 2 A.M. to study for an exam; washing my hair in a bucketful of freezing water in the freezing kitchen before heading out into the even more freezing winter to wait in the starlit night, morning after morning, to be picked up to go to school; the taxi (provided by the government) predictably getting stuck after snowstorms and the furious shoveling to get it moving again; fighting nausea while studying English grammar—and the grammar of four other languages—on the public bus (there were no school buses) that painstakingly snaked its way on the winding dirt road to my distant school; reversing the process at night to arrive at a cold room; trying to decide if the reason my room was the only one my mother didn't light a fire in after she got home from work was because she was too exhausted or because she forgot that I existed or because she didn't like me.

Clenching my jaw when I saw that my father was at home because that meant one of his tirades about how I only got good grades because I smiled at my teachers (not true), how I studied such long hours because I had to make up for being stupid (not true), how I was a dreadful writer (not true), how no one at school liked me (not true), how I had no friends (not true), how I would never amount to anything (not true), how people stared at me on the street because I was ugly (not sure about this one), and how no one would ever love me (this might be true); feeling relieved when my father's car wasn't in the yard when I got home; vigilantly listening for it all night and running up to my room the second I heard him pull up; knowing how tired he would be without being able to do anything about it.

Spending night after night, week after week, month after month, shut up in my room, grateful to be certain that no one would follow me there, that there was that unspoken agreement within the family that no one, not even my restless schizophrenic uncle, would enter my sanctuary of solitude (perhaps this is why my mother didn't heat it); sneaking downstairs when I hoped no one would be around to get my ration of bread and cheese, which I would then consume while working my way through the inevitable stack of homework; being thankful that no one from school ever made it to my village, that no one knew what went on in that house by the lake; being embarrassed whenever we—I and my elementary-school-educated parents—ran into the parents (doctors, teachers, "civilized" people) of my school friends at the grocery store in town; recoiling (in shame) from the way my mother recoiled (in shame) when she talked to such people; feeling slightly more at ease when it was my father, who knew how to sound smart (probably because he is).

There are of course also fragments of golden things: soft sunny days in July; joyfully skipping from rock to rock in the gleaming river that replenished the lake; wild strawberries on a string; watching the wheat fields sway in the wind. But mostly there's the blur of feeling acutely bad, of crying and crying and crying, of trying to cry quietly so that no one would come up to my room, hoping that someone would come but also knowing that they wouldn't and that it was better that they didn't. Sobbing especially hard—hysterically, really, and for hours on end—whenever my father had trapped me under a blanket for so long that I thought I would suffocate.

He may have thought that he was playing—he wasn't otherwise physically violent and he laughed at my screaming (which I did until I thought I was about to die and then I fell absolutely still, like a turtle caught out in the open that pulls its head under its carapace)—but it's hard to forgive a grown man who fails to realize from his daughter's screaming that what's happening is torture rather than playing. When the sobbing subsided, I always resolved that I *would* get out (and that once I did I would rise from the ashes).

After this, *America was easy.* Again, I want to stress that I'm not naïve or callous enough to think that this means that America is easy for everyone. As I've already mentioned, I recognize that I had an advantage that most deprivileged Americans don't have, namely access to a decent high school education that then became the stepping-stone to everything else. And it's not like rising from the ashes was painless.

There was terrible fear about not being smart enough for the fancy Ivies I was attending (it took me a while to realize that half the students at these schools thought, as I did, that they had gotten in because of some error at the admissions office). There was terrible overwork during graduate school when a change of fields (academic departments) resulted in the loss of funding. After graduating, there was a terrible lack of money (and immense student loans) that replicated my parents' pattern of anxiety-filled nights of worrying about money. There were terrible problems with the U.S. immigration service, which was oddly unwelcoming even after I had spent two decades in the country. There was a thoroughly miserable decade in Canada—where immigration turned out to be equally hostile (more on this in the next chapter)—and where I, ironically, felt "too American." And now that a stable income, a steady stream of publications, and a Canadian passport have eased things, I'm chronically in pain, just like my parents.

Still, the biggest challenge has been the persistent, ongoing impact of those years, before America, when bad feelings filled the day, every day. The hardships that came after immigration have felt manageable in comparison. It's impossible to live for two decades like that, materially and emotionally deprived of the slightest comfort, terrified of the next insult, of the next time someone throws a blanket over your head, and then just suddenly drop the bad feelings because a cute little Ivy gives you a full scholarship. This is why, as I mentioned in the introduction, I can't always agree with those of my colleagues who rail against neoliberalism and biopolitics with such rancor that they make it sound like these are the worst things that could ever happen to a person. I know that there are worse things. And even though it's true that even my formative experiences can't necessarily be entirely dissociated from the dominant ethos of neoliberalism and biopolitics, I don't think that they can be reduced to or fully explained by this ethos either.

Despite the fact that I've adopted a loosely Foucauldian approach in the first four chapters of this book—that I'm in many ways staging a critique of neoliberalism and biopolitics—I'm aware that the problem with this approach is that it all too easily turns everyone into a sufferer: a wounded creature whose existence is threatened by a whole host of invisible forces; it suggests that subjectivity *as such* is a matter of being traumatized.

This renders the concept of trauma so capacious that it becomes virtually meaningless. This is why I want to preface the rest of my commentary by clearly stating that I believe that there are more difficult things in the world than being brainwashed to work hard and stay positive.

LOVING ONE'S FATE (OR NOT)

Trauma in its various manifestations interests me, as does the relationship between traumatization and the singularity of who we become. Nietzsche famously argued that those who are strong love their fate, however traumatizing this fate might be. Instead of fleeing from their fate, they would choose the same fate again (and again and again) because they know that this fate is what has made them who they are. They wouldn't want to be anyone else so they wouldn't want a different past; no matter how awful this past might have been, they would want to live it again exactly in the same way in order to arrive exactly at where and who they are right now.

Here is one of Nietzsche's formulations of this love of fate, of *amor fati*: "I want to learn more and more to see as beautiful what is necessary in things; then I shall be one of those who make things beautiful. *Amor fati*: let that be my love henceforth! I do not want to wage war against what is ugly. I do not want to accuse; I do not even want to accuse those who accuse. *Looking away* shall be my only negation. And all in all and on the whole: some day I wish to be only a Yes-sayer."[6]

I remember being riveted when the charismatic Eric Downing, my spectacular professor at Harvard, quoted this passage in class. A chill went down my spine—the kind that tells you that something extraordinary is happening—and I remember thinking that being blessed enough to sit in that lecture hall that day, hearing that sentence by Nietzsche delivered so exquisitely, made up for those wretched tear-filled years before America. Even now, two decades later, when I pass that lecture hall (I've recently had an office in the same building), I vividly remember (and I remember few things vividly) Eric leaning against his desk in a relaxed way—the way professors do when they feel at ease in front of their students—and opening *The Gay Science* to read those lines in his mesmerizing voice, a voice that dropped into a half-whisper whenever he was quoting something life altering. The room fell absolutely still: fifty bodies quietly alert. I remember how at that moment everything crystallized into the realization that *this is what it means to be alive.*

Did I refunction suffering that day? Perhaps. I suspect that when it comes to fate, Freud had a better idea than Nietzsche: instead of loving your (bleak) fate, you can remake it by talking to a stranger who (mostly) listens silently—that is, by entering analysis. For me, this started the day I sat sobbing on a curb in Jamaica Plain (Boston) when my friend Doreen said, "You *have* to see someone. I'll get you some names." I didn't have the money to pay for it, but I started analysis anyway. For the first eighteen months, I cried every day, usually on the floor of my bathroom because that's where the toilet tissue was, usually having absolutely no idea why. I was paying someone, going deeper into debt, in order to cry. One day I cried so hard that I cracked a molar. But it was the right thing to do because it was the beginning of a new destiny: I remade my fate by crying so that I no longer have to cry.

The analyst who (mostly) listened silently while I, in a shaky voice, talked about the cold house by the mysterious lake died shortly after I moved to Toronto. When I—back in Cambridge—walk past her house, I thank her for her incredible gift: she didn't tell me that she was dying of cancer because this would have made my anguish look so insignificant that I would have instantly stopped talking about it.

This incredible woman allowed me to understand that trauma can be transmitted intergenerationally, that a lot of what I experienced in relation to my father he had probably experienced when he was a child, raised in poverty by an overly critical mother and a reckless, alcoholic father, and tormented by five older brothers, four of whom would end up with the sad fates I've mentioned (two died young, one was crippled in the war, and the intensely intelligent one became schizophrenic). My father was the youngest of eight children and in so many ways, he was the only one who made it, who managed to carve out a livable life for himself. There were crushing disappointments along the way. I'm sure he felt like sobbing much of the time but didn't. If someone gave me a choice between his life and mine, I would take mine.

I also realize that if my father tried to crush my ambitions early, it's probably not because he actually thought that I was stupid but because he was deathly afraid that I might follow in the footsteps of my schizophrenic uncle. I know that I don't have half of my uncle's brainpower. But this might have been hard for my father to judge, for my grades were high. And I know from an old photo of my uncle that back then I looked a lot like he did before he fell ill during his first year at the University of Helsinki (the family had invested in him to be the one to get an education; after what happened to him, no one else dared to try until I did). Otherwise too I was a lot like him after I learned to read (which, due to slight dyslexia, was late): during summer breaks from school, I rode my bike on the dusty dirt road to the library seven kilometers away to secure a stack of books that I would then devour in a couple of days, often reading late into the night.

This aggravated my father. He didn't like the bookishness. In his roundabout way, he was trying to protect me; he didn't want me to end up like my uncle. So I applied to Brown without telling him. One day I stood in the kitchen and said, "There's this college in America. It's perched on a hill in Providence, Rhode Island, which is a state between New York and Boston. It's beautiful. Lots of smart people go there. It costs more than $40,000 a year (this was the 1980s). But they gave me the money. I don't know why—they might have made a mistake—but they did. So I'm going." I have no recollection of what he said, what either of my parents said. I have no idea how they felt. But they let me go without an argument. I now know that this was a gift.

I also now know that my sudden departure was hard on my already deeply depressed mother. Her background was materially even more challenging than my father's. My father's family was poor but they owned land, which was meaningful even if making a living from that land was virtually impossible, the climate not being conducive to growing things. In contrast, my mother's parents didn't own anything. She grew up in a tiny cottage, living mostly on the fish that her father caught in a nearby lake (there's always a nearby lake in Finland). She was severely dyslexic and because no one at that time knew about the condition, the other kids in her school ridiculed her for being stupid. They used to stuff her into the communal mailbox—which was large enough for a small child—and then sit on the lid (her version of being asphyxiated). Her teachers tried to break her aversion to milk by forcing her to drink it, so she vomited every day at lunch. Her mother died of cancer when she was a teenager. She had many reasons to be depressed.

It didn't help that at the age of twenty, she met my father and immediately got pregnant with me, which more or less ruined her life. Even her body rejected me due to different blood types (rhesus factors) so that she threw up for nine months (just like she had in elementary school) while waiting for my arrival. I was an alien, poisonous entity in her body that made her sick. She then lived for seven years under the same roof as my father's censorious mother, learning to take up as little space as possible, until my grandmother's death put her in charge of taking care of my schizophrenic uncle and making sure that we had bread and cheese to eat.

Because I didn't know then about things like depression, I didn't realize that my mother's indifference toward me arose from it rather than from a lack of love. So when I crossed the Atlantic, I assumed that she simply didn't care: I rarely visited and never called or wrote, once falling entirely silent for seven years. Neither of my parents speaks a word of English, so they had no way of tracking me down through the universities I attended; for all they knew, I could have joined a convent. There were long periods, months at a time, when I callously forgot that they existed: I freed myself to live a new life by never thinking about the old one.

After my first year at Brown, I had also forgotten much of my Finnish (who wants to keep speaking the language of hell when one has been handed the keys to paradise?): it took me a few weeks back at home to speak fluently again. These days I don't forget the language but I do forget lots of words, and I speak it with a weird American intonation. This must be surreal to witness as a parent. But they never complain. Now that I have some perspective on this—now that I have friends with over-bearing parents—I know that this too is a gift.

My mother is no longer depressed, though she remains pessimistic. We get along. We chat about this and that in the sauna, just the two of us. When I took her to Thailand for her seventieth birthday (her first time to Asia), she was so excited that she barely slept the whole trip. As we walked for hours and hours in the Bangkok heat, I kept asking her if she needed to rest. "*No way*—let's go back to Chinatown!" The other day she told me on the phone (these days I call twice a year—there's still plenty of room for improvement on this) that she's been climbing the mountain at the far end of the wheat field—the one my aunt ran across with bombs exploding around her— several times a week because "one's gotta stay fit for ballroom dancing." She may be the toughest person I know. Now that I understand her better than I did even a decade ago, I know that I received a lot of good things from her, including a sizeable serving of the *sisu* that I talked about above.

Trauma is complicated. The people who traumatize you don't always mean to do so. Sometimes they can't cope because your arrival has ruined their life. Sometimes they're too depressed to care. Sometimes they themselves have been too badly traumatized. In addition to abject poverty, family tragedies, and considerable physical abuse, both of my parents grew up in environments filled with what Eve Sedgwick calls *zingers*: emotional snubs, brush-offs, or mortifications that are casually delivered but that leave the recipient reeling from pain.[7] Some zingers are unexpected, shocking in their abruptness. Others may be expected, yet no less upsetting for being predictable.

The psychoanalyst Margaret Crastnopol evocatively describes such jolts to the self as "little murders," explaining that such microtraumas tear the fabric of relationships; they corrode the quality of everyday life by communicating envy, hatred, ridicule, indifference, or abandonment.[8] Some of these little murders are intended, but others are inadvertent. Sometimes they accumulate silently, like layer upon layer of dust in an attic, the danger being that if you drop a match there by mistake, the whole building will go up in flames. Other times they are identifiable but seem insignificant: mere mild annoyances that we think we should be able to brush off easily. But when repeated over time, they bruise the psyche, eroding our self-esteem and basic sense of goodness.

Both of my parents were used to speaking in zingers because that was the language that surrounded them. Zingers can be buried in seemingly benign statements, including jokes. Crastnopol gives the example of a young man whose father delivered damning judgments under the guise of jests, such as "Watch out, kiddo—what woman will want to marry someone as clownish as you?"[9] My father had his own version of the same zinger: whenever I visited from graduate school, he told me that I would never have a boyfriend. When I told him that I actually had one, he responded with a dismissive "Sure, oh sure." The implication was that I was inventing a boyfriend because, having been deemed unlovable by the time I was seven, I obviously couldn't have one.

However, not all microtraumas are inflicted by the more powerful on the less powerful. Crastnopol remarks that children can grate on the nerves of their parents in various ways, especially when there's a difference of basic dispositions, so that, for instance, a hugely animated child can exhaust an introvert parent. I often think that this may have been what I did to my already dog-tired father when I was a child, which then caused him to lash out with accusations of uselessness in an attempt to suppress what must, from his shattered perspective, have seemed like excessive buoyancy.

Trauma isn't always a sudden occurrence that leaves us defeated. Often it's gradual, incremental. It can consist of collective forms of injustice, such as sexism or racism, that leave a permanent mark. Or it can consist of more or less acute forms of interpersonal traumatization, such as take place in dysfunctional families. Even microtraumas over time contribute to the unique texture that becomes our "personality," our default way of experiencing and responding to the world. In this sense, who we are has a great deal to do with how we have been wounded.

What critics of neoliberalism and biopolitics get right is that our society's ideology of good performance, high productivity, constant self-improvement, and relentless cheerfulness blithely ignores this. Instead, it focuses on enjoyment, touting the message that whatever else we do with our lives, we must find a way to enjoy ourselves; we must live our lives to the fullest, take advantage of every opportunity, distil the nectar out of every moment. This can lead to the paradoxical situation that we pursue enjoyment so relentlessly, moving from one site of pleasure to the next so quickly, that we lose our capacity to actually enjoy anything; we end up squandering our energies in a futile attempt to catch up with satisfactions that forever flee us. And in the process we suppress the damage done by traumas, often even falling into cruelly optimistic scenarios where we hope that a traumatizing scenario—say, a frustrating career path—will eventually make us happy.

THE ATTRITION OF LIFE

At the beginning of this chapter, I mentioned that Berlant's analysis of cruel optimism implies that there's something about our cultural moment that is unnecessarily abrasive, that bad feelings such as depression and anxiety are in part at least a response to collective forces of traumatization. On the one hand, as I've emphasized, it's part of the human condition to feel lacking, out of joint, off center, and self-alienated. From this condition, to which I'll return toward the end of this book, there's no escape. On the other hand, Berlant suggests that there's something about contemporary life that harms us in ways that are perhaps more comparable to the damage done by dys-functional families than to the damage done by the insecurities of the human condition, that add a coating of (unnecessary and potentially avoidable) discontent to the existential (unavoidable) discontent of life.

Even though I keep cautioning against drawing easy paral-lels about neoliberalism and biopolitics on the one hand and acutely traumatizing personal histories on the other, I agree with Berlant that our neoliberal moment is characterized by a general attrition of life that impacts especially those who are barely scraping by—not the least because neoliberal competi-tiveness augments social inequalities—but also those of the creative, intellectual, or professional middle class who can frac-ture under the pressures of our society's performance principle and its related utilitarian demands.[10] From this point of view, bad feelings such as depression, anxiety, sluggishness, weari-ness, apathy, and loss of meaning are less a personal pathology than affects that seem to cling to the very air we breathe and that consequently besiege people from all walks of life.

For many people, bad feelings seem to be an ordinary reality, a banal backdrop to quotidian life. Sometimes such feelings are pronounced, as is the case with acute depression; other times, they throb at a low level, as is the case with diffuse anxiety. One reason that so many of us fall into cruel optimism is that our fantasies of future rescue make our bad feelings more palatable: we're able to tolerate a dreadful present as long as there's hope that things will improve in the future.

Sometimes cruel optimism even locks us into patterns of living in which the very thing that seems to make our lives possible—a job, a lover, a way of doing things—is simultaneously a source of suffering. In such instances, we're so attached to a *form* of life (such as the ideal of intimacy) that we can't discard it even when the *content* of this life (such as a toxic intimate relationship) hurts us;[11] we're so committed to the maintenance of our ideal that we stick to it even when it causes discontent. Often this is because such a form of life or ideal grants us a sense of belonging and personal continuity (an intelligible identity), because it's socially recognized, predictable in its conventionality; the routines of everyday life, including the fantasies of the good life that we've inherited from our society, allow us to contain some of our bad feelings. At the same time, these very routines can hold us faithful to scenarios of living that in the long run actually make us feel worse.

Many of us stage a variety of ambivalent and incoherent attempts to forge a viable life in the context of circumstances that, for one reason or another, keep failing us. We repair and rebuild lives that have in one way or another been torn apart. We seek little pleasures that render our lives more bearable: food, drugs, alcohol, television, spacing out, daydreaming about a better life, and so on. Berlant offers the example of overeating, which she calls "slow death," as a common strategy of seeking gratification, noting that it's what's left of the good life for many American workers.[12] The slow death of overeating, like other forms of self-medication, can be a response to stressful work conditions and other forms of deprivation. It can also be an attempt (even if only unconsciously) to defy either the overwhelming rhythm of jobs that demand speed, efficiency, and constant vigilance or the tedious rhythm of jobs that consist of repetitive tasks and monotonous moods; it can be a way to introduce pockets of satisfaction into an otherwise tedious day.

The contemporary rate of working wears us out and erodes the quality of our lives. Many of us have accepted this as how things are—as how they're always going to be—but there are consequences to living in a society that's calculated to extort inhuman exertion from human beings. Eating is one of the only reliable pleasures we have, which is why so many people turn to it even if doing so in the end merely gives rise to more bad feelings. In this sense, it's less a sign of weakness than a fairly reasonable effort to create much-needed moments of respite. Berlant aptly describes overeating as a means of taking "small vacations" from the need to remain a responsible and conscientious person, of "coasting" in a "space between pleasure and numbness."[13]

The same could be said of many of our other coping mechanisms, such as binging on television or alcohol addiction. Indeed, as Brock Hessel points out, against the backdrop of the performance principle of neoliberal society, addiction may be less a matter of misspent time than an attempt to use time in more pleasurable ways; it's an alternative way to structure a life.[14] We're trained to regard addiction as pathological, yet if we're willing to discard our society's dominant happiness scripts for a moment, it's possible to view it as a form of social rebellion, of refusing to live in the way that modern society asks us to live: rushed, stressed out, and constantly on call.

When it comes to bad feelings, neoliberal culture is paradoxical: on the one hand, its ethos of performance, productivity, self-improvement, and cheerfulness can generate the kinds of bad feelings that exceed the "normal" malaise of the human condition; on the other, because bad feelings seem antithetical to the happiness scripts of this culture, including its valorization of positive thinking, it does everything in its power to pathologize them and to suppress their outward expression. We thus have a situation where a hyperbolic culture of positivity produces bad feelings that it then tells us are unacceptable, a misstep that needs to be fixed. But there's a point beyond which it's no longer possible to hide the contradictions of the situation: the more our culture views bad feelings as a problem that needs a solution, the more it ends up calling attention to the fact that so many people these days feel bad, with the result that its creed of cheerfulness begins to fray around the edges. This is one reason that the doctrine of positivity can feel so fake.

The doctrine of positivity arguably functions as a manic defense against bad feelings. Those who are grinning may be weeping inside. Interestingly, the opposite is usually not the case: those who are weeping are probably not grinning inside. It's easier to simulate positive feelings than to suppress negative ones. Our commercial culture in turn likes simulation: it tells us that we can hide our physical "flaws" by wearing the right makeup and clothing; and it assures us that we can hide our insecurity by a façade of confidence, our disconnectedness by the latest version of the iPhone, and our fatigue by a combination of concealer and caffeine. No wonder, then, that it also tells us that we can surmount our bad feelings by producing the outward signifiers of good feelings, that if we simply just keep smiling, eventually we'll become happy. Yet its attempts to replace bad feelings by the mantra of happiness is just a tad too adamant, a tad too desperate. This is why it strikes a flat note, why some of us are not convinced.

2

THE RATIONALIZATION
OF INTIMACY

Aparticularly pronounced aspect of our society's utilitarian pragmatism is its rationalization of intimacy.[1] This may at first glance seem like a bizarre statement, for the ideology of romantic love—of soulmates and the happily ever after—that surrounds us may appear like the very antithesis of pragmatism: unquestionably, lavish celebrity weddings, Hollywood movies, daytime soaps, teen shows, and women's magazines keep alive the most saccharine themes of fairytale romance. Yet even this emphasis on love's glittery aspects can't entirely conceal the fact that the ethos of efficiency that characterizes the rest of our society has increasingly become the status quo of intimacy as well, as is evident from the popularity of online dating sites. Indeed, the most common response to a romantic disappointment these days seems to be to join a dating site, which—as is appropriate for a thoroughly commercial culture—gives you access to hundreds of choices, allowing you to sample potential partners in the same way as you might sample ice cream flavors at a Ben & Jerry's.

It's interesting to think about this relatively recent change in our collective understanding of how intimacy works. Finding love used be something people left to chance, even if they did often try to augment their odds of finding the right person by frequenting venues where potential partners might circulate, such as gyms and bars. Romantic love as a matter of "chance" (of fate) was in fact one way Westerners distinguished their culture from cultures—frequently arrogantly coded as "backward" for this very reason—that arrange marriages. In contrast, these days online dating sites do this arranging unapologetically and with an efficacy that parents who attempt to arrange the marriages of their children can't always attain because they run into resistance from their sons and daughters. On internet dating sites there's no such resistance. Both parties eagerly agree to having their marriage arranged by a third party. This is an excellent example of how biopolitical control operates. As I've noted, it causes us to *want* the regulation it offers.

My aim is not to moralize about online dating sites. I merely want to call attention to the intensification of levelheaded rationalism in our daily lives. If in earlier times those who failed to find partners resigned themselves to the idea that it just wasn't meant to be, today there's a straightforward solution: fill out a detailed online questionnaire; once you have found someone suitable, follow a set of dating rules (devised by dating experts) that are designed to guarantee your romantic success; make sure you don't waste time on dead-end relationships that don't lead to the altar; and once you've reached the altar, work diligently to make sure that your marriage endures because if it doesn't, you'll have squandered your resources on something that doesn't, after all, contribute to the good life you're striving for.

One reason that conservative factions of our culture frown on divorce—making it sound like broken marriages erode the foundations of our social order—is that divorce makes things messy. It derails your good performance, high productivity, and plans for self-improvement (so I suppose its critics are right: it does in fact erode the social order). And it wrecks your mood, filling your mind with bad feelings rather than positive thinking. Marriage, in contrast, supposedly prevents all manner of personal disasters, keeping you on track, ensuring that you perform, produce, improve yourself, and smile regularly.

We all know that marriage doesn't always accomplish this, that it's not always the haven of harmony that our culture portrays it to be. Yet the idea that marriage will lead to the good life is among the most powerful of our society's happiness scripts. And it offers a clear illustration of the predicament I described in the last chapter, namely that we can become so invested in our favorite happiness scripts that we don't question them even when they don't deliver the happiness they promise: most people who manage to get out of a terrible marriage are eager to reenter the institution, assuming that *this time* they can make it work; most people don't question the presumed connection between marriage and happiness but merely their capacity to play out the marriage plot in the right way. This may be cruel optimism at its purest: your ex made you despondent but *surely* your new wife will make you "the luckiest man in the world" that your best man declares you to be, conveniently forgetting that he declared the same thing at your first wedding a decade ago; surely you'll prove the accuracy of the idea that married people are happier, healthier, and more balanced than single people.

MARRIAGE AS A PRIVILEGED GOAL

In every society, the promise of happiness clings to particular goals—goals that are deemed necessary for the attainment of the good life—so that those who are perceived as falling short of such goals are also perceived as falling short of happiness. In our society, marriage, with its expectation of lifelong monogamy and reproductive success, is such a privileged goal. This is why many social critics, including Foucault, have portrayed marriage as a means of producing citizens who behave in relatively predictable, relatively reliable ways—ways that facilitate the smooth functioning of the political and economic system. According to this line of reasoning, the glossy covers of bridal magazines, the extravagant wedding dress, the merry activity that goes into planning a wedding, and the mountain of gifts that accumulates on the display table on the appointed day are merely a charming front for the less attractive, rationally calculated realities brewing beneath, including the profit our economy makes not just from the machinery of weddings but also from managing to create a workforce that goes to bed early, works industriously, and—eventually—starts spending money on diapers, trolleys, model trains, and cute little frocks.

The idea that married people are more productive than single people is of course not necessarily true. I'm not saying that marriage actually generates a reliable workforce but merely that our society draws a link between marriage and high performance, at least in the case of men (with women, things are iffier in the sense that married women are often seen as a potential liability for the companies that employ them because they may ask for maternity leave and—so the worried reasoning goes—begin to miss days at work when their children get sick). This is why Foucault saw marriage as a matter of economic rationalization. He—rightly or wrongly—argued that marriage cuts the need for constant negotiation between partners. Unlike people who move from partner to partner, those who have been married for a long time can take shortcuts in communication: I pass the salt, you pass the pepper;[2] you load the dishwasher, I have sex with you.

Foucault also argued that it's in the cradle of married life that future producers are nurtured, noting particularly the assumption that children who have been well mothered are going to possess the psychological qualities demanded of today's workers. This is why the ideal of being a good mother is a major element of our society's biopolitical agenda: even a mother who is herself a producer is still expected to raise future producers. The conservative Right would prefer these producers to be men so that women can stay at home and devote all of their energies to the nurturing of future (male) workers. Those with more liberal views don't demonize women who work, but many do frown on frazzled working mothers who struggle with the herculean task of managing both work and family. This can be a sneaky means of sending women back home. The country's official rhetoric may be that women should be allowed to work, but the lack of affordable daycare facilities makes the daily lives of many working mothers so taxing that some are persuaded to give up their jobs.

The conservative Right draws the presumed connection between the stability of marriage and the stability of the social order explicitly. And it doesn't hesitate to defend this stability at the expense of women and children who suffer in patriarchal, inegalitarian—and sometimes even violent—marriages. The rest of our society is more squeamish about admitting that marriage is one of the lynchpins of biopolitical conditioning, that it's in the folds of marriage that the next generation is— usually (though no longer invariably)—taught the principles of performance, productivity, and self-improvement. If you're a girl, your daddy may also ask you to smile a lot (what your mommy thinks of this may remain undeclared). The details perhaps don't matter as much as the recognition that as much as marriage is marketed to us as the fulfillment of our romantic aspirations, it's also a way to rationalize intimacy, to channel intimacy into pathways that are politically and economically effective.

In calling attention to such practical considerations, I don't want to deny that fulfilling marriages exist: that so many people want to get married may not be entirely a matter of social conditioning; it implies that there's (at least sometimes) something genuinely satisfying about the institution. I also don't want to imply that building enduring intimate alliances is always misguided. I even agree with Todd McGowan that in the context of a consumer culture that encourages us to glide from one object of desire to the next as quickly as possible, sticking to one partner can be a spirited choice.[3]

Even though post-Foucauldian social critics tend to associate monogamy with conservative social arrangements,[4] one could argue that it can be a countercultural practice in the sense that it refuses the logic of accumulation that encourages us to privilege quantity over quality. Instead of accepting the idea that collecting more and more objects will grant us the fulfillment we're after, the monogamous stubbornly cling to their chosen object; they refuse the mentality that tells us that the shiny objects on offer "out there" are better than what we already have. I don't think that it's entirely unreasonable to assert that in a world that promises "seven times more second dates"—as one Match.com ad does—such faithfulness to one person constitutes a refreshingly steadfast act.

As much as consumer culture profits from marriage, it also likes the kind of mobile desire that can easily (and repeatedly) be redirected toward the new. This is why it markets not just marriage but also the romance, including the serial monogamy that's supposed to precede marriage, for romance almost automatically mobilizes desire. This may be one reason that our culture encourages dating a good sampling of partners before you settle down with "the one": you're supposed to test-drive the goods before you make your final purchase in order to make sure that you've made the right choice. On a recent visit to an elite New England college, a student told me that male students at the college routinely categorize their female peers as "dating material" or "marriage material," meaning that they often don't date the most desirable women because one day—in about a decade, I was told—they expect to marry these women. Talk about neoliberal efficiency having taken over even the most intimate details of people's lives!

Even when romance doesn't lead to such hunger for constant novelty (the gliding from partner to partner that's supposed to precede marriage but then miraculously come to an abrupt stop once the knot is tied), it's readily reconcilable with rampant commodification: from sappy Hallmark cards and extravagant bouquets of pink roses to expensive dates and diamond rings, consumer culture makes money from romance. It also makes money from the hypersexualization of our society. Although sexual liberation has certainly been a progressive development, and although I would never want to return to the sexual mores of yesteryear, particularly the restrictions on female sexuality that characterized those mores, it's important to acknowledge that it has been so thoroughly coopted by consumer culture—which promotes revealing clothes, glittering jewelry, sexy scents, lacy undergarments, pleasure-enhancing gadgets, and (of course) pornography—that it can hardly be considered a straightforward victory for those critical of the reach of biopolitics and consumer capitalism. As McGowan puts it, "Rather than harming capitalism, sexual liberation helped to save it."[5]

This may be a situation where consumer capitalism has figured out how to have it both ways; on the one hand, it makes money from the machinery of marriage and reproductive coupling; on the other, it sells romance and sexual liberation. As much as I hate to admit it, I see McGowan's point regarding the latter: it's true that some people consume sexual partners in the same way that I consume Lindt bars. The problem isn't that this is morally objectionable—I don't feel guilty about my Lindt bars—but that there seems to be no way to escape the commodification of intimacy: whichever way we choose to organize our relationships, consumer culture finds ways to turn them into profit.

This being the case, it's pointless to argue that getting married is somehow intrinsically more regressive than staying single (or vice versa). A lot depends on how one chooses to be married (or single). I also don't want to deny that love can add luster to our lives. Over the years, I've written extensively about the life-altering potential of love, including the ways in which it jolts us out of complacency, enables us to resist the daily grind, and allows us to stay connected to the more intense frequencies of life. I've argued, following Alain Badiou, that falling in love can be a revelatory "event," an experience that drastically reconfigures the basic coordinates of our entire being.[6] I even believe that when love summons us in this transcendent manner, the worst we could do would be to betray it by disavowing its power to transform us.

It would consequently be hard for anyone who has read my prior work to accuse me of being down on love. It's just that I'm suspicious of the instrumentalization of relationality that has overtaken our society. Furthermore, if I'm suspicious of the ways in which consumer society profits from romance and sexual liberation, I remain even more suspicious of the valorization of marriage as a privileged goal, of the idea that, sexual sampling aside, marriage ultimately is the only way to forge truly meaningful intimacy.

One of the main reasons for my antipathy for the ideology of marriage is that—as I'll demonstrate in the next two chapters— it tends to be directly linked to the naturalization of gender differences, to the notion that men are one way and women an altogether other way, that I find so aggravating. As a matter of fact, the student who told me about women who are marriage material specified that these women are the ones who, in addition to sitting on trust funds (modern-day dowries), refuse to participate in the hookup culture of his college. This immediately illustrates how antiquated gendered thinking—in this case, the idea that good girls don't (or shouldn't)—enters the picture the minute marriage takes center stage. Still, if you're happily married, I have no quarrel with you. Rather, my quarrel in this chapter is with those who stay married even when they're miserable, who continue to abide by the ideology of marital bliss even when it has become clear that this ideology has led them astray.

THE INVISIBILITY OF IDEOLOGY

I'll come back to miserable marriages later in this chapter. But first I want to provide some commentary on how ideology, including the ideology of gendered thinking that I'll criticize in chapters 3 and 4, functions. The most important thing to understand is that I'm using the notion of ideology in a way that's perhaps more common among academics than among those outside the academy: ideology as synonymous with our most taken-for-granted assumptions about what it means to be a human being and how collective life should be organized.[7] In other words, ideology is not always a repressive machinery that brainwashes us in the manner that, say, Hitler's fascism or

Stalin's communism did, or that ISIS seems to do today. Sometimes it infiltrates our minds softly, without any obvious political hullabaloo, giving us the values, beliefs, and ideals we live by.

Moreover, not all social ideologies are harmful. Some of our values—such as the idea that it's wrong to torture people, that hospitality is a virtue, or that generosity is admirable—are arguably well worth defending. Still, it's eye opening to realize that more or less every aspect of our lives, including the way we talk, walk, and carry our bodies, has been ideologically determined. This in many ways is exactly what Foucault means by biopolitical conditioning.

Many of us understand intuitively how collective values, beliefs, and ideals enter our minds; we understand that many components of human life are due to nurture rather than nature. But how is it that ideology enters even our bodies? Hilary Neroni gives a poignant example of this process when she explains that up until the middle of the twentieth century, most societies expected women to ride sidesaddle.[8] Logically, this is a preposterous endeavor: you're awkwardly trying to balance yourself on top of a horse in a weirdly lopsided manner, with both of your legs on one side of the horse. Neroni notes that this style of riding often led to injuries because it made it impossible for women to adequately control their horses. So what could possibly cause anyone to insist that women should ride this way?

Neroni rightly observes that social ideals of femininity were to blame: riding astride was considered unladylike, unruly, and overly sexual. In hindsight, it's easy to see that the sidesaddle was a material object produced by gendered ideology: it reinforced the notion that women's bodies needed to be constrained and controlled, as they also were through female attire such as corsets.

Although it may be tempting to think that we have progressed beyond such ridiculously heteropatriarchal ideologies,

today's women—myself included—routinely squeeze themselves into clothing styles and high heels that seriously restrict
their movement. There are mornings when I think, "I'm going
to have to walk a lot today so I shouldn't wear that narrow skirt
because it forces me to take such small steps." Sometimes I
wear it anyway and then later curse my decision because I can't
break into a run even though I'm late for a meeting: I'm skilled
at sprinting in high heels but draw a line at hiking up my tube
skirt in the middle of campus.

I recently gave a keynote address at a conference. The orga-
nizers had generously arranged things so that those of us who
were giving invited lectures had a driver shuttling us between
the conference site and our hotel. He was driving one of those
huge SUVs that stand high off the ground. The first morning
of the conference—the morning of my keynote—I didn't yet
know what the car was going to be like, so I was wearing one of
my narrow skirts, with the result that I couldn't climb onto my
seat. After several pathetic attempts, I asked the driver and my
esteemed colleagues—whom I had just met, so this was a little
embarrassing—to look the other way while I lifted my skirt to
my waist and clambered in.

What happened to me? I asked myself. I grew up as a tomboy,
roaming the woods of Finland, carrying a bow and arrow,
pretending—because I didn't yet know about colonialism as a
problem—to be the Tarzan of my Nordic jungle. So why the
hell was I wearing such an absurd skirt? The obvious answer is
that, despite my feminism, I haven't been able to dodge cultural
ideals of femininity, particularly of professional femininity.

Sartorial ideology may seem shallow and in some ways it is:
most of us don't find it *impossible* to change what we wear.
However, some women find it hard to wear flats even when
their feet hurt. And many women put on makeup before going
to the gym even though they know that they'll take a shower

afterward (which means that they'll have to reapply their makeup). Indeed, some women find it more or less intolerable to appear in public without makeup, even if they're just going to the corner store for some bread.

This is a banal example that illustrates the power of ideology quite starkly: consider the degree of social conditioning that is required to cause some women to spend ten minutes putting on makeup so that they can make a five-minute trip to a store where only the person who works there—and perhaps a neighbor who happens to enter the store at the same time—is likely to see them. The one thing that's certain is that no little girl came out of the womb being terrified of being caught in public without eyeliner and mascara. Only social ideology can explain this terror.

Ideology produces our culture's dominant happiness scripts, discretely closing off alternatives, so that it's not just that we end up doing things in a certain way but that we're literally incapable of doing them in another way. I had a vivid reminder of this in graduate school when a performance artist who specializes in coaching transsexuals to pass in their chosen gender visited one of my seminars. Perhaps because of my pronounced normative femininity—I was wearing heels, a miniskirt, and makeup—the artist chose me as the person who should learn the tricks of passing as a guy. My first task was to try to walk like a man. I'm not endowed with rounded hips so there was in principle nothing to prevent me from doing the straight guy walk. But I failed miserably: I simply couldn't make my body perform the expected motions.

I also failed at all other attempts to take up physical space like a guy. For instance, I didn't know how to sit with enough confidence, the way guys sit on airplanes when their elbows intrude into your space so that you end up leaving the plane with a backache because you've just sat crooked for six hours. Some of them blame their wide shoulders but I know that it's (often unconscious because it's completely taken for granted) masculine entitlement that makes them do this. I've rarely sat next to a woman, however large, who does the same. This is why I silently thank the airline gods when the person sitting next to me on a long trip is a woman. And I wonder about the anxious battle of wills that must be taking place when two men sit next to each other. Is the one who withdraws his elbow a "pussy"?

I also failed at our class experiment because I kept smiling too much. "If you don't wipe that smile off your face, no one is ever going to believe you're a guy," my coach told me. In the years since then, I've often thought about this assessment, aware that I tend to smile readily and wondering how I came to adopt this attitude. I doubt I was "born that way." And I certainly didn't pick up the habit from my grim Scandinavian family. I in fact recall that when I visited Finland after my first year in the United States, my father was horrified because— this was his damning appraisal—I was suddenly smiling like "one of those phony Americans" (to his consternation, I was also suddenly speaking with my hands). It's true that Americans smile more than Scandinavians. But American women probably smile more than American men. This is definitely not because of their female genes, as is proven by the fact that if you give an average American man and an average Finnish woman a point for every time they smile spontaneously, the guy is likely to win by a wide margin.

I'll return to women and smiling in the next chapter. For now, I want to note that American gender socialization often starts before the child is even born in the sense that many parents decorate nurseries and purchase toys based on the gender of the child they're expecting, so that when the child leaves the hospital, he or she immediately encounters either a blue and steely world of trains, Lego sets, and miniature police cars or a pink and fluffy world of Barbie dolls, stuffed animals, and miniature teacups. During a recent trip to a local store, I noticed that the woman in front of me in line was carrying an enormous collection of enigmatic pink items. When she got to the register, the clerk behind the counter said, "Oh, it must be a girl!" "Yes, I'm going to my friend's baby shower," the woman gleefully responded.

Despite what I just said about torture being wrong, I felt like decapitating and dismembering the pink-clad (I think even the miniscule shoes were pink) Barbie doll in this woman's frothy bundle of girly objects. I felt dreadful for the girl about the enter the world because I know that she won't have much of a chance against the tyranny of the cultural cookie cutter that stubbornly produces normative boys and girls, Kens and Barbies, in a society that otherwise touts an ideology of "individuality," "freedom," and "choice." Some children of course do rebel. Nor do all parents participate in the charade of coercive gendering. But, overall, it's virtually impossible to escape gender conditioning in this society. Importantly, children realize early that deviations from dominant gender scripts will be punished; they understand that nonconformity will result in social ostracism and ridicule.

As the personal anecdotes I've offered reveal, I haven't escaped gender socialization. Some of it, like my style of walking and taking up space, I must have learned in Finland. But much of it I picked up relatively late, after arriving in the United States, with the result that it's mostly limited to attire. I started wearing miniskirts in college as an angry feminist statement after a year in Tanzania, where I had constantly been told—by white American men, who seemed to be the only ones who cared—that showing my legs was culturally inappropriate. Graduate school added high heels, bold red lipstick, and plenty of black skimpy outfits to the repertoire after I realized that these were the uniform of every aspiring female theorist of the poststructuralist denomination, and certainly of every female Lacanian. One time when my cousin (by no means a prude) picked me up from the Helsinki airport, she took one horrified look at me and told me that I looked like a hooker. I insisted that I looked like a Harvard student (which I did).

My point is that I learned fairly quickly what I was supposed to look like in order to blend into my new environment. But this didn't impact the psychological, emotional, and sexual attitudes that I had developed much earlier, which means that I've managed to confuse quite a few of the American men I've dated: the usual assumption that if it walks like a duck it's a duck doesn't hold in my case in the sense that I look, talk, and walk like a (normatively feminine) woman but often don't think, feel, or act in ways that (American) woman are expected to. It has been interesting to watch men grapple with these discrepancies: some have been thrilled; others have been disappointed. My blunt assessment is that many (not all but many) straight American men may say that they want a straightforward relationship but that secretly they relish it when their girlfriends are complicated and titillatingly cryptic and elusive. Taylor Swift (whose album I'm listening to as I write these lines) neatly sums up my unofficial anthropological research among American men: "Boys only want love if it's torture."[9]

As I've mentioned, the Finnish society I grew up in didn't pay much attention to gender. Even the language, which contains everyday words (you'll need to roll the *r*'s) like *raparperipiirakka*, *kirkasääninen*, *aamuaurinkoinen*, and *kesämökkiläinen*—it's only now that I have trouble reading a Finnish newspaper that I can see how incredibly insane the language looks—is entirely non-gendered, to the point that there's only one pronoun for *he* or *she*: *hän*. In retrospect I can only marvel at how little I thought about gender before arriving in the United States.

I remember that when I was thirteen, my parents told me that they needed my help because they had guests arriving that night. They gave me a choice of tasks: do the dishes or mount the snow tires on my father's pickup truck (to this day, I don't know why the latter needed to get done that very day). I said I wanted to deal with the tires. My father showed me how and then left me to it. An hour later he returned to make sure that the bolts were tight enough. This is one of the fondest memories I have of him. He said, "Well done," and that was that. There was no commentary on the oddness of my choice. My father was far from being a feminist for the simple reason that few people in Finland, and certainly not men specializing in odd jobs in rural regions, thought of gender in those terms during the 1970s. He might be more of a feminist now that the country has become Americanized regarding gender in the same way that it has become Americanized about so many other things; to my father's credit, he has never been a misogynist. In recent years, I've heard him say some things that make me think that he might be a pretty good feminist, though he wouldn't necessarily call himself that.

My gender-neutral upbringing, which was at that time by no means an unusual upbringing for a Scandinavian girl, is what caused the culture shock about American conceptions of gender that I described in the introduction to this book. It's a culture shock that I've never fully gotten over because, really, I don't want to. I don't want to make assumptions about people based on gender for the same reason that I don't want to make assumptions about them based on race, ethnicity, or religion.

Doing so is invasive, even aggressive, as the following anecdote illustrates.

Two decades after my father showed me how to change a tire, my then-boyfriend and I got a flat on I-95 in upstate Maine. The state troopers chanced upon the scene when I was changing the tire while my boyfriend was (encouragingly) standing on the sidelines. The troopers broke into a tirade about the shame of my boyfriend "letting the lady do a man's work." Because they were carrying guns, I said nothing. But internally I was fuming not only because they were insulting my boyfriend but also because they were insulting me (the so-called "lady").

The naturalization of the ideology of gender differences is a significant part of biopolitical conditioning in most cultures, including American culture, and it contributes to the privileging of heterosexual marriage that I started to criticize at the beginning of this chapter. Because gendered codes of behavior are internalized early and largely unconsciously, they come to seem like they reflect inborn tendencies even if they're entirely learned. One common misconception about the nature versus nurture debate is that the results of nurture are easier to change than the results of nature. This isn't necessarily the case. Socially generated forms of behavior—including gendered behavior—are so thoroughly incorporated into our identities that being able to alter them would be akin to becoming a wholly different person.

That said, even Foucault admitted that biopolitical conditioning isn't entirely infallible, that dominant social ideologies aren't impermeable but contain gaps, fissures, and points of vulnerability that sometimes cause them to malfunction. Among other things, they tend to create their own resistances so that, for example, the attempt to control sexual behavior can generate a host of new sexual practices; when one pathway of sexual expression is cut off, people forge new pathways, thereby giving rise to a whole new array of sexual possibilities.[10] In this sense, every social restriction produces a set of counterforces.

This explains why we're able to question dominant social values, beliefs, and ideals; it explains why social change is possible. As a matter of fact, in large part thanks to feminism, American norms regarding gender (and sexuality) have changed so drastically in just a few decades that many of today's young women would find it difficult to fit into the gender system of the 1950s. In addition, the recent visible proliferation of alternative gender presentations, including genderqueer and transgender identities, indicates that the still dominant gender-bifurcated hetero-patriarchal order is eroding relatively rapidly right now.

While there have always been people in our society—particularly within the LGBTQ+ community—who have bravely defied prevailing ideals of gender, sometimes even risking their lives to do so, gender fluidity and gender variance are becoming increasingly common, with the result that our society's traditional ideology of gender is crumbling. It's definitely not going quietly, as I've begun to show in this chapter, and as I'll continue to show in the next two chapters. But I predict that in a few more decades it will seem as archaic as floppy discs, cassette players, and VCRs.

WHEN THE BOX FITS

I've written this book in the hope that I can, in however small a way, speed up the process of rendering gendered thinking obsolete. In this context, it's important to acknowledge that if social ideologies sometimes seem intractable, it's in part because accepting them brings tangible rewards: my willingness to wear narrow skirts, high heels, and MAC lipstick the shade of

"Cremesheen Speak Louder" makes my professional life easier because it fits the current image of a successful career woman.

The creators of this lipstick know what they're doing because I bought it, without paying attention to what it was called, at an airport right before giving a major talk: I knew that I was going to have to speak louder—both literally and metaphorically—and I was looking for the right portable phallus for the occasion; I knew that this lipstick would send the message I wanted to project, namely that I was confident and in control of my material. For the same reason, at the talk I wore my only pair of really expensive shoes: Armani boots that add two and a half inches to my height. Though some of the more frilly forms of fashion consciousness may keep women from being taken seriously in the workplace, its more streamlined forms have become the professional ideal, as is evident from the continual string of television shows—such as *The Good Wife*—that display professional women looking like they've stepped out of the pages of *Vogue*.

Walking into the ideological box that our collective mythologies invite us to enter is tempting because the box has been lined with all the goodies that supposedly make our lives meaningful. On one shelf glistens the promise of everlasting love and marital bliss, complete with a white picket fence, children's laughter, a dog, a cat, and a turtle. Those with a more modern mindset may find an upscale condo and a goldfish, but children's laughter is still a must. Another shelf strains under the weight of all the luxury items we could purchase if we became financially successful: enormous flat screen televisions, sparkling emerald necklaces, sleek designer watches, and youth-preserving facial creams distilled from the crushed testicles of oxen. Yet another broadcasts the rewards of education, exercise, networking, and hard work. And let's not forget about moderation and self-restraint: one scoop of mint chocolate chip ice cream is fine but three scoops are a prelude to a heart attack. Some passion is delightful but an excess of it can make you unhinged. And if you're going to fall in love, make sure that you don't overdo it by becoming one of those hapless people who love "too much."

As I've emphasized, our society is keen to see us cheerily boxed up because this keeps us productive. "Unbalanced" people don't make efficient workers, consumers, or citizens. Depressed people don't get out of bed in the morning. Grief-ridden people don't enjoy shopping. And people who eat too much, drink too much, smoke too much, or routinely let their passions get the better of them tax the healthcare system. Even those—usually women, the story goes—who love too much need a trip to the psychiatrist, especially when they can't keep their heads in their work; they mismanage important tasks because they daydream at their desks. But women who are so ambitious that they put their careers above love and relationships are an even bigger problem: they defy the "natural" order of things, particularly if they refuse to have children. And men who aren't ambitious enough challenge this order nearly as much because they fail at their expected role as "providers."

Musicians, artists, writers, and other creative types who don't like nine-to-five schedules are irresponsible unless, of course, they are hugely successful. Geniuses who insist on working in isolation are dangerously antisocial unless, of course, they win the Nobel Prize. Professionals who work around the clock are workaholics unless, of course, they make an obscene amount of money (here the ideal of moderation uncomfortably clashes with the ideal of constant striving).

Particularly troubling are people who fail to couple up "normally": durably, chastely, and fecundly within the sanctuary of marriage. Single women are selfish or emotionally damaged.

Promiscuous men are an unfortunate given, but promiscuous women are genuinely alarming: not only do they have an abnormal appetite for sex but they don't even require an emotional connection to enjoy it (what's up with that?). Men who "get" emotions (or worse, get excessively emotional) are almost as disconcerting, corroding the foundations of American manhood. Poor single mothers are a drain on the welfare system. Gays, lesbians, queers, and other sexual misfits are people who have refused to grow up; they're mocking God, breaking our collective backbone, and destroying the values that made America great. In sum, those who refuse to be programmed into conjugal, gender-bifurcated normalcy are seen as a social burden. They're an irritant on the national psyche, and the nation (naturally) strikes back with an impressive propaganda machine of self-help guides, inspirational speakers, religious leaders, magazine columnists, and faux scientists.

MARRIED WITH BENEFITS

Most Westerners who get married believe that they're making a free choice based on the fact that they're "in love." But from a biopolitical perspective, the decision to marry results from the invisible work of social ideology. If this were all we could say about marriage, there would be little reason to complain about it: after all, I've already conceded that getting married may, in its more innovative, socially progressive forms at least, be as good a way of going about intimate relating as any other. More generally speaking, I've admitted that some ideologies—collective values, beliefs, and ideals—are constructive, so that it would be unreasonable to criticize marriage just because it happens to be one of our society's ideals. Doing so would be like censoring the ideal of openness just because it happens to be an ideal that many

Americans uphold (or at least seemed to until the Trump administration turned it into a threat to national security).

However, the problem with the idealization of marriage is (at least) threefold. First, as I've already stressed, it's virtually impossible to dissociate this idealization from the ideology of bifurcated gender roles: the valorization of heterosexual marriage supports the naturalization of (supposedly complementary) gender differences (and vice versa). Second, when marriage is elevated above all other relational configurations, the latter are automatically devalued. And third, when marriage functions as the gold standard of personhood, as it arguably does in our cultural imagination, it's seen to complete your being, with the consequence that it brings concrete benefits that are denied single people: tax breaks, joint healthcare plans, cheaper vacation packages, and green cards.

The unequal access to green cards among married and single foreigners has always astonished me, probably because it has caused me so much personal grief. I find it odd that marrying an American gives you easy access to a green card whereas decades of work and taxation history and life building in the country count for *nothing* in the absence of an employer who is willing to sponsor your application (and could in fact work against you because these decades on various visas make you look vaguely suspicious). As I've mentioned, I've spent more of my life in the United States than in any other country. I feel thoroughly American—except for that bit about gender. However, as far as Homeland Security is concerned, this has no meaning whatsoever.

One of the most obvious manifestations of cruel optimism in my life has been that no matter how much I achieve professionally, no matter how many books I write, and no matter how seamlessly I assimilate myself into American society, Homeland

Security keeps barring any sense of belonging; whenever I cross the border, I may feel like I'm coming home, but most immigration officers treat me like I have absolutely no claim to the place. In August 2016, I was denied access to the United States (from ever-so-frightening Canada) because—even though I was carrying an offer of employment on Harvard letterhead which listed the dates of all my degrees and included a detailed account of why I was qualified to visit the university in 2016–2017—I wasn't carrying my PhD diploma. To say that this felt bad is an understatement. And it definitely doesn't make me feel better to know that asking one of my American friends to marry me would solve the problem.

I did eventually get through, after three harrowing days of collecting "documentation." Generally speaking, even though these days I carry a Canadian passport that (usually) grants me relatively easy access to the United States, I get panicky at U.S. border crossings because of my lengthy history of backroom interrogations with immigration officers who aren't legally obliged to give you any explanation for their decisions, including their decision to bar your entry into the country; it's hard to shed the dread of being kicked out of the life that I've meticulously fashioned for myself. Where would I go? Certainly not back to where I came from, as is the usual suggestion (by now I don't even know what that means—as far I'm concerned, New England is where I come from). So, yes, I get a little annoyed at the fact that as long as you can produce an American husband—however flimsily conceived because it's not like you can't fake one—they'll instantly hand you immigration papers. Note that I'm not saying that married people should be denied green cards. I'm merely saying that they shouldn't be given priority over singles who have equally (or more) valid reasons for permanent residency.

Ironically, Canada—a country that proudly advertises the benevolence of its immigration policies, constantly comparing itself favorably to its evil Big Brother south of the border—gave me almost as much trouble as the United States, initially rejecting my application for permanent residency even though I held a tenure-track position at the University of Toronto. My university-appointed immigration lawyer scratched his head, saying that in cases like mine, permanent residency was usually a rubber stamp: the university was full of foreign professors who hadn't had any trouble procuring it. So what was the issue here?

I suspected that it was that I didn't have a husband. During the year that the process of appealing the verdict was keeping me up at night—the decision was eventually overturned (predictably without any explanation)—two foreign graduate student friends of mine obtained Canadian permanent residency by using the online application system that the government makes available. I had a stable income and an immigration lawyer; my friends were students with no immediate employment prospects (they in fact left the country immediately after finishing their degrees). Yet their applications received a speedy approval while mine was rejected. The difference was that they were married (to each other).

Years later, when I was up for Canadian citizenship, my suspicion proved right: by then I was tenured and had published several books, but what Canadian immigration services fixated on was that I was unmarried and didn't have children. Fortunately, I'd had enough foresight to bring copies of my tax returns to the immigration interview. When the officer handling my case hesitated (even though I had aced my citizenship test and cleared all the other bureaucratic hurdles, so that she really had absolutely no grounds for rejecting my application), I pulled these out of my bag and silently pointed to the figure I had paid in Canadian taxes the previous year. She raised her eyebrows and signed my paperwork. So basically I bought my way into the country. This may be why I don't feel particularly Canadian. I'm a citizen of two countries to which I feel absolutely no emotional connection (Canada and Finland) and can't get citizenship, or even permanent residency, in the country that feels like home (the United States). The situation is as ridiculous as it is misery inducing. And if I—a white woman whose name most North Americans can usually (sort of) pronounce—have this much trouble, I can only imagine what things are like for those with darker skins and more difficult-to-pronounce names.

The green card scenario isn't the only instance where marriage brings substantial benefits. Married people even slip into coveted tenure-track professorships under the auspices of "spousal hires" whereas singles are asked to compete on the basis of their credentials. I understand that it's "nice" to work in the same city as your spouse. But this isn't so nice for singles who make it to the shortlist but aren't hired because a married colleague is given priority; it's also not so nice for singles who are asked to leave behind all their loved ones—which singles also do usually have—when they finally manage to get an offer from the University of the Middle-of-Nowhere.

It's because of such tangible disparities that many progressive academics, and particularly scholars in gender and sexuality studies, have long felt ambivalent about gay marriage.[11] On the one hand, we understand why gays and lesbians want marriage rights: as long as marriage functions as a signifier of full personhood, marriage rights carry an immense symbolic weight. Moreover, the problem with being denied these rights is precisely that you're automatically deprived of the kinds of benefits I've been talking about. Surely it's outrageous that straight people can obtain green cards by marrying if gays, lesbians, and queers in long-term relationships don't have the opportunity to do the same. And it's equally outrageous that gays, lesbians, and queers have been barred access to their partners' hospital rooms because their intimate alliances haven't been considered legitimate in the same way as the marriages of straight couples. For these reasons, the Supreme Court's decision to legalize gay marriage is a tremendous victory.

On the other hand, this victory merely solidifies marriage as an institution that, both symbolically and practically, marginalizes those who remain single, including gays, lesbians, and queers who aren't interested in joining the ranks of married monogamy. Historically, gay, lesbian, and queer subcultures have thrived in part because they have been able to envision alternative forms of sexuality, relationality, and kinship: "families we choose"—to borrow Kath Weston's memorable formulation[12]—has long been a motto for gays, lesbians, and queers who have fashioned vibrant communities and intimate alliances outside the ideals of straight society. Gay marriage threatens to displace these alternatives, in many ways reinforcing the notion that marriage is the only "authentic" way to build meaningful intimate relationships. It privileges white middle-class gay couples who conform to the dominant happiness scripts of our society, thereby further marginalizing those who either cannot or do not want to live by these scripts. This is why many scholars in sexuality studies have argued that gay marriage is the wrong fight, that a better strategy would be to insist on a system that grants equal rights and benefits to everyone regardless of marital status.

WORKING FOR LOVE

It may be in part because of the tangible benefits of marriage that many people work extremely hard to save their ailing marriages.

Others may avoid divorce because of the symbolic prestige of marriage. But perhaps the most important reason for the curious but common practice of fighting for a bad marriage may be the predicament I've mentioned a couple of times, namely that it can be difficult to admit that something that you thought would make you happy has made you despondent. It's not merely that you don't want to waste all the time and energy that you have put into your marriage by ending it, but also that you cling to the notion that your marriage will *eventually* make you happy because that's what marriage—at least *your* marriage—is supposed to do. This is one sense in which marriage is a breeding ground for cruel optimism.

Recall that Berlant defines cruel optimism as the obstinate conviction that social ideals, belief systems, and ways of life that hurt us will one day make us happy; like dominant happiness scripts, cruel optimism causes us to stay invested in well-worn scenarios of living, including scenarios of intimacy, even after these scenarios have (often repeatedly) disappointed us. The cruel optimism of married life often consists of the hope that what feels unsalvageable can ultimately be salvaged and perhaps even made better in the process.

This is why many modern marriages seem to replicate the logic of the American dream: the idea that hard work will be rewarded. In other words, cruel optimism turns some married people into emotional workaholics who believe that they can make their marriages work through unfailing willpower and relentless exertion.[13] One of the main paradoxes of modern American intimacy is that, on the one hand, we're told that love will conquer all obstacles, but on the other hand, we're taught that intimate relationships take an immense amount of tending.

Many people are willing to work on their marriages to an almost absurd degree, hoping against hope that the effort they pour into their relationship will in the end make up for all the mortification, hardship, boredom, or tension they have endured. Some are even willing to stay in marriages that they experience as deadening and suffocating; they're willing to put up with withered libidos, constant bickering, endless fighting, and recurring disenchantment for the sake of their alliances—or more precisely, for the sake of an ideal of marriage that they can't bear to discard.

Equally strangely, our society depicts this type of labor-intensive intimacy as the mature, even noble way to go about relating, so that those who dare to complain about their marriages are told to accept the grim realities of adulthood and learn to expect less from their marriages. That is, our society's message is that enduring marriages are better than short-lived alliances regardless of how wretched these marriages are; longevity has become associated with relationship success to such an extent that a marriage that lasts is almost automatically deemed a success, whereas an intimate alliance that ends is considered a failure regardless of how revitalizing and electrifying it may have been.

Marriage is presented as an institution that heals our wounds, making up for all the bad relationship choices (and perhaps even the bad existential choices) we may have made in the past; finding our "one and only" is supposed to redeem the agonies of earlier romantic dead ends and failed alliances. As my colleague Michael Cobb observes, our cultural imagination envisions singleness "as a conundrum to be solved by coupling off, and as soon as possible."[14] I've admitted that these days it's acceptable, even desirable, to date extensively before one settles down. Still, there's little doubt that we're trained to view singleness as an obstacle to (eventually, when the time is right) be surmounted, as a kind of antechamber of "real life," and this is the case even for those who have no interest in getting married.

I fall within the latter category, so I know from personal experience that those around me (except for my closest friends and colleagues) more or less automatically assume that I'm waiting for the right person to come along because obviously no one is "fundamentally" single (which in turn implies that everyone, deep down, is "fundamentally" coupled). Though young singles are sometimes envied for their freedom, remaining permanently single in our society still carries the stigma of undesirability and unhappiness. When singles are not portrayed as incomplete—desperately searching for the person who will complete them—they're deemed to be lonely. When they declare themselves content in their solitude—as I genuinely am—they're told that they're deluding themselves, that they just haven't yet met the right person ("*Then* you'll realize how lonely you really have been").

Alternatively, like queers, singles are judged to be immature, selfish, and narcissistic, unwilling to grow up and only interested in their own wellbeing. This is the case even when they have enduring friendships, extensive social circles, flourishing careers, and deeply held political beliefs. The tacit consensus seems to be that if you haven't managed to lure a mate, there must be something wrong with you. Surely you aren't *choosing* to be alone! Admittedly, increasing numbers of people, including straight women, are these days opting out of marriage (more on this shortly).[15] But singleness still remains a state that needs explanation, as I'm reminded every time that someone I barely know asks me why I'm "still single." I feel like responding, "Why are you still married?" But I know this would be impolite.

THE TYRANNIES OF LOVE

If singles are often judged to be leading an empty existence, it's because they seem to be lacking the one ingredient that's supposed to redeem all of our struggles: love. As much as I appreciate the inspiring aspects of love, I can't deny that the ideology of romantic love can take a tyrannical tone: the notion that (enduring) love is the pinnacle of happiness is so strong in our society that it trumps all other attempts to forge a life that feels worth living. The implication of this way of thinking is that those who choose to focus on other things besides permanent intimate alliances are choosing badly.

It is, then, worth emphasizing that many of those who have made the biggest imaginative contributions to our culture—intellectuals, researchers, inventors, composers, painters, writers, poets, actors, and so on—have shunned permanent relationships (which of course doesn't mean that they haven't had love in their lives but merely that this love hasn't taken enduring—that is, socially recognized— forms). It's possible that some of them have been incapable of such relationships. But it may also be that they have rated other aspects of life higher than the rewards of marriage; they may have had other priorities, have found other things more interesting.

There's no question that love can give us an enormous boost: many of us pursue romantic relationships because few things in life make us feel as fully alive and self-connected as falling in love. When we're in love, things that usually bother us suddenly don't. Tedious tasks become easier to endure. The self-doubts that nibble at the edges of our consciousness miraculously recede. Even the guy who snatches the last strawberry Danish at our coffee shop can't get under our skin. But as we all know, this elevated state fades relatively quickly. In contrast, the satisfaction gleaned from creative activities such as writing or painting can last a lifetime. This is why I'm not sure it's accurate to believe that romance, or even love, is an essential ingredient of the good life. It seems to me that there are many other things that bring satisfaction, enrich our existence, much more reliably.

The cult of relationality that governs our society implies that without enduring intimate relationships our lives are devoid of value; it idealizes relationships to such a degree that other avenues of fulfillment get sidelined. Yet it's also the case that this cult can't quite conceal the cracks in its edifice, such as the torments of bad marriages, with the consequence that some people these days are rejecting the marriage script. This in turn prompts the heteropatriarchal status quo to strive even harder to present marriage as the holy grail of happiness.

Straight women in particular are targeted with the message that marriage, more than anything else, is what they should wish for and work for. Feminists are admonished for having duped women into privileging their careers over their marriages. Career accomplishments are deemed meaningless in comparison to the rewards of family life. Female independence is declared overrated. At the same time, marriage is depicted as a refuge of warmth, safety, comfort, and responsible citizenship; it's portrayed as an antidote to the coldness of our performance-oriented lives. It's not that we're told to stop performing; rather, we're told that performing will be easier when its wearing aspects are counteracted by the support of family life (I can't tell you how many times I've been told—sometimes by doctors—that my back wouldn't hurt so much if I had a husband).

I recall a visit I once made to a psychoanalyst's office in order to determine whether he was the right fit for me.[16] When I mentioned that I wasn't in a relationship, he asked me if I had been in one previously. When I said that, yes, I had had quite a few relationships, he, visibly relieved, responded, "Well, in that case, we have nothing to worry about." The implication was that my history of intimate relationships meant that there was probably nothing *seriously* wrong with me, that whatever my issues were, they could probably be fixed by therapy; I could learn how to have healthier—that is, enduring—relationships.

Although this analyst didn't exactly blame me for being single, he subtly communicated that he assumed that I didn't want to remain so. He presumed that my prior relationships had failed rather than been voluntarily relinquished. I remember thinking, "If I tell him that I've never had much interest in being in a long-term relationship—if I mention that critical observation has led me to believe that most married people are much less satisfied than I am—he'll think I'm crazier than I actually am; he'll think that I'm putting up defenses, that I'm fleeing from the pain of past relationship failures, that I have fortified myself with the impenetrable walls of a false self in order to protect the vulnerable core of my true self, and so on." So I didn't say anything. But I also didn't go back to that analyst.

The idea that we should all want enduring intimate relationships is a peculiar one, given how much disappointment they can bring. As I've argued, many people hope that being coupled up will complete them in some essential way. Yet the very opposite seems to often be the case: many people seem eroded, depleted, and torn up by their relationships. This is why I'm skeptical of the idea that people who choose to concentrate on other aspects of their lives, such as their careers, are "compensating" for what they can't get (love). I think that it's equally possible that they have found an alternative (and arguably more dependable) way of dealing with the fact that, as I've explained, it's an intrinsic (unavoidable) part of human life to feel lacking, decentered, alienated, and always to some degree incomplete.

Let me stress, once again, that I don't wish to vilify those who find their marriages fulfilling. I don't want to suggest that there's something intrinsically better—more dignified, interesting, inspiring, or uplifting—about remaining single. I'm merely questioning the notion that even a bad marriage is better than no marriage. And I hope to have illustrated how the ideology of marital bliss reaches so deep into our lives that it becomes a form of biopolitical conditioning. It takes cultural hype of impressive proportions to convince people of the virtue of staying in relationships that render them jaded, numb, wretched, or depressed. Given how obviously agonizing marriages frequently end up being, it seems miraculous that marriage is considered the hallmark of psychic health, that it supposedly ends the turbulence and insecurity of single lives.

It would be difficult to demonstrate that married people, on average, are more fulfilled than singles, so that one has to wonder what the collective pity directed at the latter is meant to conceal. What degree of marital dejection is being brushed under the rug by the social portrayal of singles as isolated and forlorn creatures? Why are domestic dinners of silent treatment better than dinners of lively conversation with lovers who share your bedroom only when they really want to or with friends with whom you share everything but your bedroom?

Many people in our society are overly invested in love. Many are so focused on romance that they neglect other aspects of life, with the result that when their relationship crumbles, their entire world collapses. The cultural celebration of love's healing potential does not help such people. Our society's sentimental portraiture of eros drastically underestimates its destructive frequencies. The fact is that eros—passion in its undisciplined form—is far from benign: it's much more likely to shatter your life into tiny sharp-edged pieces than it is to bring you an enduring sense of completion and contentment.

This doesn't mean that people shouldn't fall in love (they certainly will and this might be a wonderful thing). But those who buy the idea that love is meant to make them happy—as so many couples walking to the alter seem to—misunderstand something fundamental about its character, namely that as long as it's intertwined with desire, it's inherently unreliable for the simple reason that desire can't be rationally controlled: we can't talk ourselves into desiring what we don't want (any longer). And when love is not (no longer) intertwined with desire, it easily attracts unpleasant sentiments such as boredom, irritation, and aggravation (which is why those we love also often drive us crazy). This is why working for love can be a waste of emotional resources that could be better spent elsewhere—an instance of cruel optimism and therefore an impediment to flourishing.

3

THE OBSESSIONS OF GENDER

As I've explained, the idealization of marriage tends to go hand in hand with a gender-bifurcated worldview that assumes that men and women complement each other by "natural" or even "divine" (Adam and Eve-esque) design. The battleground regarding gender in American society seems to be divided into three main factions: those defending a dichotomous gender order on "scientific" (often evolutionary) grounds; those defending it on biblical grounds; and those who just want to see the damn thing collapse.

I obviously fall into the last of these factions, which is where scholars in the critical humanities, including feminist and queer theorists, tend to dwell. But outside the academy, the two other factions often still dominate, although feminist, LGBTQ+, and other progressive activists are putting up significant resistance. As I've mentioned, I trust that the defenders of gender binarism will ultimately lose. But at present, they keep fanning what I've called a gender obsession disorder: an excessive, even pathological concern with making sure that men and women remain discernibly different.

The 2016 uproar about transgenderism, when scandalized state officers unapologetically spewed anti-trans (and anti-queer) rhetoric, when brawny white men guarded bathroom entrances in Texas, and when women (trans or not) who didn't look "properly" feminine were insulted in public bathrooms, revealed how deeply invested many Americans are in upholding a clear distinction between men and women. The hatred directed at those who blur this distinction was shocking to witness, even for those of us who weren't surprised by it.

In recent decades, the United States has advertised its "liberal" attitudes regarding women and homosexuals as a virtue that makes it a more tolerant and democratic society than some of its enemies; it has sometimes even justified its military interventions with the idea that it's helping liberate women in places like Afghanistan.[1] Likewise, after the massacre at the LGBTQ+ club Pulse in Orlando, Florida, just weeks after the transgender controversy erupted, the American administration and media alike resorted to an "us" versus "them" rhetoric that implied that only "they"—radicalized Islamic jihadists—would ever commit such an act of barbarism whereas "us" consists of an open and accepting nation.

I'm not saying that there's no value to the fact that on July 4, 2016, the Canadian prime minister, Justin Trudeau, marched in the Toronto Pride parade, in part to memorialize the victims of the Orlando massacre but also, generally speaking, to show support for the LGBTQ+ community. President Obama's strongly worded condemnation of the massacre was also noteworthy. At the highest levels of North American official rhetoric, we briefly witnessed a shift in attitudes that felt historically significant. But this shift was short-lived, quickly replaced by the logic-defying election of a foaming-at-the-mouth misogynist, homophobe, and racist as the next American president. Moreover, the transgender controversy—which brought to the fore not only immense transphobia but also immense homophobia—demonstrated that there are plenty of ordinary people on the side of "us" (on the side of mainstream Americans) who abhor the LGBTQ+ community.

If the Orlando gunman had wanted to look for justification for his actions from within the fabric of American culture (rather than in the ideology of ISIS), he would have found ample evidence for extreme bigotry. Consequently, portraying the United States as tolerant about gender and sexuality (in contrast to "enemies of the state" like him) could only be done by sidelining the hostile attitude of many American Christians toward trans and other LGBTQ+ people in the months (and decades) that preceded the Orlando tragedy—a tragedy that revealed how very tenuous LGBTQ+ rights (and lives) in this country really are.

American fanaticism about gender and sexuality may take different forms from the fanaticism of other cultures, but the transgender controversy and other conservative attempts to turn back the clock on progress on issues related to gender and sexuality make it difficult to claim that the United States is more relaxed about these matters than other parts of the world. The gender obsession disorder that infects so many American minds—and that ultimately can't be entirely dissociated from the mentality of the Orlando gunman—has serious consequences, including psychical violence and psychological abuse, *particularly* for the transgendered. This makes it all the more maddening that the reasoning of those who want to keep trans women out of women's bathrooms is that trans women could (supposedly) pose a threat to the "real" women using these spaces.[2]

Many women, trans or cis, feel threatened walking the streets of America's major cities. They worry about their basic safety. Their movements are restricted insofar as they're forced to avoid certain parts of town. And it's definitely not trans people who make them feel this way. Rather, it's men who murder them, rape them, whistle at them, and provide a constant public commentary on their appearance (more on the last phenomenon in the next chapter). As a result, those who defend the rigid male-female dichotomy succinctly symbolized by the icons on bathroom doors aren't defending the safety of women (trans or cis). They're defending a heteropatriarchal social order which is predicated not only on the privileging of heterosexuality but also on the disparagement and the physical, emotional, and psychological terrorization of women, the gendervariant, and visibly LGBTQ+ individuals.

The gender obsession disorder is an instance in which biopolitical control doesn't even bother to conceal itself. When I needed to use the bathroom at my grocery store on Cape Cod during the transgender debate, I noticed that the store had suddenly glued life-sized pictures of men and women onto the respective doors: clearly they wanted to make sure that no one could claim to have made an innocent mistake when the gender police came for them. On a more positive note, at a Canadian grocery story in the summer of 2017 a woman pushed a cleaning cart out of the men's bathroom, saw me waiting in line outside the women's bathroom, and said, "I've just cleaned the men's room, so use that one." When she saw my hesitation, she smiled and said, "Go ahead—this is not Trump's America." For once, I was happy to be in Canada.

Those most obsessed with gender differences seem to believe that the slightest blurring of the binary between men and women will result in the end of civilization. This is why the "gendervariant" pay such a high price, why they're scrutinized not just at high-security venues such as airports and subways, but also at work and school, in restaurants and locker rooms, and in the general flow of daily life. What's more, weirdly enough for a society that prides itself on being so welcoming of diversity, America's hatred of gendervariance and homosexuality is frequently completely out in the open.

I want to argue that these explicit forms of prejudice rest on a taken-for-granted sexism (including preposterous assumptions about gender differences) that has become so naturalized that few people in our society see it as an injustice. In this sense, while some parts of America's obsessiveness about gender are highly charged (and periodically flare up into political crises, as the transgender debate did), other parts sit on the surface of our cultural landscape without causing much of a stir because most people are so used to them that they look right through them. What interests me in this chapter is the latter type of sexism: gender fanaticism that hides in plain sight.

THE PROBLEM THAT HIDES
IN PLAIN SIGHT

A few years ago when I was looking for a literary agent for what became my 2015 *The Age of Scientific Sexism*—in which I criticize evolutionary psychology for its habitual practice of "gender profiling," for making enormous faux-scientific statements about people based on gender—a prominent agent in New York rejected my pitch because she thought that I was exaggerating, that gender discrimination can't be compared to racial discrimination because it's not institutionalized in the same way. Although I understood her reticence about drawing parallels between racial and gender profiling—and although I want to limit the term *gender profiling* to scientific and related contexts that officially endorse a stark distinction between men and women—I disagreed with her assessment that gender discrimination in our society isn't institutionalized. I think that its institutionalization takes the peculiar form of being so widely accepted that many people don't recognize it as discrimination.

Many Americans like to believe that gender equality has been achieved, that sexism isn't a big enough problem to make a fuss about. But I think that it is, and one reason for this is precisely that sexism persists in modern science in astonishingly crude ways, in ways that are reminiscent of the obscene "science" of those who once measured skulls in order to prove the inferiority of black people. My survey of popularized versions of evolutionary psychology—which serve as a foundation for many relationship and self-help guides as well as for a great deal of mainstream commentary on men and women—revealed the following litany of gender clichés: while men are aggressive, women are nurturing; while men are autonomous, women are relational; while men need space, women need intimacy; while men are productive, women are reproductive; while men like sports, women like to cuddle; while men are attracted by youth, beauty, and feminine vulnerability, women are looking for men with power, status, and financial resources; while men are hardwired to cheat on their partners, women are the faithful sex; while men are aroused by porn, women need a lengthy courtship—flowers, conversation, expensive dinners, and flashy displays of devotion—to feel the slightest quiver of the needle.[3]

Evolutionary psychologists present these "findings" with utmost earnestness, with solemn claims to scientific "objectivity" even though it's very easy to illustrate that they lift them straight out of cultural ideology; they strive to make social mythologies about gender sound like hard science. Unfortunately, this creates a vicious cycle of mystification: such faux-scientific arguments sound right to many members of our society precisely because they replicate cultural ideology, precisely because we have all heard these arguments countless times before.

For instance, it's easy for scientists to convince the general public that men are more sexual than women, and that women are more emotional than men, because these stereotypes are already a prominent part of our social mythology: we have been bombarded with them for so long that when scientists assert that they are "proven" facts, many people robotically nod their heads. "We all know that the ladies like to weep, particularly when it's that time of the month," seems to be the general consensus, except among those of us of the female gender who haven't cried in years. (Interestingly, a *New York Times Magazine* reporter recently found through extensive interviews with married couples who have opted for open relationships that it was usually the wives who had requested the opening up of the relationship, who seemed most interested in sexual variety.[4])

Sexism, then, is so deeply naturalized that many people view it as entirely reasonable. This in turn leads to the odd situation that many people in our society, including many women, are intensely proud of their sexism. This is one of the main differences between racism and sexism. White police officers who brutalize black men and white supremacists who want to reinstitute segregation (or ship all black people to Africa) may flaunt their racism, but it would be difficult to find a black person who proudly endorses negative stereotypes about black people. In contrast, it's easy enough to find a woman who uncritically buys our society's stereotypes about women and even vehemently defends them. Likewise, if it would be hard to find a black person who vilifies the civil rights movement, a woman who ridicules feminism can be found on every street corner.

I don't wish to suggest that sexism is a bigger (or deeper) problem than racism. Ta-Nehisi Coates's account of what it's like to be a black man in America—constantly afraid, subject to street violence and police harassment, and in danger of being imprisoned for no good reason—confirms that maleness is not always enough to empower a person in our culture.[5] It may in fact be that exhausting hypervigilance in public places is something that black men, many other racialized men, the gender-variant, the transgendered, and many women of all races have in common, even if the reasons for this vigilance differ. In addition, racism, sexism, and transphobia can intersect in sinister ways: recall the infamous cartoon that, during the 2016 presidential campaign, depicted Melania Trump—who had been made to look like a curvaceous Disney princess—"trumping" a muscular Michelle Obama who had been stripped of her harmonious physique in order to transform her into an offensive caricature of a trans woman. This cartoon fed not just on transphobia but also on age-old stereotypes of black women as overly bossy, brassy, and "masculine."

As a consequence, the last thing I want to do is to argue that sexism is more damaging than racism. Rather, I see sexism and racism as intertwined problems, as products of a system that serves (some, though not all) straight white men before it serves anyone else. And my point in the current context is merely that sexism is endorsed by large numbers of women, and that it is, moreover, *officially* (openly) condoned by our public and scientific institutions in ways that racism mostly no longer is (even if on the practical level it remains a tremendous problem in places such as many police departments). This is because differentiation based on gender seems more natural to many people than differentiation based on race.

For instance, evolutionary psychologists frequently attempt to explain every aspect of human sexual behavior—including our romantic choices—purely on the basis of the "natural" imperative to reproduce, as if cultural conditioning played no part whatsoever in how people behave in intimate relationships. According to their reasoning, the romantic strategies of men and women clash because men are primarily interested in spreading their seed (which is why they're promiscuous) whereas women are primarily interested in finding the best possible father for their children (which is why they're sexually choosy). It doesn't seem to matter that this depiction doesn't hold up to even a cursory glance at what's actually happening in our society, where more and more people enthusiastically (and explicitly) embrace the idea that there are lots of reasons to have sex that have nothing to do with having babies. Perhaps it's the specter of "useless" sex—sex that doesn't produce anything—that appears so frightening in our performance-oriented culture, with the result that fundamentalist Christians and fundamentalist Darwinians are tripping over each other to defend traditional gender arrangements, the former in the name of God, and the latter in the name of Nature.

I'm not hostile to science as such. And I'm not saying that humans aren't animals. I (obviously) believe in evolutionary development. But as I argued at length in *The Age of Scientific Sexism*, humans live in an intricate cultural world of governments, economies, skyscrapers, universities, nightclubs, elevators, websites, movies, books, and so on. Even our most basic bodily functions, such as eating and peeing, have been subjected to social control (the Bathroom Police have left us no doubt of this). When we sit down to have dinner with others, we usually use plates, forks, and knives and don't drop chicken bones under the table. And unlike other animals, we usually close the bathroom door when we have dinner guests. On a trip to Tokyo, I even discovered high-tech bathrooms where you could push a button to make noise to discreetly obscure the activities taking place in the cubicle. There were in fact so many buttons to choose from that I couldn't figure out how to flush the toilet.

Against this backdrop, the idea that human sexual behavior hasn't been touched by culture is preposterous. For starters, most people don't choose to have sex in broad daylight in the middle of a busy street, which would be the equivalent of how many other animals go about the task. Furthermore, even though evolutionary theory tells us that men want to spread their seed as widely as possible, I'm yet to meet an American man who wishes to spawn a hundred, or even a dozen, children. And given that more sexual activity in today's America may be taking place on online porn sites than in people's beds, the much-touted evolutionary link between sexuality and reproduction seems fragile at best. If the point is to produce children, I can't think of a less efficient method than . . . clicking the mouse.

Recall that there was a time in our society when it seemed like part of the "natural" order of things that black people worked for white people without getting paid for their labor. Many people, including some scientists, justified this system on evolutionary grounds, arguing that different races were destined for different roles, so that whereas white people were designed to think, invent, and govern, black people were designed for physical labor. This ideology persists as a feature of our economy to this day in the sense that blacks still perform manual labor for low wages much more often than whites. However, my sense is that most people—except for die-hard racists—these days consider this to be a consequence of structural factors such as the historical legacies of slavery and lack of equal opportunity rather than as a phenomenon caused by *natural* racial differences. In contrast, our society's thinking about gender is overtly premised on the idea that there's something about the shape of people's genitals that determines who they are and what their place in the cultural order should be.

THE FANTASY OF COMPLEMENTARITY

Even those with otherwise liberal social views seem to find gendered thinking reassuring because it implies that men and women are destined to complete each other in harmonious unions. On the one hand, evolutionary psychology fans the battle of the sexes by suggesting that the reproductive, and therefore romantic, agendas of men and women diverge; on the other, it suggests that when men and women are able to overcome their differences, they "naturally" balance each other out.

I've already noted that a cultural mythology that envisions women as embodiments of lack, of "castration," immediately implies that they need men to fill this lack, both literally and figuratively. This is one way in which our society has arrived at the idea that a woman without a man is in a fundamental sense unfinished. A man, in contrast, is deemed to be self-sufficient and autonomous to start with, which is why we're constantly reminded that men don't need relationships as much as women, that sometimes they even find relationships a nuisance (ergo: commitment phobia). That said, our society begrudgingly admits that men might benefit from a "woman's touch," that women might, for example, ease men's burden of competing in the public sphere.

Traditionally, it was thought that women, by staying in the private domain, would soothe away the anxieties that accrued to men in the public domain; woman was to be the caretaker, the redeemer of man, who, without her humanizing influence, might become overly callous. Today, too many women participate in the workforce to make their role as the angel of the hearth tenable. Yet even this has not eradicated the notion that it's their task to salvage men emotionally, to provide warmth as a corrective to our society's general pragmatism. According to this mentality, men may not "lack" anything essential—they do wield a penis after all—but they still have needs that women can fulfill.

In this manner, heteropatriarchy perpetuates the idea that men and women are capable of rescuing each other: women, supposedly, are supported by men's ambition, activities, and protection whereas men are saved by women's tender sensibilities. This fantasy of mutual rescue in turn helps present marriage as a space of unalloyed satisfaction, thereby—as I've argued—naturalizing it as the most legitimate form of intimacy. In the same way that a screw that fits a hole stabilizes a chair, the image of a man and woman "fitting together" sexually, emotionally, psychologically, and existentially offers a seductive vision of nature's plan having been fulfilled.

We all know that the seductiveness of this vision doesn't render it reliable: many married people eventually experience the return of the emptiness that they hoped their marriage would banish, unless of course they're able to find other ways to occlude it, such as focusing on their children or working so hard that they don't have time to think about anything beyond their next task. However, the more frequently the mantra of gender complementarity is repeated, the more deeply it becomes embedded within our collective imagination. It's in fact so entrenched that it's imposed even on relational failures that should in principle instantly discredit it: when men and women can't get along, our relationship gurus don't call into question the ideology of "natural" complementarity, but instead claim that relationship glitches arise because men and women have ceased to respect their distinctive (gendered) ways of relating.

This way of thinking is misleading because it fails to acknowledge that there are countless reasons for which two people with different unconscious motivations, histories of suffering, existential struggles, and points of vulnerability may find it difficult to get along. By fixating on gender differences, it overlooks the fact that relating is such a complex endeavor that there's never any guarantee that two idiosyncratic individuals can build a union that will work in the long run.

The gendered mentality of mainstream culture seeks to conjure away this complexity by insisting that misunderstandings of gender are to blame for most relationship difficulties. The extent of the problem is obvious to anyone willing to spend five minutes on Google: if you use keywords such as "love," "romance," and "relationships," you'll be inundated by headlines such as these: "The Ten Mistakes Women Make with Men," "How to Keep Your Man from Cheating," "How to Satisfy Him in Bed," "How to Get Him to Pop the Question," and "The Secret to Holding onto Your Man." This online culture is a good example of the kind of labor-intensive intimacy I've criticized: it makes women feel like love takes endless effort, cunning, and self-discipline. Indeed, it gives the impression that women have nothing better to do than to worry about all the ways in which they are failing with men.

Sadly, the advice offered is usually not based on anything more tangible than the stereotypes that have circulated in our culture for longer than anyone can remember. The young women who cruise the internet for guidance on how to back off when their boyfriend needs space, and the young men who are being told that the trick to making a woman happy is to listen to her attentively, may not be aware that they're reading the same advice their parents were reading more than a quarter of a century ago when John Gray published *Men Are from Mars, Women Are from Venus*.[6] And they may also not realize that they're being gradually brainwashed to hold beliefs that may not in any way reflect reality: surely it's not the case that men somehow inherently need more space than women; nor can it be true that men always find listening to women such a tedious chore that they must constantly be reminded of the necessity of doing so. And even if these were detectable social trends, would they really be the result of *natural* (rather than socialized) gender differences?

Some of the things that our society attributes to gender could be purely circumstantial, due to historically specific social arrangements. Let's assume for a moment that Gray was correct in arguing, based on his observations as a therapist during the 1980s, that men like to retreat to their "caves" whereas women crave connection. If so, I would look for an explanation in the fact that, a few decades ago, men more often than women spent their days in social work environments where they talked all the time, whereas many women spent their days mostly in the solitude of their homes (and perhaps with their young children).

I can well imagine that the result of this pattern might have been that men didn't want to talk when they got home from work, whereas women were eager to chat. This is not about gender but about how one spends one's days. I understand this intuitively because the tone of my work varies considerably from day to day. On days when I'm at the university, things are overwhelmingly social, with the result that when I get home, the last thing I want to do is talk. But on days when I work alone at home all day, I would be pleased to have a conversation in the evening. Translating such structural factors into the idea of natural gender differences is intellectually shortsighted.

THE PERSISTENCE OF GENDER STEREOTYPES

Obsessing about gender differences isn't a specifically American phenomenon. Most of the world's cultures insist on differentiating between men and women, and many of them do so even more firmly than Americans. My goal, then, is not to accuse Americans of being more sexist than the rest of the world but to ask why we're still sexist at all. Given how drastically our society has changed in recent decades, the stubborn persistence of gender stereotypes is remarkable. Even those who acknowledge that each individual is a singular creature with singular psychological, emotional, and sexual predilections, and who therefore realize that stereotypes are a pitifully reductive—and usually unfair—way of approaching others, often appear entirely complacent in the face of gender caricatures; the same people who oppose stereotypical thinking based on race, ethnicity, religion, and income frequently readily accept the rhetoric of gender differences that surrounds us.

As I've suggested, the only logical explanation for this contradiction is that these people don't view the rhetoric of gender differences as an instance of stereotypical thinking, that they see it as either truthful or perfectly benign. What they don't recognize (or want to admit) is that the naturalization of gender differences cannot be separated from the denigration of women, for whenever people are being systematically grouped based on presumed biological differences, discrimination is virtually unavoidable.

This is why I believe that Freud was onto something fundamental when he fixated on the genitals as one of the main organizing principles of our society. He recognized that our collective imagination has spun an elaborate cultural edifice around the simple fact that men have a penis and women have something else. That the penis has traditionally, perhaps due to its sheer visibility, been the defining organ of sexual difference—the norm in relation to which women have been deemed to have "something else" (or even more insultingly, nothing at all)—is ultimately the foundation of heteropatriarchy: what academics call phallocentrism. Until relatively recently, the lack of a penis kept women from voting, working for wages, owning property, going to school, participating in the arts, writing books, doing sports, and even walking alone in public places. In this sense, the privileging of the penis was definitely not Freud's invention (as some have argued); it was a social reality he diagnosed and analyzed.

The differentiation of people based on whether they have a penis or not was responsible for the—thankfully now largely defunct—division between a masculine public sphere and a feminine private sphere, including the notion that men should be warriors, leaders, orators, and authors whereas women should cook, sew, and mend socks. It also contributed to the—unfortunately much less defunct—idea that men are active creatures who produce things whereas women are passive creatures who receive things: penises, flowers, boxes of chocolate, and engagement rings, among other things. Among other things, American culture appears to assume that sexual penetrability equals receptivity, which is in turn coded as being equivalent to obedience, vulnerability, and submissiveness. The result is that this culture is governed by a sexual imaginary of masculine aggression and feminine violation, as if straight intercourse were a matter of women being conquered by men. I'm not talking about how straight people actually have sex; I'm talking about the American collective sexual imagination. And I can honestly say that before I arrived in the United States, it never once occurred to me to think of sex this way. When I realized that this is how many people in this country envision things, I kept saying, *But why? What makes you think that penetrability equals passivity? Aren't there a lot of active things that women do sexually?* Now that I read American queer theory, I find the same bizarre equation between penetrability and passivity in the pages of books that otherwise promote sexual transgression, so that gay men who prefer to be penetrated are characterized as "feminine," "passive," and "submissive" bottoms whereas lesbians who prefer to penetrate are deemed to be active—read, "masculine"—tops. In this sense, mainstream American notions of straight sexuality have "penetrated" (pun intended) even the most radical of academic thinking about queer sexuality. For me, the whole thing is just plain maddening.

What complicates things is that the penis *can* be used as a tool of domination; it *can* be used to rape women (or other men). Conversely, what complicates things for straight women, including straight feminists, is that even misogynist men can sometimes be a source of sexual fulfillment. This is one reason it has been difficult for women to present a cohesive political front. Their relationship to men is different from the relationship of racialized individuals to white people in the sense that, for them, the oppressor is also sometimes the source of some pleasurable things.

Furthermore, sometimes the oppressor himself is oppressed, as is the case when he's poor or a target of racism. Poor and racialized women often face the very difficult dilemma of having to choose which form of subjugation they'll resist most resolutely: poverty, racism, or sexism. Ideally, they would resist all three, but the situation may at times appear impossibly thorny. If your boyfriend is terrified to walk the streets because he's afraid of the next cop car that turns the corner, are you going to lecture him about feminism? Or are you going to comfort him? I can see why doing the latter might feel like the better option.[7]

Because sometimes it's easier—or feels necessary—to go along with our society's gendered thinking, many women honor gender stereotypes even though the world is full of examples of people who don't fit these stereotypes. Take the widespread notion that because women physically bear children, they're automatically more nurturing than men. From personal experience, I know that this is a bunch of hogwash: I can easily name two dozen men of my acquaintance who are more nurturing than my mother was when I was a young girl.

I've mentioned that getting pregnant made my mother's life wretched, with the consequence that she would definitely not have won the Mother of the Year award. But this doesn't keep her from being one of my favorite people: sprightly, intelligent, determined, tough as nails, and capable of fixing the roof at the age of seventy-three. Yes, I might have benefitted from having a mother who paid more attention to me, who sometimes gave me a hug. But over the years I've come to reassess things because I now recognize that my mother was a better role model for a young girl than, say, the overly nurturing mothers of today who treat their children as the center of the universe, who teach their sons and daughters (particularly sons) that they're invincible so that—and the influence of positive thinking is obvious here—their children come to believe that if they just have

enough faith in themselves, they'll be able to accomplish anything they want to.

I once knew a young man who told me he was going to travel
to a far-away country by rail and boat. When I asked him how
he was going to finance his trip, he said that he wasn't worried
because money had always "found its way" to him (I assumed
that this meant that his parents had always given him money).
He left on his trip with plenty of confidence but very little
money. When I ran into him a year later, he admitted—
obviously still confused about the matter—that "things didn't
work out in the end." He had only made it to the closest city
before he ran out of money and, shockingly, no one approached
him on the street with a wad of hundred-dollar bills.

In hindsight, I'm glad that my mother didn't feed such pipe
dreams. I don't mean to suggest that mothers should become
forbidding in order to toughen up their children. But it seems
worth emphasizing that one of the consequences of our society's gender stereotyping enterprise is to make many mothers
feel that in order to be "real" mothers (or even "real" women),
they must be so excessively nurturing that their children enter
the world with the expectation that all of their needs will automatically be met.

LETTING MEN OFF THE HOOK

Gender stereotyping undermines both men and women. But
it would be hard to deny that it hurts women more. Consider
the idea that men are inherently more sexual—and more
promiscuous—than women. This idea is merely a thinly veiled
attempt to let men off the hook for cheating on their partners,
the reasoning being that if men are biologically programmed to

philander, they can't help themselves even if they want to. This in turns implies that they can't be held fully responsible for their lapses (so that, really, women shouldn't complain and should maybe even learn to look the other way).

It may of course be that many of us, men and women alike, are prone to promiscuity. But the *gendering* of promiscuity—the notion that it's a specifically masculine predilection—puts extreme pressure on straight women to be forgiving about male sexual behavior that they may experience as devastating. Likewise with other "masculine" lapses, such as commitment phobia, amnesia about anniversaries, and lack of emotional intelligence: women are supposed to cut men slack because . . . well, they're *guys* so they can't be expected to be good at these things. For instance, the idea that men aren't "built" to understand emotions is a perfect excuse for insensitive behavior. Though it may sound like a compliment to women to say that they possess more emotional intelligence than men, in fact it's just a way to make women work harder than men at intimate relationships: women are asked to figure out how to navigate emotional complexities because men supposedly don't know how.

One manifestation of this predicament is that women sometimes put up with men's emotional ambivalence even when they experience it as hurtful. I'll discuss this theme—which leads to a lot of bad feelings among women—in greater detail in chapter 6. Here I merely want to observe that women have been trained to think that their emotional intelligence should give them the psychological resources to tolerate men's emotional opacity, to interpret enigmatic clues, to respect (and even to expect) romantic hesitation, to avoid making demands, and to prolong strained intimate connections in the hope that they might eventually right themselves; they have been trained to enter into a cruelly optimistic process of negotiating with men's desire. Essentially, many women are conditioned to believe that masculine emotional ambivalence can be conjured away by sheer perseverance. Unfortunately, this is rarely the case, which means that women spend immense amounts of energy on relationships that will never give them the fulfillment they're after.

It seems to me that if men feel emotionally incompetent, they should learn to be more competent in the same way that I've had to learn to be competent in various areas of life that are important to me. Emotional competence is not something any of us—women any more than men—are born with; it's not a genetic given. It's something we have to learn, and the difference between men and women in our society is that women are asked to learn it whereas men are not.

Let me express the matter as follows: if you spend your teen years watching online pornography and playing video games—as many young men have done—there's a good chance that you're going to be "emotionally incompetent": you're going to totally suck at emotional understanding, not only in terms of not knowing how to relate to others but also in terms of not knowing how to interpret your own emotions. This has happened to millions of young men. Older forms of heteropatriarchy—such as the model of the tough guy who would rather kick a garbage can than talk about his feelings—produced the same effect in older men. But instead of dealing with the problem, our society resorts to the comforting idea that women are just "naturally" better at relating.

It's doubly convenient that while young men are watching misogynistic porn (a topic I'll return to in the next chapter), young women are watching romantic comedies and television shows that teach them to accept the idea that men just don't "get" emotions and that they are consequently likely to act in hurtful ways—even though, deep down, they mean well so please have some sympathy. Sometimes I think that the recent epidemic of Asperger Syndrome as a specifically masculine pathology is merely the latest in the long list of excuses for why men are destined to wound women. I don't mean to say that the syndrome isn't real and debilitating to those who suffer from it. It just feels like its sudden prevalence has become yet another way to give men permission to mow women down with emotional insensitivity.

Women in turn are taught to think that it's their job to overcompensate for all the ways in which men (supposedly) don't know how to relate. This is one reason that some women keep working at their relationships until they're too tired to tell the difference between a good relationship and a bad one; and through their exhaustion, they do their best to keep reminding themselves that it's not the guy's fault because, well, it's just so *hard* for men to deal with the emotional side of things.

In the last chapter, I argued that many people slide into labor-intensive forms of intimacy. I would now like to add that this tends to be a gendered phenomenon, that it's often women who drain themselves emotionally, who keep trying to resuscitate relationships that are well beyond the point of rescue. Our popular scientists and other relationship "experts" add their venom into the mix by telling women that they're up against an immutable gender difference, that there's nothing to be done but to endure male emotional incompetence. Yet there's a great deal that *could* be done: if much of masculine callousness, coldness, insensitivity, and inability to judge the consequences of one's statements is caused by gender socialization, including a misogynistic world in cyberspace, then obviously the problem is not untreatable.

Our society's basic message to straight women is: boys will be boys, so you'd better make the best of it. This message permeates our romantic and self-help culture, but it's obvious in numerous other areas of life as well. Take, for example, our society's casual attitude toward street harassment: women are expected to simply just ignore it as a benign component of masculine behavior. But it's far from being benign, as becomes immediately clear if you replace women with any other social group, such as bald white men. If the latter group was suddenly subjected to constant commentary about their appearance from strangers on the street, I think we would quickly start to hear about the inappropriateness of this commentary, about how it's offensive and disruptive, and so on. We might even get an address from the president of the nation asking us to curtail our urge to tell bald white men what we think about their bald spots. Well, no such address is forthcoming about the incredibly offensive and disruptive ways in which many men harass women in public places.

Even the seemingly more generous aspects of street harassment, such as the command to smile, eat up a lot of energy. "Smile, beautiful!," "Why so grim?," "You'll be prettier if you smile," "Did your granny just die?" There are endless variations on the theme. It's like these guys are asking us to reassure them that everything is well in the world by forcing us to beam even when we're having a dreadful day. The command to smile may appear innocent enough—better than being told that there's something wrong with your ass, right?—but it's a good example of the coerciveness with which our society tries to impose cheerfulness on lives that aren't necessarily feeling that joyful. That (some) men feel like they have the right to dictate women's moods in public places tells us a great deal about power differentials. Our society may not officially insist that women's place is in the home, but it nevertheless manages to bully some women into wanting to stay there.

Undoubtedly, the burden of relentless cheerfulness in our society falls more strongly on women than men. I can't imagine walking up to a rushed businessman—or a random bald guy—on the street and demanding that he make my day better by pausing to crack a smile. Yet men routinely interrupt the lecture plans I'm devising in my head during my walk to the university with this very request. When I say, "Do you realize that you've just cost me forty minutes of thought?" they look genuinely bewildered. Thought? "You were *thinking*?" What do they suppose I'm doing? Do they believe that I left my apartment just so that I could smile at them?

The demand that I smile doesn't end on the streets. No matter how much my back hurts, I know that if I don't show up to my lecture with a convincing Julia Roberts smile, my undergraduates—at least those at the University of Toronto, Harvard being a different (much easier) case—will read me as intimidating, forbidding, and overly demanding. This would result in bad evaluations, which in turn would reflect badly on my professional reputation. Though my male colleagues are to some extent subjected to the same demand for good humor, their lapses are more easily forgiven because they aren't expected to soften their authority with reassuring displays of feminine solicitude. The emotional labor that female academics, like women in so many other jobs, are asked to perform is considerable. But it's rarely talked about. Like most of my colleagues, I usually don't have time to talk about it. So I take painkillers and force a smile.

But having to smile when I walk into the classroom moments after some guy on the street has ruined my lecture plans feels like I've jumped from the frying pan into the flames—that is, very bad indeed. There's nothing good that comes out of such a bad feeling. Its most productive result is anger. But usually it simply poisons my mind, causing me to anticipate the next command, to recoil from public life so strongly that my body starts to ache. When I search for causes for my constant back pain, decades of street harassment make it to the short list (just below childhood terror and adult overwork).

This is yet another demonstration of how biopolitics—cultural ideology—infiltrates not only our psyches but also our bodies, why even our biological constitution cannot be separated from social power. Consider, then, the pernicious impact of a life-time of hostile racist gazes, of eyes gliding over one's being with a barely suppressed disdain. And consider the combined effect of such disdainful eyes and the gendered injunction to keep smiling. Add to this the erotically charged demeanor of those with the power to look, judge, and tell you exactly what is attractive or repulsive about you, and it becomes clear why bad feelings accrue to some individuals more than others.

This makes it all the more irritating that our culture's gender stereotypers—including self-help authors advising single women on how to catch a husband—persistently try to sell straight women the most retrograde cavemen under the sun, as if there were no decent men, men who don't harass women on the street, who do their share of emotional labor, and who remember your birthday, in the world. Some of these gender stereotypers may genuinely think that they're helping women but it feels to me like they're merely wasting women's time, for what can women possibly gain from dating (or marrying) the kinds of emotionally unavailable, boorish men who are the darlings of the self-help industry?

WHY AREN'T WOMEN PROTESTING?

Women usually get the short stick of gender stereotyping: As I've illustrated, even negative stereotypes about men get spun in such a way that women are expected to good-naturedly cater to them. The way heteropatriarchy works in the romance department is that a woman who replicates dominant stereotypes of femininity is a damn good partner—sexy, sweet, caring, considerate, faithful, emotionally competent, and willing to compromise (though perhaps excessively chatty)—whereas a man who replicates dominant stereotypes of masculinity is a dating nightmare: brooding, selfish, arrogant, ambivalent, unfaithful, and emotionally clueless. So why aren't women protesting?

The naturalization of gender differences that I've criticized is a major reason. But another reason is that our gender stereotypers have been busy recoding traditionally "feminine" traits as signifiers of female empowerment. The example of emotional intelligence I've highlighted offers one such instance of recoding, recasting empathy, compassion, altruism, and intuition as desirable traits. Similar arguments have been made about women's nimble fingers, attention to detail, and patience to excel at repetitive tasks. I'm not saying that it's bad to be good at these things—not at all. But given that these traits have throughout the ages been used to justify the idea that women's place is in the home, taking care of the young, smoothing over ruffled feathers, and scrubbing the stove, we might think twice about their renewed vitality as specifically "feminine" traits.

Hanna Rosin's *The End of Men and the Rise of Women* stands as an example of the phenomenon I'm referring to.[8] At first glance, Rosin appears to be on the feminist side, on the side of those who would like to see women thrive, for she argues that our economy has shifted in such a way that traditionally "feminine" traits, such as the capacity to communicate, read emotions, build social networks, and create collaborative work environments, are now in high demand, which means that women for the first time in history have an edge in the professional world. This may sound promising, but the fundamental problem of a gender binary—the ideology that tells us that men are one way and women another way—persists.

If the traditional Mars-Venus universe is one where men are presumed to possess the qualities for professional success, in Rosin's universe women are the ones who (supposedly) come out on top. If this were actually true—and I'm not sure it is— one can see how this could seem like a victory for women. But from the perspective of those of us who would like to put an end to gender stereotyping altogether, it's an empty victory: rather than challenging the status quo of gender, it cedes ground to those who insist on the validity of gender stereotypes. Equally problematically, it makes gender stereotyping more palatable to women: now that such stereotyping seems to work in women's favor, they have even less incentive to complain about it. Yet there's something quite chilling about the idea that women might now be rallying around the very sexist mythologies that have for centuries been used to keep them down.

In this context, it helps to remind ourselves that feminism is not an attempt to defeat men, as it is frequently mistakenly portrayed to be. Most academic feminists and scholars of gender and sexuality distinguish between heteropatriarchy as a system of male domination and individual men—who may or may not support this system—and view progressive men as allies in their struggle to undo toxic gender stereotypes that force all of us to accept an impoverished definition of what it means to be a human being. Transcending these stereotypes would mean that all of us—cismen, ciswomen, the gendervariant, trans people, and everyone else—could lead more multidimensional lives.

From this viewpoint, those who understand feminism to be a matter of women outwitting men—of women outmaneuvering men professionally or in any other way—are working at cross-purposes with feminism; they're choosing to reinforce the very rhetoric of divisive gender differences that feminists have sought to dismantle. They may think that they're doing women a favor, but in some ways they're merely locking both men and women more securely into a system that has always pitted them against each other and that cannot, therefore, be good for anyone.

If we take gender stereotyping as a sign of heteropatriarchy's strong grip on our culture, it seems like things are actually sliding backward in our so-called postfeminist world in the sense that women, who a few decades ago tended to complain about gender stereotypes, are now sometimes on the front lines of arguing for their resurrection. Writers such as Rosin have convinced women that they can make gender stereotyping work for themselves, that they can beat men by learning to use gender-specific traits to their advantage; they're no longer asking for recognition of their equal humanity but rather for appreciation of their "feminine" specificity in the understanding that this specificity has been redefined as valuable.

This type of female "liberation" is a lost cause. I don't think that the attempt to recast "feminine" traits as the foundation of female empowerment will be able to erase the long-standing stigma associated with many of them. Indeed, I believe that as long as men and women are deemed to be inherently different, women will be considered inherently inferior. I say this in part because of our historical experience with other divisions, such as the one between whites and blacks: it may be benign enough to talk about cultural differences, but the minute people start to insist on innate racial differences, racism rears its ugly head. It seems extremely unlikely that insisting on essential racial differences would defeat racism. I don't see why things would be any different with sexism. However, many women find the idea of celebrating "feminine" specificity appealing because— let's be honest—many of them experience components of the heteropatriarchal definition of femininity as pleasurable. This is what I was getting at when I said, in the introduction to this book, that women have been taught to eroticize their own subordination.

I'll resume a more thorough exploration of this theme in the next chapter. In the present context, I want to offer a less complicated explanation for the popularity of gender stereotyping among straight women, namely that many women remain compelled by the idea that learning to interpret men accurately will deliver them to the gates of romantic fulfillment (this is arguably one form that positive thinking takes among straight women). Inasmuch as they agree with self-help authors that relationship problems result from the misunderstandings of gender, and inasmuch as they feel responsible for making their relationships work, they may come to trust that figuring out what makes guys tick is the surest way to solve these problems. Even women who don't recognize themselves in the portrait of femininity that our society holds up to them can be convinced that there's a grain of truth to the masculine portrait, that it offers a convenient shortcut for the ambiguities of relating.

Along related lines, our culture's gender stereotypers are skilled at implying that deviating from dominant blueprints of femininity will result in the lack of love. Even self-help authors who are nominally rooting for women routinely imply that any woman who refuses to abide by normative definitions of femininity—who, say, is too ambitious, competent, or self-sufficient—risks losing her man; the punishment for not performing one's gender correctly is loneliness and desolation. This can be a successful antifeminist terror tactic, for the prospect of being unlovable is a daunting one for most people; it can pull even the feistiest of women back in line. This is why I think that gendered codes of romantic behavior are—along with economic disparity—among the main strongholds of heteropatriarchy in our society, that they are a means of feeding otherwise confident women a hefty dose of submissiveness when their defenses are down.

Women who place their faith in gender stereotyping are ensnared in cruel optimism—as Berlant defines it—in the sense that they believe that what is bad for them (limiting, coercive gender models) is their ticket to the good life. Insofar as romantic fulfillment seems to depend on performing one's gender correctly—and on reading men's gender correctly—many straight women enter into a downward spiral of repeated disappointment where they're willing to work extremely hard at perfecting their relationships (and their gender performance) even when there's no evidence that their exertions are bringing them any closer to satisfying relationships.

The hope that their efforts will eventually pay off keeps many women loyal to relational paradigms that are extremely unlikely to reward them with the kind of intimacy they're looking for. Yet they can be so seduced by the mirage of impending romantic fulfillment that they stay patient even when they shouldn't. They consent to a retrograde narrative about gender even when the price of doing so is a big chunk of their dignity. In this way, they end up participating in a system that guarantees their misery at the same time as it relegates them to a secondary status.

THE ALLURE OF THE QUICK FIX

On a basic level, gender stereotyping is so alluring because it panders to the pragmatic tenor of our society that strives to offer simple solutions to all of life's problems. As I've emphasized, such pragmatism assures us that every facet of our lives can be reduced to a formula that increases our efficiency. Gender stereotyping is an attempt to arrive at such a formula in the realm of relationships: it provides a quick fix for relationship dilemmas by (seemingly) bypassing the murkiness and complexity of intersubjectivity.

People resort to hackneyed gender stereotypes in part because it's faster to make assumptions about others than to start from the premise that every individual, and every relationship, is going to be unique. Unfortunately, this approach is misleading because it places the emphasis on largely superficial aspects of relating, such as who is supposed to do what (drive the car; bake the cookies) in a given situation; it makes it more difficult for us to do the actual work of relating, thereby thwarting the very possibility of a genuine human connection.

Gender stereotyping supports the idea that we should be able to control our romantic destinies, that we should be able to streamline our relationships in the same way as we streamline all other aspects of our lives. This is why popular culture tries to distil dating into a set of rules, why it constantly recycles the dos and don'ts of romance. Straight women in particular are told that their romantic success depends on taking the right steps at the right time: toss your hair, tilt your head, touch his shoulder, don't forget to smile, let him pick up the bill, don't talk about your ex, don't talk about your problems, don't let slip that you fixed the leak in the bathroom sink yesterday, and above all, don't have sex on the first date (men don't marry sluts, do they?). The list is as familiar as it is pathetic. And it assumes what I criticized in the last chapter, namely that everyone—and especially every straight woman—wants to get married.

Nothing has destroyed my romantic relationships more often than male partners insisting that deep down I must be looking to get married even when I've told them that I'm not; the idea that women want dates, and particularly sex, to lead to marriage is so ingrained in our culture that even otherwise wonderful men sometimes accuse me of lying when I say that I have no fondness for the institution. What's doubly vexing about this is that it makes it impossible for them to appreciate the relationship for what it has to offer in the present; they become so fixated on the idea that I must want marriage—that I'm just not admitting it or that I'm even trying to trick them by pretending that I don't want it when in reality I do—that they can't allow themselves to relax into what is wonderful about the relationship that day. As much as I try to say that what I'm looking for is vitality in the moment, they dig for an ulterior motive.

I've even had men break up with me because *what's the point if marriage is off the table?* Annoyingly, these were men who had no interest in marrying me or anyone else in the near future. What I view as liberating—being freed from the marriage script—they view as too confusing *even when they themselves don't want to get married.* A woman who doesn't want to get married is so mystifying, so far outside the norm, that these men prefer to date a woman who wants to get married even when they know all along that they will one day have to disappoint this woman by telling her that, actually, she's not the one.

I meet a man who has no interest in getting married. I say, *Great, me neither!* He says, *That's too weird,* and turns to another woman who does want to get married. After a few months he breaks her heart by telling her that he's not looking to get married. This is just plain stupid. And it's a good example of how dominant happiness scripts keep people from pursuing alternative modes of life: those who think of a relationship as a linear process that leads from the first date to the altar automatically stifle other relationship possibilities. Gender stereotyping is obviously in part responsible for this mentality: if it had not been pounded into the psyches of straight men that all women want to get married—and especially those who say that they don't because that's just a ruse, a way to put men off guard so that they can furtively tighten the noose—everyone in the straight world would be having a lot more fun (and quite possibly, a lot more sex).

The gender stereotyping enterprise cannot tolerate the idea that when two people—straight, queer, or anything in between—bring their eccentric personalities, motivations, and histories of traumatization into an intimate encounter, things are likely to get messy. Instead, it insists that gender differences explain why our attempts to relate to one another can be so convoluted, why even our most devoted loves can be so fragile. Essentially, it tries to neutralize love's power to ravage us by turning it into yet another rational endeavor; it offers a reassuring illusion of control over love's illogical passions. Yet a moment's reflection should reveal that this is a moronic way of going about relating, for obsessing about gender differences covers over the idiosyncratic doubts, desires, anxieties, insecurities, and aspirations of others, thereby making it all the more difficult for us to build meaningful relationships with them; it causes us to assume that we understand others when in reality we don't.

Desire is never wholly predictable; it's never just a matter of physical impulses but includes bits of social conditioning, cultural imagery, personal background, and unconscious fantasy.

The attempt to impose clarity on this complex reality by gender stereotyping is a fool's errand. Although I understand the wish to avoid pain, to protect oneself against love's power to devastate and disillusion, I can't think of anything that's more antithetical to the ethos of eros than the idea that it can be tricked into submission. If anything, the more we try to control it, the less likely it is to reward us. Gender stereotyping strips romance of its power to genuinely transform us, forcing us to live in a bankrupt romantic culture devoid of any real adventure. This is why it's part and parcel of the rationalization of intimacy that characterizes our neoliberal society. It's a quick fix that doesn't actually fix anything.

4

THE REINVENTION OF
HETEROPATRIARCHY

That women are trained to work harder at intimate relationships than men is related to another pronounced social trend: many straight women translate our culture's ideal of constant self-improvement into the idea that it's their bodies in particular that need improving.[1] Women are of course also engaged in other types of self-improvement projects: career progress, for instance, is important to many. But being female in twenty-first-century American culture is so centered on the body—on physical appearance and desirability—that female self-esteem is often directly linked to having the kind of body that men find attractive. This is yet another reason that the female body as a site of discipline and punishment is a particularly good example of Foucault's notion of biopolitical control.

Because the body is always imperfect—because it could always be more beautiful—there's in principle no end to the process of improvement it can be subjected to. Consider, in this context, the importance of "the makeover" to contemporary feminine culture. Makeover shows such as *America's Next Top Model*, which elevate the manipulation of the female body to an art form, are only the most obvious manifestation of a collective attitude that tells women that their happiness depends on being "made over" (which in turn implies that the "original" doesn't deserve happiness or isn't good enough to procure it).

The makeover is a standard feature of romantic comedies, television shows, and women's magazines, which routinely deliver detailed instructions on how to do your makeup, style your hair, and shop for accessories to attain a whole new you (in some magazines these instructions sit nicely next to instructions on how to give the perfect blowjob). This makeover mentality implies that a physical transformation is what women need to land the perfect man, the perfect job, and the perfect life. It teaches women that to be successful in today's society—professionally as well as romantically—demands the ability to regulate, manage, and constrain their bodies. In this sense, not much progress has been made since the days of the corset and the sidesaddle.

I recently visited a makeup store catering to young women's beauty concerns because I needed a birthday gift for a fourteen-year-old girl. It was startling to see how much more complicated things have gotten since I myself started to wear makeup: besides the overwhelming array of colors and precision tools on offer, particularly striking were kits that are designed to recontour your entire facial structure by the clever usage of different shades of foundation. I've always known that makeup artists employ this strategy on actresses about to enter a scene and models about to enter a photo shoot. Seeing that teen girls are now expected to undertake this task in their everyday lives was telling. There may be pleasure in the process—a point I'll return to shortly—but there's also a lot of pressure, for within this mentality, no obstacle is insurmountable, no imperfection is beyond repair.

If feminists during the 1960s and 1970s demanded freedom from gender discrimination, today's postfeminist women seem more focused on freedom from bodily flaws.[2] Freedom from wrinkles, cellulite, body hair, and other forms of physical "deficiency" is presented as a prerogative that women should claim—you guessed it—by spending loads of money on expensive products. For many women, the commercial construction of femininity has become a way of life and perhaps even a means of bandaging the foundational discontents of human life; feeling desirable not only offers an antidote to bad feelings such as depression or insecurity but also promises a solution to the general malaise of existence. Finding the right props for femininity in the commercial realm brings a temporary sense of satisfaction, healing wounds, concealing inadequacies, completing what appears incomplete. Unfortunately, this means of alleviating existential anxiety is inherently precarious, threatened by every slice of blueberry pie, every pint of ice cream, every bag of cookies, and every bowl of pasta that crosses your path.

For many women, anorexia, bulimia, and pervasive body anxiety are the painful underside of today's appearance-oriented society. Even those who escape acute distress can feel ashamed and frustrated by the fact that their bodies rarely become as flawless as they would like them to be. Indeed, so many women are in the habit of monitoring every aspect of their physical being that it seems reasonable to argue that there's something compulsive about contemporary female subjectivity. It's not just the random guy on the street who is assessing women's looks: women themselves are constantly judging their appearance, constantly comparing themselves to other women and worrying about their desirability to men. Notably, such self-surveillance tends to be primarily self-critical: instead of focusing on the pleasing aspects of your being, it lingers on all the ways in which you're falling short of the feminine ideal. In this sense, women's self-scrutiny can adopt a masochistic tone, eroding their confidence at the precise moment in history when they're being told that they're fully liberated, that they've never had it so good.

In our culture, (straight) men are programmed to look at women. And women are programmed to be looked at: they see themselves as being seen, through the eyes of the men (real or imaginary) looking at them. This means that their relationship with themselves is mediated by what film scholar Laura Mulvey in 1975 famously dubbed *the male gaze*: an assessing gaze that explicitly positions women as objects of male desire.[3]

This isn't to say that men aren't these days presented as objects of female desire: modern media culture often breaks the dichotomy between man as the bearer of the look and woman as its object by presenting us with gorgeous male bodies to admire; a quick survey of television shows—particularly ones aimed at young audiences—immediately illustrates the mass appeal of the shirtless man (it's not just for the fight scenes that I watch *Arrow*). In this sense, media culture normalizes the objectification of both men and women. But in the case of women, there's a greater emphasis on conscious self-fashioning: many women adopt a third-person perspective on their bodies, deliberately objectifying themselves.

We know that the images of femininity that stare at us from the pages of fashion magazines, roadside billboards, and television shows are manipulated. But we still frequently can't keep these images from insinuating themselves into our psyches in ways that make us feel intrinsically defective; many women are fully aware of the degree to which contemporary body ideals are unrealistic and punishing, yet they're unable to shed the power of these ideals; they see through the ruses of media culture but buy its products anyway. There are obviously women who are either explicitly rejecting the accouterments of femininity or not really thinking about the matter a whole lot. But unquestionably, "looking hot" is one of the main priorities of many women, sometimes even their main goal in life.[4]

THE MASQUERADE OF FEMININITY

I don't want to deny that many women enjoy what Freud's disciple Joan Riviere in 1929 called "the masquerade of femininity": the art of producing a seamless façade of femininity.[5] I grant that deploying the props of femininity can be lighthearted fun; the artifice of self-fashioning can be a genuine pleasure. Many women love the process of altering their facial structure by the skillful application of makeup; changing the shape of their body by wearing a padded bra, stiletto heels, and tummy-flattening underwear; and adding volume, shine, and curls to their hair with the right products and styling. I'm not saying that there's something inherently wrong with these actions. I myself would never walk into a classroom without wearing *some* makeup even though I know that by the end of the lecture most of my mascara will be running down my cheeks, possibly creating an effect closer to *The Adams Family* than *Pretty Woman*.

I have a smart graduate student who runs a blog on feminism and floral fashion.[6] And I have hyperfeminine feminist friends who are skilled at combining their badass politics with their Jimmy Choo shoes. So I'm definitely not proposing that women should stop wearing makeup, dressing up, and trying to look attractive. But I don't think that there's any way to deny that the commercial construction of femininity—and the attempt to squeeze female bodies into restrictive molds—is one of the main ways in which heteropatriarchy is reinventing itself: women may have made political and economic gains, but the emphasis on appearance that has always been one of the burdens of female subjectivity seems to have merely intensified in the aftermath of feminist victories. On some level, this is a backlash against feminism. At the very least, it's a means of compensating for increased gender equality in other areas of life: I know that many young postfeminist women experience looking hot as empowering, but from a more critical perspective, this component of contemporary culture looks like an attempt to assure men that women haven't gotten too powerful.

This was Riviere's explanation for the masquerade of femininity already in 1929, for she argued that professional or intellectual women sometimes choose to wear an exaggerated version of femininity—an excess of femininity, as it were—as a mask to compensate for their usurpation of "masculine" power. In other words, Riviere described a defense mechanism that's familiar to many successful career women: the attempt to alleviate the sting of female ambition on the male ego by flamboyant displays of femininity, including a girly demeanor, sexy appearance, and a flirtatious attitude.

For women, adopting the mantle of power, grabbing the portable phallus, too convincingly can result in retaliation from men who feel cheated of their birthright and from other women who don't appreciate women who meddle with the established gender order. The masquerade of femininity seeks to offset such retaliation by reassuring onlookers that the gender system hasn't been irreversibly altered, that the successful woman hasn't *actually* usurped masculinity (or masculine prerogative) but remains a woman.

Riviere explained that much as a thief turns out his pockets to prove that he hasn't stolen anything, competent women can resort to the masquerade of femininity in order to prove that they haven't stolen the power that in heteropatriarchal society belongs to men. This is one reason I opt for a short skirt and high heels when I'm about to give a talk in a male-dominated domain, such as a philosophy department, and I do so especially if I know that I'm about to challenge some of the ideas that this domain cherishes. As ridiculous as this feels, it's better than the aggression that ensues when colleagues suspect that I might have nicked the golden phallus from their display cabinet and am now trying to smuggle it out of the department underneath my skirt. I know that if my skirt is short enough to make this untenable and my heels are high enough to make it clear to everyone that I won't get too far before I'm caught, they'll like me more.

This is a sad state of affairs, isn't it? It's a way that I keep apologizing to my male colleagues for having made it into the ranks of academic professionals. Likewise, I find it hard to read contemporary female makeover culture as anything but a massive apology that women, collectively, make to men for the successes of feminism. On some level, the makeover craze is of course just an aspect of the generally narcissistic tenor of neoliberal society, a society that markets self-expression—taking the right selfie, posting it online, getting noticed, standing out from the crowd—as the epitome of empowerment. In this system, looking good becomes a way of getting validation for one's uniqueness, a way of being "somebody." Even those who are struggling to make ends meet can buy into this mentality in the sense that they keep hoping—in a cruelly optimistic manner—that one day they might be able to join the hordes milling around the mall in search of the inner glow that comes from finding just the right item for one's arsenal of self-fashioning. Still, I can't help but interpret our society's emphasis on female attractiveness—its attempt to reduce female subjectivity to its physical manifestations—as a means of asking forgiveness for increased gender equality in other arenas of life.

WANTING TO BE WANTED

In some societies, heteropatriarchy takes the form of suppressing outward signifiers of female sexuality through practices such as veiling. In contrast, Western heteropatriarchy has long displayed female sexuality for male consumption. Within older versions of this paradigm, men were explicitly portrayed as active subjects of desire—as individuals who get to "own" their desire—whereas women were portrayed as its passive objects. Until recently, the only form of desire that was available to women was the desire to be desired, to be the pleasing object of male desire. In this sense, women's desire was indirect, so that the closest they came to expressing desire was by desiring men's desire; essentially, they wanted to be wanted.[7]

As I already noted, things seem to have changed: even if our society still reads female sexual penetrability as a signifier of passivity and submission in the manner that I discussed in the previous chapter, it's now acceptable for women to look at men, assess them, and desire them. If anything, acknowledging active female desire has become one of the main advertising tricks of the twenty-first century, used to sell us everything from clothes, makeup, and perfume to cars and condos. However, the makeover culture I've just described illustrates that traces of the old order of things still linger, and arguably quite emphatically, in the sense that many women are still working overtime to elicit male desire; they still primarily want to be wanted.

If one wished to insist on the accuracy of the mythology that tells us that men are more sexual than women, one could point to this predicament as the reason for this phenomenon: being asked to desire one's own objectification is much more complicated than the process of objectifying another person. According to this interpretation, it's not biology that might make some women hesitate in the face of their own desire but rather the psychological contradictions of having to eroticize their subordination as passive objects of someone else's desire.

Granted, the play of desire can take unpredictable forms. For example, it's possible that the bearer of the look fails to dominate the object of the look but is instead flustered by it. Being able to capture another person's attention can be a form of power, so that it's legitimate to propose that the one whose gaze is arrested by a beautiful object—whether animate or inanimate—in many ways surrenders to that object, allowing himself, his desire, to be disoriented by it.[8] This is why contemporary movies and television shows repeatedly offer us women who use their sexuality to manipulate men, why the guy who drops his stack of business documents when a stunning woman walks into his office is such a familiar trope.

Yet in the world of straight romance, women are still in many ways expected to signal their desirability rather than to approach the object of their desire directly; they're expected to send (usually discreet) signals of availability in the hope that the man they're interested in will act on these signals and approach them. Although women obviously feel desire, many of them conceal its outward manifestations because they're afraid to come across as unfeminine or too aggressive. Indeed, I've always thought that those who believe that men are "naturally" more sexually eager than women are letting themselves be duped by the dexterity with which many women hide their desire. As a result, as much as we might want to think that the days of relegating women to objects of the male gaze are over, the imprint of this dynamic persists: in most instances of budding straight romance, a woman is expected to (more or less) passively wait for a man to decide if she's desirable enough to be pursued.

Street harassment is one of the many ways that our society tells women that when it comes to the male gaze, they don't ultimately have any choice but to submit to it: any man, at any time, appears to possess the right to publicly assess a woman's desirability. Obviously not all men participate in this charade. Many consciously reject it, wanting nothing to do with the heteropatriarchal legacies that still shape our culture. Moreover, there's no doubt that women often deliberately play into the male gaze, that women sometimes feel empowered when they know that they're activating this gaze, as when they walk into a party knowing that they look great.

But the flipside of such moments of empowerment are the moments in public places when a male stranger feels that it's his unquestionable right to appraise your physique. One only needs to make a trip from Harvard Yard to South Station—the Boston bus station—to know that what's empowering in one environment can be hugely disempowering in another, that, for instance, the style of clothing that professional women use to their advantage in work environments can elicit a deluge of sexual (and often even hostile) commentary on the streets, in the subway, and in bus station staircases. This is why I use my office in the same way that Clark Kent uses a telephone booth: at the end of the work day, I shed my miniskirt and heels (the Harvard Yard superwoman uniform) for jeans and sneakers (the South Station everywoman outfit—an outfit that's less likely to attract unwanted attention when I'm rushing to catch the bus).

THE EROTICIZATION OF OBJECTIFICATION

At the beginning of this book, I suggested that if so many women fail to protest their denigrated status under heteropatriarchy, it may be because they have been taught to eroticize, to take pleasure in, their subordination. I hope that you can now see how easily this can happen. And I hope that you can see how confusing things have gotten: on the one hand, I think that I'm not wrong in proposing that female self-objectification (hyperfemininity) on some level (and at least in some instances) functions as an apology for increased gender equality; on the other, many women genuinely experience it as empowering. As is the case with Rosin's attempt to recast formerly denigrated "feminine" traits as desirable ones, postfeminist culture strives to transform sexualized images of hyperbolic femininity that have historically been used to disempower (objectify) women into signifiers of female empowerment.

This explains why so many postfeminist women eagerly participate in their own objectification. Some even reject feminism on grounds that it robs women of the power of femininity, not to mention the pleasures of the masquerade of femininity. Those of us who are familiar with the history of feminism, who recognize the ways in which today's women are the direct beneficiaries of feminist victories, find this attitude baffling, for it implies that young women believe in the justness of heteropatriarchy; it suggests that women think that men should be politically, economically, and socially superior to them. I can't imagine that this is what they actually think. Yet somehow things have developed in such a way that many women recoil from feminism as hopelessly outdated: prissy, bitter, uncool, aggrieved, forbidding, and miserably frumpy.

It's in part because they see feminism as hostile to femininity (and to sex with men) that some postfeminist women end up implying that if their choice is between heteropatriarchy and feminism, they'll choose heteropatriarchy. What they don't realize is that contemporary feminism doesn't see feminism and femininity (per se) as antithetical. It merely criticizes the damage done to women when the worship of (commercially constructed forms of) femininity is taken to an extreme; it asks women to develop a greater degree of self-awareness about their complicity in the very system that oppresses them, that causes them to feel uncomfortable in their skin. Nor are most of today's feminists the dowdy anti-sex advocates that the media have portrayed them to be. Indeed, the notion that feminism opposes sexuality is utterly wrong: even feminists who criticize misogynistic aspects of pornography—as I'm about to do— aren't opposed to sex or pleasure; if anything, female sexual pleasure has long been an important feminist goal.

For feminists such as myself, the battle is—and should be—between feminism and those who uphold rigid gender stereotypes rather than between feminism and femininity (or sexuality). Still, I can see how things can get perplexing, given that women who adhere to hyperbolic forms of sexualized femininity are on some level doing exactly what gender stereotypers want them to do. In addition, when women try to manipulate men erotically in an effort to gain power, they participate in the instrumentalization of intimacy I've criticized. I—naïvely perhaps—adhere to the notion that relationships, particularly intimate ones, shouldn't be approached with the calculating mindset of a war strategist, that they should be a matter of forging meaningful connections (however short-lived) rather than of striving to control one's partner, either sexually or otherwise. Furthermore, women's erotic power over men can fade over time, so that women who have built their self-esteem primarily by brandishing this power may one day find that they don't have a whole lot left.

Don't get me wrong. I'm definitely not among those who believe that a woman's erotic life ends at the age of forty. One of the many things that irritate me about evolutionary psychology is the field's insistence that older women hold no appeal for men, that only women in their twenties can arouse a man's desire. My point is merely that any person who develops one dimension of their being at the expense of all others risks feeling impoverished when the privileged dimension no longer brings the rewards it once did. In *The Second Sex*, Simone de Beauvoir offers a piercing commentary on this predicament, pitying women who have been so focused on fanning men's erotic fantasies that they have failed to develop other aspects of their lives, with the result that in the absence of sexual adventures, their existence feels empty.[9] The problem is part and parcel of the overvaluation of romantic love that I called attention to at the end of chapter 2: those who bank everything on romance close off alternative avenues of fulfillment.

A related dilemma is that postfeminist femininity offers an illusion of power without challenging the systematic devaluation of women that characterizes heteropatriarchal society. In the same way that the American dream—and related happiness scripts—silence political opposition by promoting individualistic solutions to social inequalities, postfeminism implies that it's each woman's personal responsibility to tackle all the obstacles on her path, that the only thing holding women back is their lack of exertion. If a woman can be the attorney general or the secretary of state, what's keeping you from climbing up the career ladder?

You want to complain about the glass ceiling, the lack of childcare, or your boss's assumption that you don't deserve a promotion because women don't perform well under pressure? People in our postfeminist world don't want to hear about it. They want *you* to find a way around the impediment. Whining about obstacles won't solve anything, so get over it. Adjust your attitude. You're not one of those uptight *feminists*, are you? Don't you know that gender equality has been accomplished? Haven't you heard that feminists keep women down by making them insecure about their ability to compete as men's equals? They are a defeatist bunch, complaining about minor issues. Surely *you* won't let trivial hindrances conquer you! Surely *you*'ll find a way to make something of yourself. Surely *you*'ll beat the odds.

As media scholar Susan Douglas remarks, today's media present an endless parade of savvy female doctors, lawyers, detectives, and corporate executives, which might give you the impression that feminism is obsolete—that there truly is nothing but your own lack of effort that can keep you from thriving.[10] The female go-getter—the woman who overcomes impossible obstacles on her way to the corner office (while still looking appropriately feminine)—has become the ideal that women are asked to emulate. This is by no means entirely bad: Alicia Florrick (*The Good Wife*) in a courtroom is nice to watch. But the downside of the spectacle of female competence is that it suggests that structural impediments have been overcome, that those who are still lagging behind are to blame for their lack of accomplishment. Contemporary media images that imply that sexism has been superseded—and that feminists therefore belong in the dustbin of history—obscure the fact that, when it comes to gender (and racial) relations, we're still far from an equal playing field.

THE LATEST EDITION OF HETEROPATRIARCHY

Today's postfeminist women want to retain basic feminist political, economic, and social victories without calling themselves feminists. Opportunistically, they appropriate the successes of feminism while simultaneously rejecting feminism as too grim. In this sense, heteropatriarchy hasn't been defeated; it has merely reinvented itself. It has mutated into stealthier, more elusive forms that are harder to fight because they're harder to detect.

The latest edition of heteropatriarchy is much better at hiding its inegalitarian underpinnings than older, clumsier versions of male dominance.[11] It even manages to make heteropatriarchy enjoyable to women for the reasons I've outlined: it exploits the fact that women have been taught to eroticize their own objectification by convincing them that it's through sexual display that they'll attain true power, the kind of power, moreover, that men won't resent; true power, according to this reasoning, is a matter of getting men to lust after you and other women to envy you. This is heteropatriarchy made palatable to women; it's female "empowerment" stripped of its feminist bite.

What could be better than female empowerment that men find just as agreeable as women? This version of female "empowerment" suggests that now that gender equality has (supposedly) been achieved, it's safe to resuscitate sexist stereotypes.

Douglas explains that this attitude is frequently accompanied by a "knowing wink": the idea that guys are such idiots, such salivating slaves to their crotches, that the objectification of women is actually a joke on them.[12] Hypersexualized women may appear objectified but they're actually the ones with power because in choosing to objectify themselves, they manage to reduce men to ogling, stuttering nitwits. It's all done in an ironic, self-reflexive tone that implies that it's not to be taken seriously, that it's all tongue-in-cheek, so what could possibly be wrong with it? It announces that a girl is confident, not embarrassed about her sexuality. Only prim, old-fashioned feminists would condemn this—right?

In her critique of this phenomenon, Ariel Levy proposes that in today's American society women have two alternatives: either they must accept a hypersexualized culture that tells them that being fuckable is their most important asset, or they must consent to being read as being prudish and uncomfortable about their sexuality.[13] Understandably, the second of these alternatives is hugely unappealing.

I grant that bold female sexual display can be a way of rejecting the idea that men are intrinsically more sexual than women, that women find sex vaguely distasteful, a chore they undertake merely to please men; it can be a way of rejecting obsolete models of female sexual passivity. At the same time, in uncritically embracing their own objectification, women may overlook the fact that the parameters of this objectification are still set by a heteropatriarchal society governed by a heteropatriarchal sexual imagination. As one of my students summed up the matter, it feels a bit like women have simply given up—discarded feminism—because they have realized that they can't defeat the heteropatriarchal system; neoliberal pragmatists that they are, they have decided that since they can't beat the system, they might as well join it.[14]

All things considered, the hypersexualization of women may be a better option than the curtailment of female sexuality. I certainly wouldn't want to go back to the repressed female sexuality of earlier eras. Yet I also sense that our victory over archaic views about female sexuality is not as clean as it could be, that somewhere along the line, major compromises were made, and that it may only be now, in hindsight, that we're starting to understand something about these compromises.

The issue for me is not female sexual display, let alone female sexuality. Nor am I saying that sexual objectification is always wrong, for being an object of desire for another person, and wanting to be as enticing an object as possible, may simply be a part of human sexuality (not just for straight women but for everyone). Rather, the problem is that today's postfeminist women rarely seem free to express their eroticism in ways that deviate from the dominant heteropatriarchal script. Stated more strongly, the problem is that the only style of female sexuality that gets a serious hearing in our society is the one that has historically been favored by a notoriously misogynistic porn industry: an industry that, at its most aggressive, disseminates images of women being gagged, bound, raped, pissed on, and otherwise humiliated.

I need to be precise: I don't think that porn is intrinsically immoral. I don't think it should be banned. I don't even think it should be censored. I know that many women enjoy it as much as men do. I also know that alternative, feminist, and queer porn exists, and I'm glad it does. It's possible that the most effective antidote to misogynistic heteroporn would be to expose more people, including straight women, to different types of porn.

As a result, what I'm about to say has little do with the ethics of porn as such. Rather, I'm interested in a more specific problem, namely that (straight) female sexuality has become more and more difficult to dissociate from pornography.

I'm equally interested in the fact that many straight women today find themselves in a porn-related predicament that can be as confusing as it's painful, namely that now that they're sexually liberated rather than repressed, they're asked to tolerate men's porn usage even when this usage involves types of porn that demean women, and even when this usage deprives them of sex with their partners. In other words, some straight women are up against a peculiar quandary that has yet to be clearly articulated: they're faced with sexually reluctant men; they find themselves in the bizarre situation of being entirely secondary to the sex lives of their partners.

These two arguments may at first glance seem mutually contradictory: on the one hand, female sexuality has become pornified but, on the other, some women aren't getting enough sex. But a closer look reveals that these problems are interrelated: today's straight women are literally competing with porn images for the attention of men. Sometimes they lose even when they do their best to pornify themselves, which is how they end up pornified yet deprived of sex.

In addition, there's virtually no cultural space for them to complain either about the misogynistic inflection of heteroporn or about the fact that many straight men seem to prefer the world of such heteroporn to sex with them. It may not be too much of a stretch to say that one of the main dilemmas that straight Western women face today is that they don't have a whole lot to do with their sexually liberated bodies because men are looking elsewhere: women may have gained their sexual freedom but in the process some of them lost men to the enticing entrails of online sex.

THE DILEMMAS OF PORNIFICATION

Much of the porn that straight men consume (and I would place the emphasis on that word: *consume*) is undeniably sexist, which means that the sexual culture straight women are forced to operate in is inherently sexist. To be sure, contemporary porn culture includes images of whip-wielding women who dominate men. But its most common trope remains the woman who either eagerly worships at the altar of the penis—who just can't wait to give that blowjob—or who invites male sexual aggression. This produces the following paradox for those women who equate female empowerment with emulating the dominant sexual symbolism of our culture, who believe that embodying the ideals of this culture is what will earn them parity with men: in order to feel empowered, such women have to adopt a misogynistic attitude toward their own sexuality; they, essentially, have to learn to appreciate their own sexual degradation.

This is an extreme manifestation of the phenomenon of women being taught to take pleasure in their own objectification that I've analyzed. And sadly, the history of academic feminism is in part to blame for the fact that many straight women feel like they don't have the right to complain about either the content or the prevalence of heteroporn in our society.[15] Academic feminism in the 1980s, during the so-called "sex wars," saw an enormous rift open up between those who criticized the misogyny of heteroporn and those who emphasized the fantasy aspects of sexuality, arguing that these aspects could (and should) not be policed. The latter camp came to be known as "pro-sex," while the former, problematically, got labeled as "anti-sex" even though most of its supporters were looking to liberate women from misogynistic forms of sexuality rather than to argue that sex in itself is evil.

Admittedly, vehement critics of pornography such as Catherine MacKinnon sometimes gave the impression that they believed that all forms of heterosex are a matter of patriarchal violence—that heterosexual intercourse is invariably a matter of men raping women—which understandably irked those feminists who enjoy sex, sometimes even the kind that puts men on top.[16] But despite the "anti-sex" tag that was pinned on them, most feminist critics of misogynist porn didn't hate sex. In retrospect, I would say that they merely wanted more interesting sex lives than what the heteropatriarchal imagination made available for straight women; they wanted better sex and they didn't think that mainstream heteroporn was the way to get it.

Like most sex-positive feminists, I've always carried the flag for the "pro-sex" side. I've been among those who insist that heterosex can be dissociated from patriarchy and male aggression. And I've been wary of the rapidity with which the critique of pornography can lead to a moralistic condemnation of sexuality as such. This is why, when a student asked me after a presentation I gave on the topic of this chapter why I was so cautious in my critique of the content of heteroporn, I didn't have a good answer: I could only say that I'm so aware of the history of the feminist porn wars that I'm afraid that any critique of heteroporn will instantly earn me a reputation for being anti-sex (which couldn't be further from the truth).

The fact is that my intellectual formation took place during the rise of queer feminism in the 1990s,[17] which tends to be emphatically "pro-sex," and vocally anti-MacKinnon, with the consequence that for two decades I flinched at the very mention of MacKinnon; like many pro-sex feminists, I thought of pornography as a way to sidestep a 1950s type of sexual prudery. It was interesting for me to discover that the twenty-something feminist (some of them do still exist!) who challenged me on this point was much more critical of the content of heteroporn than any of my closest colleagues have been willing to be—or that I myself have been willing to be.

In recent years I've had to reassess things, not because I want to endorse an anti-sex agenda but because I've come to see that the fact that the pro-sex side won the sex wars has contributed to a sexual culture that tells straight women that it's never cool to grumble about porn (because supposedly it's invariably sexually liberating and socially progressive). In other words, I've come to see that *unqualified* sex-positivity—the kind of feminism that, out of allegiance to the idea that erotic fantasies are intrinsically beyond reproach, celebrates all forms of sexuality—has closed off important critical avenues: it has made it virtually impossible to criticize heteropatriarchal sex culture without immediately being labeled puritanical and sex-negative. I've even known straight men who use "feminist" pro-sex arguments to bluntly silence their female partners who are bothered by their porn consumption.

The contemporary feminist nonchalance regarding the misogynistic (and racist) aspects of heteroporn is weirdly out of step with the generally critical attitude that academic feminism takes toward other components of mainstream culture. Notably, the same feminists who adamantly refuse to criticize porn adamantly criticize more or less every other aspect of biopolitics (in the same way that I've done in this book). This, I believe, is the biggest flaw in their thinking: it's not logical to use Foucault's theory of biopolitical conditioning to pick apart every element of present-day culture without admitting that the straight guy who cruises misogynistic porn on a nightly basis is getting an education on what sex is supposed to look like and on how he, as a sexual being, is supposed to act. It's not intellectually plausible to exempt sexual fantasies from otherwise intense critiques of the biopolitical fashioning of human subjectivity, for it seems incontestable that today's multibillion-dollar porn industry is one of the most powerful tools of this fashioning, fundamentally shaping the sexuality, and perhaps even the entire modality of being, of new generations of people, especially young men.

Paul Preciado may be right in speculating that if critics of biopolitics discreetly leave porn out of their analyses, it's because they're among its avid consumers.[18] Preciado, who otherwise adopts a queer- and trans-feminist approach, stands virtually alone on the pro-sex side in having the guts to call a spade a spade, admitting that the mainstream porn industry—which he calls "the porn factory"—revolves around women servicing the cock, of making this cock hard.[19] All the talk about the (supposed) liberation of sexuality that porn accomplishes can't change the fact that much of heteroporn is designed to get men off on the abjection of women; it's designed to make men feel powerful in relation to women whose main role is to serve them sexually.

Much of heteroporn folds the denigration of women into its basic understanding (and portrayal) of sexuality, which explains why some women—myself included—find it extremely difficult to watch; the truth is that I've always been bothered by the visuals of (not all but a great deal of) heteroporn but too afraid to admit this for fear of being called a bad (MacKinnon-esque) feminist. Again, I don't mean that all porn is condemnable. And if couples like to watch porn together, I couldn't care less.

I'm not making an argument against all porn. But I'm no longer willing to pretend, out of an allegiance to a certain type of feminism, that all of it is beyond reproach, let alone invariably an instrument of sexual liberation. I can see how for some, such as queer individuals isolated from queer communities, pornography can function precisely as such an instrument. But that's not what's happening with straight guys who tell their girlfriends to shut up about the objectification of women in mainstream heteroporn. As is the case with most cultural phenomena, how one interprets pornography is (should ideally be) contextual and related to questions of social power (to questions about who has this power and who doesn't).

Misogynistic heteroporn that men consume alone in large quantities reinforces the pillars of traditional—and for me unquestionably objectionable—heteropatriarchy by locking men and women all the more securely into the binary of the desiring man and the woman who is relegated to the position of the (often passive) object that titillates this desire. Online porn sites in fact give men absolute control over the images they consume: although they may lose control sexually, the women they "interact" with have absolutely no say in the way in which sex unfolds: porn images of women can't talk back, which means that they're the ultimate sexual "object."

Porn may also participate in the biopolitical creation of productive workers. Consider the common practice of using online pornography to take a break from work, to recharge one's ability to tackle the next task or to endure the dullness of the day. This is the epitome of neoliberal efficiency: it's quick and clean, devoid of the messiness that often characterizes "live" sexual encounters. You take your break and then you go back to work, back to performing. The libido, in this scenario, is not repressed, as it was in earlier models of sexuality, but instrumentalized in the service of increased productivity. The sad fact is that, at the very moment when we experience ourselves as sexually "free" (better off than earlier generations), we're getting a very precise tutoring in how to desire. We're being taught to desire in ways that allow the system to make money off our desire, whether directly through pornography or indirectly through our improved productivity.

Many of the young men at the presentation I mentioned above admitted to viewing porn on a regular basis. One of them was amused by the irony of being able to turn to some feminist texts to justify his porn consumption (he didn't appear to view it as a profeminist act). All the women in the group acknowledged that they know that the men they date or hang out with as friends spend a lot of time on porn sites. Most found this disturbing, though a few did not. Some of the men complained that porn was complicating their real-life sexual interactions (more on this shortly). But many seemed to view it as a largely pragmatic matter: a way of saving time and effort.

Since the 1950s at least, progressive social critics have equated sexual freedom with rebellion, with countercultural transgression, resistance, and subversion. For a long time, this equation made sense: it's not a coincidence that sexual liberation in the United States took place at the same time as antiwar protests, the rise of second-wave feminism, and general public unrest. But by now, capitalist consumer culture has coopted sexual liberation to the extent that these days sex, including sex that used to be considered "perverse," often merely facilitates our ability to successfully participate in the game of keeping up with a multitude of psychological, emotional, and work-related pressures; it props up rather than challenges the status quo of our competitive culture. Furthermore, the very practice of picking and choosing from among a profusion of online sexual scenarios—akin to the practice of picking and choosing from among the profusion of pasta sauces at the grocery story—reinforces the capitalist mentality that presents consumerism as a solution to all of our problems; it explicitly promotes the idea that it's our inalienable right to "enjoy" the offerings of our affluent societies.

Online porn consumers exercise "choice" like any other capitalist consumers in the sense that they can cherry-pick their favorite sexual scenarios. On the one hand, most of the scenarios they have access to have been produced by global conglomerates, which means that their choices have been largely predetermined; on the other, because capitalism thrives on the proliferation of goods and services, porn consumers are given the same illusion of choice as the consumers of pasta sauces who browse among a large array of jars whose labels make them seem distinctive even though they all contain more or less the same ingredients. In addition, porn consumers are trained to think that their satisfaction should be immediate, constant, and without exertion, which seems a whole lot like yet another iteration of the capitalist creed. This is a mentality that tells us that everything should be readily available to us, that we should not be asked to make any sacrifices, to set any priorities; it tells us that our options are infinite, which is one way of producing people who think that they're entitled to everything.

I feel the effects of this reality concretely—in ways that make a difference in how I feel (often pretty bad)—whenever I walk into an undergraduate classroom: I'm aware that I'm standing in front of dozens of young men, some still teenagers, whose principal sexual engagement with women has been through porn images that I would most likely find troubling. The idea that this formation has no bearing on how they approach women in the real world, including their female professors, is unrealistic. I don't think that it's possible for people to move in and out of online venues without carrying traces of those venues into their offline lives.

I find it hard to dispel the mind-altering fumes of spending fifteen minutes on Amazon.com. So I can't imagine that the young men who started watching misogynistic porn when they were ten haven't been in any way impacted by this practice. Generally speaking, online porn has changed my relationship to men: whereas a couple of decades ago progressive men seemed like allies, friends, intellectual buddies, and potential lovers, these days I mostly want nothing to do with them. Something in their eyes has changed.

Some men I've talked to admit that there are unwanted results to their porn usage. Some admit that they feel ashamed of having enjoyed watching pornography that humiliates women, that they don't quite know what to do with the images that saturate their imagination, and that they consequently find real-life sexual encounters challenging and bewildering; they find it difficult to reconcile the female-degrading images that they have relished with the reality of being attracted to women they admire, with the result that their offline sexuality is timid and self-conscious. This conflicted attitude seems common among profeminist men who want to treat women well but who simultaneously find online porn too seductive to resist.

Among such men, guilt about their online activities can even give rise to a desperate effort to idealize their partners, to see women as virginal creatures who are entirely divorced from the "dirty" images they see online; it can give rise to an attempt to redraw the age-old heteropatriarchal dichotomy between virgin and whore as a line between offline and online sexuality. One man even mentioned that he would rather receive a kind smile from a woman than have sex with her; his desire is sublimated into gentleness, an idealizing love that flees from the disorganization of passion. Though this attitude may seem protective of women, it undermines women who would prefer robust sex lives, who would like to actually have sex with their partners rather than be worshipped as icons of purity.

It's surely an irony of ironies that at the same time as the cultural hype about men always wanting sex is ongoing, pornography is creating a generation of men that, actually, don't seem to much want it. Having constant access to online porn can be sexually numbing: people who open their laptops the minute they feel the slightest stirring of libido may after a while no longer know what desire feels like. If I've just demolished an industrial-sized bar of chocolate, I'm not going to want to turn around in thirty minutes and devour another such bar. At a certain point, I start feeling nauseated. So I can only speculate about the libido-killing effects of a constant stream of wet pussies on one's computer screen.

A French colleague of mine told me a few years ago that he's haunted by the vague impression that the young men sitting in his classes are largely drained of desire—perhaps because they are. I've also had young men tell me point blank—because I'm curious enough to ask—that they experience sex with real women as a tedious chore because it's never as fuss-free or good as sex on the internet: it takes too much effort—you have to try to actually please the woman—and it's less exciting because there's a limit to what you can do. Plus you have to worry about your performance. So why bother?

THE SAME OLD STORY

I trust that this is not how all men think, but I'm not surprised that some of those whose entire sexual formation has taken place online do reason along these lines. And what's certain is that the basic message our society is sending straight women is that they have no choice but to learn to live with porn. You catch your husband looking at girly pictures on his laptop? Look the other way and count your blessings that he's not watching hardcore rape porn.

One man I talked to—let's call him Rick—attempted to convince me that men simply can't live without porn: supposedly it's as necessary to them as breathing, water, and food so that, really, there's nothing to be done but to accept it. I find this argument, which we increasingly hear in our public culture, including in advice directed at straight women, absurd in the sense that there are many things in life that we may want but can't have. For starters, I would like a shorter working day, a higher salary, quieter neighbors, and students who know the difference between *it's* and *its*. But I've learned to accept that I can't always have these things. So it seems to me that the idea that porn is the one thing that men simply *can't live without* is part and parcel of the heteropatriarchal mythology that naturalizes the male sex drive as intractable (while pretending that women have no trouble suppressing their urges, that they don't much care either way).

This is one way in which antifeminist evolutionary (pop "scientific") arguments enter mainstream culture, for nothing is more important to conservative evolutionary psychologists than the idea that male sexuality is the kind of force of nature that nothing can stop (whereas female sexuality barely merits mention). Rick told me that he once forgot about porn for *two whole weeks* because he fell madly in love. He reported being shocked that he could go for that long without an online fix. He also revealed that he doesn't choose girlfriends on the basis of their sex appeal—he knows he can get instant satisfaction online—but rather on the basis of their "presentability" to his parents. Essentially, he assesses the suitability of his partners by using a 1950s measuring stick: he's looking for a Wife rather than a sexual partner, a woman who is respectable, who will be a good mother, and who reassures his parents.

The idealizing attitude I referred to above here takes a decidedly retrograde inflection: if some of the guilt-ridden men I talked to feel conflicted about sex with women they admire, Rick wants his girlfriend to act like one of the virtuous wives of bygone eras. He has stepped back into a time when men didn't sleep (much) with the women they loved (and married) and didn't love (much) the women they slept with. Rick is also among those who admit to finding real-life sex lackluster in comparison to its online counterpart. This seems to directly contradict his claim that his girlfriend shouldn't be bothered by his porn usage because "it doesn't mean anything." Clearly, if online porn satisfies him more than sex with his girlfriend, it means *something*.

That Rick's girlfriend isn't allowed to complain about his online activities is (for him) a given. When I pressed him on what he thought his girlfriend should do with her sexuality, it took him a while to understand what I was asking, because he assumed that women's level of desire is not very high: "Everyone knows that they only fuck to please men." When I said that I didn't think that this was necessarily true, that I knew many women who liked "fucking" just fine, he finally seemed to grasp the dilemma: "So, you're saying that if I get most of my sex from the internet, my girlfriend might feel deprived of sex that she thinks she deserves as my girlfriend?" *Yeah, that's what I'm saying.* "Ah," he said, as the lightbulb went on.

My conversation with Rick gave me my first, and thus far only, panic attack. To say that I felt bad is an understatement (even though I had absolutely no interest in dating this guy). I felt utterly defeated as a sex-positive feminist. Even though I know that Rick isn't Mr. Every Guy, I don't think that he's entirely unusual either, and this terrifies me, for I recognize that when men like Rick tell their girlfriends that complaining about their porn consumption is prudish, heteropatriarchy has found yet another way to tell the same tired story: *men get to have what they want (in this case, porn) whereas women's preferences, including their sexual preferences, are deemed insignificant.*

Heteroporn perpetuates a gendered economy of sex that unapologetically reinforces the notion that men's desires come first. It really would be convenient for men like Rick—and for the entire system of heteropatriarchy—if women just learned to "live with it," if they simply just stopped quarreling about it. Indeed, when I floated the possibility that Rick's girlfriend might be complaining about his porn consumption because she feels slighted by it, he said that he didn't care. He clearly expected her to accommodate his needs, whereas it didn't even occur to him to try to accommodate hers: in this case, the need for a porn-free sex life. He expected her to respect his way of taking his pleasure, whereas he had no interest in catering to hers. Essentially, he expected her to admit the superiority of his needs without question. For Rick, there seemed to be no such thing as active female desire.

When I finally told Rick (because the conversation was making me livid—this was not a "controlled" interview) that I didn't care what he did with his sex life but that I would never want to date a man like him, a man with no regard for my preferences or feelings, Rick insisted that, like his girlfriend, I don't have a choice because every guy out there is like him (even if they don't like to admit it). Fortunately, I know that I *do* have a choice. Even though I certainly recoil from men more than I used to, I haven't found it impossible to find ones who are willing to enter into the give and take of negotiating a mutually satisfying sex life.

Rick's unwillingness to accept the idea that I have some say about the kinds of men I date came across as an attempt to erase my subjectivity and to make his sexual attitude more palatable by claiming that all men, by virtue of being men, are like him. Rick also clearly assumed that he should not be asked to make any choices in life, that *of course* he should be able to have his girlfriend's love at the same time as he gets to keep his porn. This mixture of entitlement and pure gluttony characterizes many aspects of our consumer society. I learned a long time ago not to be surprised by the fact that it's frequently expressed by young men of anticapitalist, in this case explicitly Marxist, inclinations.

For all these reasons, I'm not convinced that our postfeminist sexual culture is taking place on women's terms. Men like Rick silence women who seek to voice their bad feelings about pornography, sometimes even—if they're clever enough—claiming that being critical of porn turns a woman into an antiquated antifeminist. These are men who tell their girlfriends that if they're feeling bad, they should learn to feel differently. This is one of the oldest tricks in the heteropatriarchal handbook: if you do something that makes a woman feel bad, make sure that she feels terrible about feeling bad, so terrible in fact that she'll do her best to suppress that bad feeling. Gendered thinking that tells us that men can't live without porn whereas women don't mind going without sex merely puts a new spin on this old trick: it implies that women's desires are so trifling that, really, instead of complaining, they should feel relieved that men are getting their satisfaction elsewhere.

There are some women who are genuinely okay with their partner's porn habits. Others may say that they're okay with these habits when in fact they aren't; they may say so because they feel cornered or because they don't want to appear uncool. If so, they probably can't keep up appearances indefinitely, in which case their relationship will eventually run into trouble. When this happens, men like Rick are likely to try to turn the tables by telling their girlfriends that they're being too sensitive or straitlaced or both; they'll try to make them feel bad about feeling bad.

Many men are getting away with this strategy. But fortunately, more and more straight women are becoming aggravated. Some of them are starting the protest ("I'm sex-positive but still . . ."). The contradictions of pornification—the contradictions of a culture that presents itself as female-friendly at the same time as it tells women that they have no choice but to reconcile themselves to men's fascination with misogynist porn—are becoming too immense to ignore; they're making it impossible for the world of heterosex to fully conceal its paradoxes. Perhaps one day things will truly explode. Perhaps there will be another wave of feminism. I hope it's going to be a tsunami.

5

THE SPECIFICITY OF DESIRE

The Foucauldian line of reasoning I've been following may seem deterministic, giving the impression that we're hopelessly entangled in dominant ideological structures, that in the final analysis, there's no way out of oppressive social configurations such as heteropatriarchy. Even though Foucault admits that biopolitical conditioning is never entirely successful, that there are holes in the ideological net that traps us, his conviction that this conditioning is both endemic and invisible doesn't leave much space for freedom or autonomy: personal agency doesn't make much sense in the context of a theory that assumes that our coming-into-being as human subjects, as well as our long-term viability as such subjects, cannot be dissociated from collective values.

This far in this book, I've adopted a broadly Foucauldian perspective because I believe that his analysis of biopolitics gives us important tools for understanding the ways in which bad feelings can be socially generated. However, I have to admit that, more generally speaking, I've never been a devout Foucauldian precisely because I find his outlook too deterministic. I've always also been drawn to philosophers such as Hannah Arendt and Jean-Paul Sartre who argue that human beings have the capacity, and even the ethical obligation, to critically examine their existential choices.[1] And I've been even more strongly influenced by the Freudian-Lacanian psychoanalytic tradition that I introduced at the beginning of this book.

At first glance, it may seem that it would be impossible to reconcile Arendt and Sartre—who place a strong emphasis on conscious self-reflexivity—with the psychoanalytic tradition, which focuses on the unconscious determinants of human life. Indeed, one could point out that if the Foucauldian approach risks coming too close to social determinism, the psychoanalytic approach risks coming too close to the idea that our destinies are determined by unconscious forces over which we have no control. However, although psychoanalysis shies away from the post-Kantian rationalism that Arendt and Sartre are sometimes criticized for, it shares with these thinkers the ideal of being able to take a degree of critical distance from our lives, including the social currents that condition our beliefs and choices. It even believes in the possibility of gaining some critical distance from the unconscious currents that shape our lives (determine our destiny). Why else enter into analysis?

Like Arendt and Sartre, the Freudian-Lacanian tradition suggests that we have the ability to take ourselves as objects of contemplation, with the result that we have the potential to resist components of collective life that we find banal, coercive, or oppressive. We also have the ability—albeit a limited one—to intervene in our unconscious predispositions. The price we often pay for this ability is anxiety: the anxiety that arises from knowing that even though many components of our lives—such as illnesses, accidents, sexism, racism, and the enigmatic workings of the unconscious—are beyond our control, we do have some say over how we're going to live, although we might not always be able to make the right choices, let alone stay faithful to these choices when things become difficult or some-how go awry.

During my career, I've repeatedly struggled with the fact that this emphasis on existential choices is hard to reconcile with major trends in posthumanist theory (my field), which has been vehemently critical of notions of freedom and autonomy derived from the Enlightenment.[2] I've found myself in an intellectual bind. On the one hand, my survival in that devastating house by the mysterious lake depended on my capacity to believe that I had a way out, which means that I've never been able to entirely discard humanist (Enlightenment) ideals of choice, agency, and self-determination. On the other hand, I'm deeply supportive of the reasons for which critics from the Frankfurt School and French poststructuralism to postcolonial studies, deconstructive feminism, and queer theory have accused the Enlightenment of an excessive celebration of choice, agency, and self-determination. The critics of the Enlightenment are correct in arguing that this celebration resulted in both political and epistemological violence—the kind of violence that, among other things, sought to rid the world of (destroy, repress) the irrational, the affective, the feminine, and the "othered" (the racialized, colonized, dispossessed, marginalized, and so on).[3]

The Enlightenment—once considered a revolutionary defender of reason and equality against mysticism, prejudice, and tyranny—has in recent decades (rightly) been reproached for upholding an image of straight white masculinity as fully agentic, self-governing, and masterful and for denigrating every other subject position as falling pitifully short of this image. It has also (rightly) been charged with promoting an overly individualistic vision of subjectivity. Against this backdrop, the idea that it's up to me as a self-reflexive being to figure out the meaning and direction of my life may seem to replicate some of the most problematic principles of the Enlightenment. Post-Foucauldian critics in particular might argue that the ideal of self-reflexivity is nothing but a crafty ruse of biopolitical conditioning—a ruse that gives me the impression that I'm free when in fact I'm not.

Along related lines, those intent on dissolving the distinction between human beings and other animals or between human beings and inanimate objects such as rocks or lakes[4] might argue that the Freudian-Lacanian approach privileges the human at the expense of other entities. I concede that there's no way to effectively contest this charge. And in principle I'm sympathetic to attempts to shift our focus from the human to the nonhuman, for such attempts are often motivated by the wish to arrest the exploitation of the nonhuman by the human. Nonetheless, I don't see any reason to deny that one of the many things that clearly *does* distinguish humans from other entities is precisely their capacity to take their existence as an object of contemplation.

Contemplation doesn't automatically lead to exploitation. Nor does self-reflexivity equal seamless agency or self-mastery. It is merely one of the few defenses we have against social determinism. This may be why even Foucault, toward the end of his career, started to investigate the power of self-interrogation: having built his reputation on explaining how biopolitical conditioning—what he also called *disciplinary power*—shapes our subjectivity, including our sexuality, he ended up analyzing ancient Greek notions of the care of the self that relied on the ideal of active self-fashioning.[5]

Much of post-Foucauldian theory has emphasized biopolitics over active self-fashioning, the early Foucault over the later Foucault. I'll return to some of the conceptual problems that ensue from this choice in the conclusion. Here, in preparation for shifting to the Lacanian psychoanalytic register that I'll foreground in this chapter and the next, I want to note that although Lacan, like all psychoanalytic thinkers, values self-reflexivity (the practice of taking one's existence as an object of contemplation), he doesn't valorize the ideal of a fully agentic self. As a matter of fact, Lacan was an early and prominent critic of the autonomous Enlightenment subject.[6] As a consequence, although his psychoanalytic approach advocates self-examination, it nevertheless emphasizes the ways in which human beings inevitably fall short of self-mastery.

The lack of complete agency or self-mastery, however, doesn't mean that we possess no agency, willpower, or self-control whatsoever. Quite the contrary, the Lacanian subject is often thoroughly stubborn and rebellious. One reason I'm drawn to Lacanian theory is that it manages to resolve the intellectual bind I referred to above: it shuns Enlightenment notions of freedom and autonomy without thereby implying that human beings have no capacity for self-reflexivity or self-determination. Or to state the matter slightly differently, Lacan recognizes that human subjectivity is socially conditioned, and that none of us can therefore fully control our destinies, without falling into social determinism. Perhaps even more importantly for my purposes, he sidesteps biological determinism—the kind of determinism advocated by sexist (and racist) evolutionary thinkers—without denying the kinship between humans and other animals.

One way to bypass biologism is to interrogate the difference between sexed bodies and the cultural mythologies of masculinity and femininity that have been imposed on those bodies. As I illustrated in the introduction, Lacan was among the first to undertake this task. He was also among the first to break the hold of biologism by highlighting the difference between human desire and animal instinct.

This difference between human desire and animal instinct interests us in this chapter, not the least because desire, understood in the Lacanian sense, offers the key to sidestepping not just biological determinism but also the social determinism implied by Foucault's analysis of biopolitics. In other words, desire provides a way of thinking about what agency might look like after the demise of the sovereign (fully agentic, autonomous, and self-mastering) Enlightenment subject. It's not a coincidence that both desire and self-reflexivity—self-reflexivity as a means of interrogating desire and desire as an opening to self-reflexivity—fall within the main preoccupations of psychoanalytic practice, for both are connected to the quest to reconceptualize agency in the posthumanist (post-Enlightenment) moment.

Lacan demonstrates that because human biology cannot escape the imprint of culture, of socialization, there's nothing natural (or "reproductive") about the functioning of desire; he demonstrates that because socially intelligible subjectivity demands the disciplining of bodily drives, desire is not an instinct that we can satisfy straightforwardly by having sex but rather an amorphous and unpredictable force that puts pressure on us, much of the time causing us to feel disharmonious, even tormented. I don't want to be mistaken for saying that human beings have no instincts at all, for obviously they do, such as the instinct to withdraw a hand from a hot burner or to recoil from aggressive men on the street; the instinct to survive (and maybe even thrive) seems pronounced enough. I'm merely saying that desire is too convoluted, too socially conditioned, to be an instinct in this semi-automatic sense.

One could say that there's always something off the mark about desire: there's too much of it, too little of it, or it's aimed at the wrong object. In addition, although it has been shaped by social norms, it also chafes against them, which is why Freud thought that there is a fundamental conflict between desire and civilization (note that there isn't a similarly inevitable conflict between animal instinct and animal societies).[7] This is why post-Freudian critics such as Lacan (and his followers) have tended to regard desire as a defiant, countercultural force. That is, even though desire is socially conditioned, it tends to push against the constraints of that very conditioning. My analysis of pornography in the last chapter shows how easily desire can be subjected to biopolitical control. But I still have faith that some of it will always elude this control, which is why I trust that Lacan, and psychoanalysis generally speaking, is correct in suggesting that the specificity of desire—while often a cause of tremendous suffering—is also potentially an opening to a degree of self-determination.

BAD, PAINFUL CHOICES

I'll return to the connection between desire and self-determination toward the end of this chapter. But I want to begin with the observation that the specificity of desire can cause tremendous suffering (bad feelings). In this context, my emphasis will be less on collectively generated bad feelings than on ones arising from intimate relationships: in both cases, the causes of our bad feelings are at least partially external, but the scale is different in the sense that even though the disappointments of desire can certainly have a broadly cultural source, it's usually the ones that have a very specific cause, such as the loss of a lover, that sting the most.

The specificity of desire—the fact that it tends to fixate on a specific object even when this object (sometimes repeatedly) disappoints us—is one of the strongest arguments against evolutionary thinkers who endeavor to equate desire with reproduction, for from the point of view of reproductive success, such obstinate specificity is an impediment: it can cause us to make relational choices that cannot possibly bring us any reproductive benefit, that end up being painful, and that are therefore detrimental to our overall wellbeing.

Evolutionary explanations for human romantic behavior fail to account for several agony-inducing realities about desire: (1) we often desire people who are unavailable; (2) we often desire people who wound us; and (3) we often find it impossible to get over our romantic losses, and this can be the case even when our partner has coldly abandoned us. In all of these instances, our sadness can persist for long stretches of time, sometimes even years, paralyzing our desire and making it impossible for us to shift our attention to new lovers. Although other animals may also have their preferences, they don't seem nearly as neurotic—as obsessed with particular objects of desire—as humans do.

Desire can cause bad feelings even when we leave specificity out of it: when we fail to attain what we want—say, a coveted job—it's hard not to feel morose; it's hard not to feel heavy in the legs when we climb the steps to our current, utterly unsatisfying job with the knowledge that we might be stuck in it for the rest of our lives. In such situations, the main difference between ourselves and the six-year-old at the supermarket who throws a temper tantrum because her daddy refuses to buy the chocolate bar she craves is that we seethe in silence, at least as long as we know that our colleagues can hear us. What we do in the privacy of our homes or over drinks with our friends may come closer to a tantrum.

Ironically, when we manage to get what we want, we're often instantly anxious about losing it, hoping that no one steals our chocolate bar, wondering how we'll feel once we've eaten the chocolate bar, and so on. Alternatively, we might start to doubt that the bar we've managed to procure is in fact the best available bar; we start to scrutinize other chocolate bars just to make sure we haven't settled for an inferior one. This is why loss is intrinsic to every pleasure and why happiness is such a precarious state: when we're happy, we tend to worry about becoming unhappy, sometimes because we're afraid of losing what we have, other times because we're afraid of discovering that what we have isn't that great after all.

The existence of desire on some level depends on the unavailability of its object, so that there's an inherent contradiction that haunts desire: getting what we want tends to diminish the value of what we want. As a result, to the extent that we want to keep wanting, we may find various ways of making sure that we don't obtain what we want. Even more ironically, desire can be vexing even when it's satisfied. We may find it so impossible to tolerate getting what we want that we engage in various forms of self-sabotage in relation to whatever it is that we (seem to) want: a person, a vacation, a career goal. We may even try to actively render our object disappointing.

This is the predicament of those who cannot take pleasure in anything they have—say, a house—but must move to a new object of desire, a new house, as soon as the old one has become even a little bit familiar. The same restlessness can obviously apply to lovers, which is why some of us move from one lover to the next at predictable intervals. Even when it's in no way the case that the new house, or the new lover, is superior to the one we have discarded, there can be a perverse satisfaction to moving along the chain of desire.

The inability to find a resting place for our desire can be traumatizing. However, the opposite scenario is an even bigger source of torment: perhaps the most prominent among the bad feelings caused by desire is the anguish that ensues from losing a person (though it could be a house, a job, or something else) who feels irreplaceable. Let me put it this way: one of the most excruciating things about human relationships is that we often feel like we simply aren't capable of giving up a specific person, yet we have to find a way of doing so anyway; we have to relinquish the very person who means the most to us in the world and we have to do so even when we, on some level, can't. Usually, the reason for this predicament is that the person we experience as irreplaceable doesn't feel the same way about us, which means that, short of turning into a stalker, we have no choice but to replace (or at the very least release) him or her.

Losing a person we consider irreplaceable can freeze our desire so completely that even when we chance upon someone new that evolutionary psychologists, our dearest friends, and our eighty-something aunt would all characterize as an outstanding choice, we can't get interested; we can't force ourselves to want this person. Instead, we spend our time fantasizing about the lover we've lost, trying to guess whom he or she is spending time with, regretting the mistakes we've made, wondering what's wrong with us, trying to figure out why we always get wounded in the same way, and aspiring to find a better way of doing things in the future. We complain about our problems to our friends until they get so tired of our story that they throw a muffin at us. Sometimes we hire therapists because we know that they get paid to listen to us, which means that they'll have to eat their blueberry muffin in silence while we blabber on.

My point is that there's a startling irrationality to human desire that our so-called "rational" sciences, such as evolutionary theory, haven't been able to elucidate. Indeed, to the extent that our sciences keep denying this irrationality—to the extent that they, for instance, insist that our romantic behavior neatly follows the logic of reproduction—they confuse things even further, misleading people into thinking that there's an easy answer to their relationship problems when this is far from being the case. This is why this chapter is devoted to offering an account of desire's irrationality, starting with its misery-inducing fixations.

Yet I also want to propose that the fixations of desire can be valuable, that they can (paradoxically enough) augment the self-determination that I've claimed psychoanalysis wishes to protect. They can for example cause us to resist the capitalist mentality that constantly asks us to replace things, to impatiently move from one object of desire to the next, one person of interest to the next. We'll see that in the context of consumer culture, the fixations of desire, our fidelity to the objects and people we love, can be a sign of courage and perhaps even an ethical attitude.

THE PARALYSIS OF DESIRE

Freud called the paralysis of desire that results from the loss of a loved person melancholia, which he defined as the kind of mourning that doesn't come to a timely end. Usually in the aftermath of a romantic loss we mourn for a while, but eventually we get over our disappointment; we become capable of desiring new people. Melancholia, in contrast, is the kind of sadness that continues indefinitely because our faithfulness to our lost object renders the idea of new objects intolerable.

Melancholia is particularly likely to arise when the loss that we have experienced is premature so that—and here I paraphrase Freud—even though we know whom we have lost, we don't know "what" we have lost:[8] we know the identity of the person we have lost but not the details of the future we could have had with that person; in addition to the person, we have lost the relational and existential avenues that we might have been able to pursue with him or her. These possibilities include the person we might have become as a result of loving the person in question, so that we have, in a way, lost a potentially desirable future edition of ourselves. This hurts. And not having a good sense of how things might have unfolded makes things worse, with the consequence that our mourning may go on indefinitely.

Melancholia drains the world of its allure, causing us to retreat into a solitary province of private grief. Objects (beyond the one we have lost) become unenticing. In a sense, our sadness becomes our primary object of attachment. This isn't necessarily entirely bad, for melancholia can generate a clarity of vision, an accuracy of perception, that more sanguine individuals lack. As Freud remarks, the melancholic may have "a keener eye for the truth" than those less racked with grief, adding that the melancholic may in fact have "come pretty near to understanding himself."[9]

To the extent that melancholia shatters our cruelly optimistic hope that things will improve in the future, it generates a pessimism that may in some instances be more accurate than the rosy picture painted by positive thinking. In addition, melancholia forces us to confront our lack-in-being (the ontological lack that interested Lacan), demonstrating that the attempt to heal this lack through objects, including the object of our love, is treacherous; it dissolves the fantasies that, through desire, attach us to a world of objects. In saying this, I don't mean to suggest that all objects of desire are devoid of value (quite the contrary, as we'll see below). But sometimes a degree of distance from objects is the precondition of heightened self-understanding.

When in the grip of melancholia, it may also feel like pursuing new objects of desire would be a betrayal of the one we have lost; even when it's our lover who has severed the bond, it may feel like replacing him or her would break a sacred covenant. Rejecting new lovers may seem like the only way to cherish the memory of the old one. For the melancholic—the person stuck in mourning—even a sad recollection of the lost object is better than the irrevocable loss that would ensue from replacing that recollection by a new passion, a new object of desire.

Moreover, our sadness may cause us to vow that we'll never again allow ourselves to desire because we have learned that desire leads to unbearable suffering. Over time, we usually discover that our vow doesn't hold, that even a prolonged melancholia does in due course lift. And even if we never fully cease to mourn what we have lost, the intensity of our pain will diminish over time. Either way, we're likely to desire again. Unfortunately, this often means that we *are* likely to get hurt in the same way again. Freud explained this sad state of affairs through his notion of the repetition compulsion: our tendency to fall into painful patterns of desiring that stubbornly resist our attempts to alter them.

The repetition compulsion is worth pausing on, for the repetitive nature of the ways in which many of us keep getting hurt by our desire is distinctively human, arguably one of the most pronounced differences between humans and other animals, who don't seem prone to repeat the bad mating choices— or other bad choices—they have made in the course of their lives. The repetition compulsion is also one of the ways in which we're forced to grapple with bad feelings as an ongoing component of our lives in the sense that over time it becomes hard to ignore the fact that we repeatedly manage to end up in painful relational, professional, or other life-shaping scenarios that are made all the more maddening by being so familiar. It may even start to feel like it's our destiny to end up in such scenarios, that they're how our lives are supposed to proceed. The more curious among us are likely to wonder why.

Throughout this book, I've argued that many of our bad feelings are socially generated. We have seen that depression and anxiety, for instance, can be reasonable responses to precarious circumstances, such as poverty. The repetition compulsion can also have external causes in the sense that it may have its origins in a difficult family history or some other kind of trauma. But because it has a strong unconscious component, it comes to be lived as something that seems to enigmatically arise from our own choices and actions, from the mistakes we keep repeating, rather than from challenging external factors.

It would be nice if we could learn from our mistakes, if our missteps resulted in the kind of clarity that allows us to avoid similar missteps in the future. But often this isn't the case. Quite the contrary, sometimes it feels that the more resolutely we seek to avoid a painful pattern, the more nimbly it catches us in its net, leaving us stunned and breathless. Freud's explanation for this was that, in its twisted way, the repetition compulsion is trying to help us heal our most formative wounds, particularly the ones we carry from childhood. It reflects our unconscious hope that if we repeatedly place ourselves in the same distressing scenario, one day we'll learn to master it so that we won't get hurt.

This is an unconscious version of cruel optimism: something in us that causes us to trust that practice makes perfect, that *this time* things will turn out differently. Unfortunately, this is rarely what actually happens; unfortunately, it's more likely that we'll keep repeating the same pattern until the end of our days. In this sense, the repetition compulsion does in fact determine our entire destiny, over time shaping us into the person we are. Even those who grow up in loving families cannot entirely avoid the feeling of being bruised, for a child's demand for love always exceeds what any caretaker—no matter how caring— can offer; even the most devoted upbringing cannot avoid inflicting a degree of mortification. In addition, those whose caretakers did not take good care of them—who were treated coldly, callously, aggressively, or otherwise violently—have been exposed to intense suffering, the kind of suffering, moreover, that they were powerless to fend off for the simple reason that their survival depended on those who inflicted it; the tragedy of childhood abuse is that children are physically and emotionally tied to the very people who injure them.

Freud hypothesized that such childhood traumas, whether slight or acute, imagined or actual, leave behind an unprocessed emotional residue that we spend the rest of our lives trying to process. The repetition compulsion is one way in which this processing happens. This is why, according to Freud, there's no such thing as a completely normal psychic life, why all of us are in one way or another neurotic. Freud built an entire therapeutic practice around this insight: even those who ridicule him cannot deny that contemporary psychotherapy can be traced back to his invention of the "talking cure." Nor can we deny that the majority of those who enter therapy do so because something is not working in their love lives. Desire, in short, is routinely derailing, even deforming, making it difficult for us to get things "right" in intimate relationships.

LACAN'S THEORY OF LACK

If Freud's genius (among other things) was to recognize the difference between how human desire works in contrast to the instincts of other animals, it was the genius of Lacan (among other things) to elucidate the link between the social character of human subjectivity and the fact that we tend to feel lacking, as if a part of us were missing.

I've explained that Lacan thought that the reason for this feeling is that during the process of socialization, children encounter a symbolic world of meanings that exceeds their cognitive capacities, leaving them feeling inadequate and alienated (existentially, ontologically humbled). It may in practice be impossible to distinguish clearly between such (ontological) lack-in-being and the more specific modalities of interpersonal mortification that Freud connected to the repetition compulsion; these two forms of deprivation may reinforce each other in life-defining ways. But what interests us in the present context is Lacan's hypothesis that our (ontological) lack-in-being is what gives rise to desire as a specifically human experience.

It's because we sense that some essential part of ourselves has been chopped off and lost (misplaced) that we want things, it being our (unconscious) hope that these things will make us whole again. From this viewpoint, it's because children are exposed to a social world that they on some level experience as intrinsically wounding (even when no one is intentionally trying to hurt them) that there is, later in life, no such thing as a straightforward desire, desire devoid of traces of loss, let alone a straightforward reproductive instinct that would guide our romantic choices in a logical manner. The scandal of Lacanian theory was to describe this all-too-human quandary, and moreover—and here I return to a theme from the opening

pages of this book—to insist that "castration" (lack) is foundational to the human condition rather than a sign of a specifically female deficiency.

That our society has historically insisted on pushing the
stigma of lack onto women is an indication of the desperation
with which (many) men have fled their lack (woundedness), for
if men felt genuinely secure, they wouldn't feel the need to dis-
parage or oppress women. As female intellectuals from Simone
de Beauvoir and Virginia Woolf to contemporary feminists
have argued, women have throughout the ages been asked to
personify lack so as to reassure men of their wholeness; women
have been coded as passive objects so that men could have faith
in their status as active and agentic subjects.

In the next chapter, we'll see that Lacan thought that, ironically, nothing symbolizes castration more unmistakably than
the penis in the sense that (premature) flaccidity is the repressed
twin, and predictable result, of every erection. In this chapter, I
want to focus on the idea that nothing holds the promise of
regained plenitude more strongly than the person we love, the
person we believe is our soulmate. It's in fact conceivable that
our society's entire romantic edifice—its preoccupation with
the "one and only," its emphasis on marriage as what completes
a person, and its vision of the nuclear family as a protective
cocoon whose integrity needs to be respected at all costs—
might have formed in response to the simple fact that human
beings don't feel whole.

Lacan's account of desire also goes some distance toward
explaining the heteropatriarchal notion that men and women
complement each other, each offering the other what he or
she "lacks." I've noted that our society recycles the idea that
women—who, according to cultural mythology, possess more
warmth and emotional intelligence than men—are able to

rescue men from their sterile existence; through their sensitivity, patience, and generous care, women are supposed to humanize men. Men, in turn, are urged to offer women protection and practical support; they're asked to provide the voice of reason when feminine irrationality threatens to unsettle things. Such beliefs are central to the gender stereotyping practices I've criticized. In contrast, Lacan emphasized their fantasmatic, purely ideological underpinnings, elucidating the ways in which our yearning for wholeness can mislead us into placing the burden of providing it on others, particularly on those who seem to "naturally" possess what we lack.

One reason that desire is not reproductively efficient is that it doesn't focus on children but rather on the sexual partner as a site of regained wholeness. By this I don't mean to say that the wish to reproduce plays no part in human life. Obviously it does. Indeed, for some people, children function as a means of coping with the very lack Lacan diagnosed: undoubtedly, some people use their children to plug the hole within their being. As a matter of fact, even if this is not what parents intend, children can offer an effective distraction from this hole.

Who has time to worry about feelings of existential deficiency when your children demand this and that? As a friend of mine with three young children said the other day, "I'm still alive, ain't I?" Clearly, the hole at the heart of her being was not at the top of her list of priorities. Nor was it a priority for the harried mother I recently met in the locker room of my gym. She said that she had come there just to take a shower—"no time for a workout"—so that she could wash her hair without having to listen to her two-year-old scream at the top of her lungs. She had forgotten her towel. I handed her mine, thinking that this woman's need for a shower superseded mine, that I could take one later at home while contemplating the meaning of life in my calm fortress of solitude.

My point, then, is not that people don't want to reproduce. Rather, it's that reproduction isn't desire's main goal. If it were, desire would function more rationally, with more attention to attaining its goal expediently, without all the agonies that humans experience in intimate relationships. The reason desire causes so much consternation is that it covets something that's intrinsically impossible, namely self-completion, the undoing of lack.

Western philosophy has known this since its beginnings, for Plato already expressed this idea in *The Symposium*, where Aristophanes explains that humans were once rounded creatures with four arms, four legs, and two faces, looking in opposite directions; that one day Zeus got so angry at their arrogance that he split them in half in order to weaken them; that since then they have been looking for their lost half; and that whenever they happen to find it—which isn't very often—they're so overjoyed that they throw their arms around each other and vow never to be separated again.[10]

Lacan reasons along the same lines when he suggests that humans suffer from a gnawing sense of lack and that they look to objects of desire, particularly other people, to alleviate this suffering. Other animals are presumably not burdened by this problem; their desire is presumably not motivated by the wish to conjure away their existential insecurity. Human desire, in contrast, often is, which is why this desire can't be reduced to the instinct to propagate the species.

MORE IN YOU THAN YOU

That no loved person can in the end fill the nothingness within our being doesn't keep us from hoping that he or she can. Lacan's playful way of expressing this idea is to say that when I fall in love with you, it's because there's something in you that's "more than you."[11] There is you. And then there's an element—a *je ne sais quoi*—in you that's "more" than you in the sense that it seems to enigmatically contain the key to my completion. It's as if you contained a little morsel of what I've lost, the piece of me that I thought I would never recover. In your eyes, I discern a glimmer of what I'm missing; in your voice, I hear a faint echo of my lost voice; in your touch, I sense the coming alive of what has become deadened in me. This is why I feel that you—and only you—can add a special glow to my life.

Countless novels, poems, movies, and songs chronicle both the inspiring and pathetic aspects of this experience. On the pathetic side, I'll only mention in passing the all-too-common narcissistic outcome of this setup: it's easy to see how the fantasy of self-completion through a loved one can give rise to an attempt to turn this loved one into a mirror that reflects back an illusory image of perfection.[12]

An incisive depiction of this attempt can be found in David Henry Hwang's play, *M. Butterfly*, where a French diplomat, Gallimard, believes that a Chinese male spy pretending to be a demure and sexually reticent woman is the woman of his dreams because s/he massages his ego in just the right way, allowing him to feel manly and important.[13] The play suggests that the spy is able to perform a woman so perfectly, so convincingly, because he knows how to produce the masculine fantasy of femininity, a fantasy that reflects back to Gallimard the self-aggrandizing image he's looking for. At the end of the play, when Gallimard discovers his lover's (male) identity as a spy, he kills himself because—and this is explicitly stated—he would rather have the fantasy (the woman as a fantasy object) than reality; reality is unbearable after the fantasy because it spells the collapse of Gallimard's narcissistic vision of himself. The same theme of a man making a fantasy object out of a woman—often literally assembling her to meet the parameters of his fantasy—runs from Ovid's *Pygmalion* to *Pretty Woman*.[14]

On the inspiring side, let us briefly return to Alain Badiou's account of love as the kind of transformative "event" that changes the basic coordinates of our being, making it impossible for us to go on living as we hitherto have. Love as a life-altering event of this kind is the very antithesis of narcissism, for it forces us to reorganize our entire existence so as to accommodate the arrival of the loved one; it asks us to surrender the modes of the life that we have devised as solitary beings in order to create space for another person as an unpredictable entity that we by definition can't control or even fully understand. From this moment on, the enigma of the other will excite us, incite us, arouse us, and sometimes even drive us crazy.

This is why Todd McGowan argues that love is rarely "a good investment."[15] It doesn't necessarily yield a profit of calm contentment, nor does it grant us the wholeness that we're looking for. It's much more likely to derail us. If our romantic culture tries to tame love, to render it safe and convenient, the event of love can be tremendously unsafe and inconvenient in the sense that it interrupts the usual flow of life and not always in a manageable way; the event of love can be as traumatizing as it is uplifting.

The event of love, as Badiou theorizes it, doesn't allow us to invest in the fantasy that the other will complete our being. Indeed, because it forces us to view the other as a subject in her own right (rather than as an object designed solely for the pur-pose of making us whole), it also forces us to acknowledge that the other is just as much a creature of lack (castration) as we are. This means that we have to come to terms with the process of loving a flawed person. This may explain why the event of love may not always be brought about by a person who on a superfi-cial level meets the socially accredited attributes of desirability—such as physical attractiveness or professional success—but by a person who touches some deeper chord in us.

For the event of love to be ignited, we must encounter a per-son who meets the idiosyncratic contours of our desire without allowing us to fall into the narcissistic pattern I sketched above. He or she does not serve as a mirror as much as he or she inter-rupts our complacency, infusing our being with new energy in ways that can be both vitalizing and disconcerting. Instead of the serene surface of a pleasing mirror, such a person offers us the turbulence of feeling fully alive (sometimes too much so, agonizingly so).

There aren't too many people who are capable of mobilizing our desire on this level, which is why human desire tends to be much more discriminating than the reproductive instinct of other animals: though we can be attracted to many people, finding one who moves us in this manner is not that common. Although we meet countless people during our lives, and although we may find many of them engaging and appealing, usually only a few contain an aura, feature, or attitude that fully activates our desire. This is why—as Roland Barthes argues—the trait that captivates us about another person is fre-quently some seemingly insignificant detail, such as the way she bites her lip, tilts her head, or lifts her glass.[16]

The account of lack generating desire I've given clarifies why falling in love is so intoxicating, so full of longing. It also clarifies why we experience some of our loves as irreplaceable: once we have (irrationally) decided that a particular person has the power to conjure away our lack, to redeem our alienation, this person becomes virtually impossible to relinquish, for in giving him or her up, we would automatically also give up any hope of wholeness. At stake is not only our beloved and those of his or her attributes that we love but our entire being. This is why our desire for some people feels nonnegotiable.

It's easy to see the danger that this type of desire poses, how vulnerable it makes us, how easily it can devastate us, for losing a person who feels irreplaceable means that we also lose the promise of self-completion. This is one reason that romantic failures so easily usher us into the depths of melancholia: we're not only mourning the person we have lost but also the collapse of the possibility that our lack could one day be healed. This is why replacing a person who feels irreplaceable is one of the most difficult psychological feats for us to accomplish.

The specificity of our desire can therefore devastate us. Desire at its most singular—at its most dogged—is too honest to resort to techniques of romantic manipulation, which in turn means that it retains the power to ravage us. This type of desire doesn't allow us to control our romantic destinies; it's immune to all attempts to safety-proof relationships. It even knows that it may at some point have to replace the irreplaceable; it knows that there can be no event of love without the specter of loss. If our culture's relationship advice tries to reassure us that we can avoid loss by taking the right steps, desire in its specificity recognizes the possibility of losing what we feel we can't afford to lose; it recognizes the possibility of the kinds of bad feelings that have the power to break us, yet it takes the gamble anyway.

THE TWO FACES OF DESIRE

Human desire arguably has two different faces: one is generic and complacent, the other specific (reflective of the singularity of our subjectivity) and at least potentially defiant. In earlier chapters, I've talked mostly about the generic side. In chapter 1, I argued that consumer culture directs our desire toward predetermined existential goals, modes of life, and bundles of commodities. In chapter 2, I analyzed the rationalization of intimacy that characterizes neoliberal society. In chapter 3, I criticized the reductive account of desire offered by evolutionary psychologists and other cultural authorities hung up on gender stereotypes. And in chapter 4, I looked at the manner in which straight women are socially conditioned to turn themselves into objects of desire for men and examined the commercial production of desire in pornography. This chapter, in contrast, has focused on the idiosyncratic, and therefore nonconformist, frequencies of desire.

Foucault's account of biopolitical conditioning has helped me analyze the generic and complacent side of desire. Lacan was also attentive to this side, often talking about the ways in which our embeddedness in collective social ideologies (what he called *the symbolic order*) causes us to lose track of the truth (specificity) of our desire. But as a psychoanalytic thinker, Lacan was perhaps even more interested in the potentially defiant frequencies of desire; as a theorist who was also a clinician, he was invested in loosening the hold of the symbolic order on desire. He wanted to see what his patients would do with the specificity of their desire if they were able to access it, if they were able to peel away the layers of cultural conditioning that concealed it.

This explains why I've shifted from a Foucauldian to a Lacanian register in this chapter. And looking back at my overall trajectory as a writer, I realize that this is why I've always been more drawn to Lacan than to Foucault, even if I also have a great deal of respect for the latter. Even though I'm interested in how consumer culture makes money from the conversion of desire into sentimental romance (chapter 2), and even though I'm equally interested in how this culture makes money from the conversion of desire into pornography (chapter 4), I'm even more interested in the fixities of desire—in desire's crystallization into the kind of irrational faithfulness that treasures its object even when doing so is inconvenient—because this type of desire functions as a paradoxical site of self-determination in the sense that it remains one of the few things about human life that stubbornly resists biopolitical conditioning.

Let me sum up the matter as follows: if biopolitical conditioning suspends contemporary Western subjects between sentimentalism and pornography, only the kind of desire that cuts through these modalities—what some might call love (the event of love)—has any chance of breaking the spell of this conditioning.

Self-determination—freedom, autonomy, agency, and choice—interests me more than it has interested most progressive (or feminist) critics of my generation. This is why I've always been slightly out of step with my field, sounding too quaintly "humanistic," too invested in questions about existential meaningfulness and self-reliance that appear outdated and perhaps even ideologically questionable (in the sense of touching on concepts that are associated with the Enlightenment, with the very mode of thought that has been deemed to be politically and epistemologically violent). As I've mentioned, one reason for my fascination with such questions is a personal history that made me want self-determination: the feeling that I wouldn't survive without having some say over how I was going to live.

But the intellectual reason for this fascination is that I read Lacan not as a theorist of social determination—as many have[17]—but as a theorist of self-determination (of freedom, autonomy, agency, and choice).

Undoubtedly, Lacan's analysis of the impact of collective ideologies on psychic life—of the symbolic order as a site of disciplinary power—is in many ways comparable to Foucault's analysis of biopolitics. But what is much more original—and interesting—about Lacanian theory is its emphasis on what (however incompletely) eludes the symbolic order and what consequently lends our being the kind of unruly singularity that cannot be accounted for through an analysis of social ideology (biopolitics).[18] Desire in its specificity is one of the entities that is capable of such evasion.

On the one hand, the cultural machinery that disciplines desire is powerful enough to produce general tendencies, such as the prevalence of reproductive heterosexuality and the tendency of straight women to see themselves as objects of male desire. But on the other, it's never seamlessly powerful: queers rebel by displaying same-sex desire, women rebel by displaying active desire, and so on. Despite relentless social efforts at normalization, pockets of desire always remain disobedient; some of it routinely spills over the borders that are supposed to contain it. This is why it can take forms that cannot be predicted ahead of time. It's why we end up desiring people we're told we shouldn't desire, why we end up dreaming at our desks, too disoriented to work, having imprudent affairs, and squandering our energies on extravagant fantasies that will not in any way help us lead balanced and reasonable lives.

While the neoliberal ethos of good performance, high productivity, and constant self-improvement I've analyzed often manages to highjack our desire, causing us to desire exactly what it wants us to desire, our desire can also derail this ethos. It can make us frivolous and unfocused. And the disappointments of desire can paralyze us in the way that I described in the context of melancholia. In this sense, desire couldn't care less about good performance. Nor does it honor the creed of positive thinking: it's just as likely to make us despondent as it is to put a bounce in our step. This interferes with the smooth functioning of collective life, which explains why social critics have long fixated on desire as a socially subversive force even as they recognize the various ways in which it can be made to serve the dominant cultural ideology.

In the last chapter, I concluded that the hegemony of commercial heteroporn has to some extent eroded our ability to see desire as a rebellious entity. I don't think that there's any way to deny that today's capitalism knows how to harness our desire. Heteroporn is an index of this know-how, as are the countless consumer items beckoning us from store windows, television commercials, and magazine spreads. Every time I leaf through a duty free magazine on an airplane, I'm struck by the insistence with which capitalism elicits our desire, sometimes with items that are entirely predictable, such as anti-aging creams or French perfumes, other times with items that seem far-fetched yet must still somehow be effective.

An example of the latter is Finnair's attempt to market Tove Jansson's most fierce-looking *muumipeikko*—a little punk of a girl troll (*peikko* = troll) with furious eyebrows and a piercing scowl named Pikku Myy—to Japanese tourists flying from Tokyo to central Europe via Helsinki. This is an instance in which I must admire capitalism's capacity to sell what at first glance seems like the very antithesis of desirable femininity.

The same trend is evident in recent television shows such as *Homeland*, *The Killing*, and *The Bridge*—the last two, perhaps not coincidentally, are Scandidramas—whose heroines, though physically attractive, fall outside of the feminine norm in being bipolar, on the autism spectrum, antisocial, nonmaternal, overtly (and often clumsily) sexual, and so on. Clearly, our society is grappling with the rapid transformation of gender norms. And clearly, capitalism has found a way to translate even this grappling into a profitable enterprise.

This phenomenon confirms that capitalism knows how to turn even efforts to resist its norms into profit, converting what in principle should seem undesirable into something that masses of people suddenly find desirable. Still, when desire makes us frivolous or unfocused, or when it disappoints us, it can cause us to act in ways that undermine the goals of consumer capitalism. The bad feelings caused by the disillusionments of desire—such as depression resulting from romantic rejection—in particular remain among the few ways in which human beings remain resistant to dominant happiness scripts.

When we have been spurned in love, the last thing we want to do is to perform, produce, improve ourselves, and smile. Over time, once the initial sting has abated, these things may reenter our lives, sometimes even coming to function as manic defense mechanisms against our discontent, as is the case, for example, when we work nonstop so as to be able to push our bad feelings to the margins of our consciousness. But when the wound is fresh, it can render us more or less incapable of living in the way that our pragmatic society would like us to live.

The agonies of disappointed desire can deliver a severe blow to the levelheaded attitude of our culture, for they can make us utterly irrational and sometimes even a little unhinged. In this sense, the setbacks of desire may be even more difficult to domesticate than desire itself: we can be cajoled into wanting what the social order wants us to want; but once our desire has fixated on a specific object, we can't be ordered not to want it (even when we can't have it). Unquestionably, we're often forced to give up what feels irreplaceable. But we can't be forced to declare the irreplaceable easily replaceable; we can't be forced to love anew before we have had time to mourn what we have lost.

THE ETHICS OF DESIRE

Here we meet up with the ethical potential of desire that I alluded to at the beginning of this chapter, for surely there can be something admirable about desire's tendency to deem certain people (or objects) irreplaceable and to cling to such people (or objects) even when reason—or the surrounding world—tells us that we should relinquish them.[19] From this viewpoint, there can be something ethically laudatory about desire's tenacious fixations, for these fixations can make us insubordinate in relation to collective cultural demands: they can induce us to defend our idiosyncratic choices against the pressure to desire like everyone else.

For example, those around us may attempt to convince us that we have fallen in love with a person of the wrong age, race, gender, ethnicity, religion, social class, or educational level. Alternatively (and sometimes simultaneously), they may tell us that the life choices we have made are imprudent. In such situations, the specificity of our desire can give us the courage to stand our ground; it's robust enough to resist the warnings of the social order, making it possible for us to desire in rebellious ways.

Desire therefore contains a clandestine defiant streak that under some circumstances leaps into visibility. This is exactly what happens when we insist on staying with someone we love even in the face of external opposition. In such cases, the specificity of our desire gives rise to an ethics of relationality that assesses the value of those we desire not on the basis of the pragmatic criteria of our society but rather on the basis of how well they match the inimitable silhouette of our desire. When this happens, we judge a person who resonates on the singular frequency of our desire to be more important, more worthy of our loyalty, than one who is merely convenient or socially appropriate.

Consider the following: our commercial culture works overtime to produce sparkly lures to distract our desire. And it thrives on our lack of commitment to the choices we have made: it banks on the expectation that we'll readily discard what we have bought the moment an updated model arrives on the scene. This is the logic that produces a new stock of cars every year, a new version of the iPhone faster than you can blink, and a new—usually inferior—edition of Microsoft Word just when you have finally figured out how to use the old version.

Against the backdrop of such enticing commodities, insisting on the specificity of our desire can become an ethical stance, making it possible for us to appreciate the preciousness of what we may be encouraged to cast aside (or not even recognize as valuable). Essentially, when we deem a specific object irreplaceable, we signal that as far as our desire is concerned, only this object will do. In this manner, we refuse to participate in the capitalist mentality that tells us that every object is disposable; we refuse to participate in the frenzy of consumption that demands that we float from one object to the next without regret.

Such faithfulness to desire's specificity is perhaps most noticeable in relation to the people we love. But it can apply to

inanimate objects as well: we bypass consumer culture's exulta-
tion of the new whenever we decide that the object we already
possess—say, a chipped plate—is good enough, that we don't
need to replace it with a pristine one. We also bypass capitalism's
enthusiasm for excess when we decide to lead pared-down,
uncluttered lives, as I've sought to do.

I like spare living spaces, spare cupboards, closets, and fridges.
I try to only own what I actually need—and consistently use—so
as not to encumber my life with unnecessary items. Whenever I
attempt to decide whether to purchase something new (which
is rarely), I pause to assess whether the item is in fact superior to
the one I already have and whether it will in any way enhance
my life. Most of the time, the verdict is that it isn't and it won't.

This may be a habit that formed during the decades when I
had no money, when I routinely borrowed money from friends
during the last week of the month—when my paycheck had run
out—just to buy food. I might also have picked it up from my
parents during their years of poverty: my mother is still making
coffee in the same pot that she used before I was born. But even
if the habit arose from scarcity, it feels enriching, for it feels
that the fewer things I have, the fuller my life is. The stacks
of clothes I see in the closets of some of my friends make me
slightly queasy, not because I judge these stacks morally but
because they overwhelm me affectively.

I can happily live out of a medium-sized suitcase for a year
(and have done so more than once). I wrote most of my books
on a laptop that most people would have considered a dinosaur.
I even kept it for more than a year after one of its hinges broke
so that I could no longer close it. At the end of the writing day,
I would carefully place it on a dresser, cover it with a towel to
keep the dust off the keyboard, and hope that it wouldn't collapse during the night. I reluctantly gave it up when the need to

travel with a laptop made keeping it completely unfeasible. Now that I'm typing on my shiny new laptop, I still miss the old one: it used to overheat nicely, warming up my fingers in the winter, whereas the new one stays cool no matter how many hours I use it. When my fingers start to whiten at the tips, I curse the new and hanker for the old.

When I was forced to buy a new laptop, I asked a friend who knows about computers to strip it of all the clutter, including online access (these days this takes serious expertise and the best you can apparently do is to hide the internet link in a place that someone like me can't find). I specified that "a glorified typewriter" was what I was looking for. Likewise, when my ancient cell phone broke beyond repair, I told the bewildered sales person at the phone store that I wanted a phone that just makes calls, nothing else. It took him fifteen minutes to dig one up at the storage facility. For me, what's often irreplaceable is the *absence* of things, of distractions.

It's fortunate that the human quest for wholeness can find (always partial) satisfaction in a variety of ways, that it's not only romantic objects of desire that fulfill us but also ancient laptops and faded pairs of jeans. If love were our only source of fulfillment, many of us would be chronically miserable, given how often it devastates us. Indeed, as I've suggested, a mistake we routinely make is to focus too many of our emotional resources on romance, in part because our society reinforces the notion that love is the zenith of life, that without love our lives are unfinished, and in part because, as I've argued in this chapter, nothing promises self-completion more than the person we love.

I've conceded that there's something about the event of love—love not as mere romance but as a wholesale reorganization of being—that may in fact be incomparable. I've conceded that when we chance upon a partner who manages to instigate such an event, we may indeed be transported to a transcendent place. But it's helpful to keep in mind that we—again, unlike other animals—possess the capacity to reach into the world in search of a whole array of objects, activities, ambitions, and preoccupations that might also gratify us. The fact that these objects and these pursuits can never fully satisfy us doesn't mean that they don't satisfy us at all; as partial as our satisfactions sometimes are, they are simultaneously all important.

Sometimes we're forced to replace the irreplaceable. Fortunately for us, usually even the most prolonged melancholia, the most persistent paralysis of desire, over time lifts so that we're able to direct our desire to new objects. If this wasn't the case, our lives would eventually lose their meaningfulness (as in fact happens in chronic depression). By this I don't mean that melancholia can't have its own beauty, even its own enchantment, in the sense that there's a special kind of sweetness to holding onto an object we have lost even after its recovery has become impossible. Melancholia keeps rejecting the reality of loss in favor of a memory of what once was (or a fantasy of what could still be); it sacrifices the present for the sake of the past, and sometimes this sacrifice may feel worth making.[20] However, continued life usually demands that we find a way to dig our way out of the crypt of melancholia.

Even so, if our loss was significant, if what we have lost feels irreplaceable, its trace will persist within our psyche, animating our inner world, making a contribution to the kind of person we are. In a way, one could say that our character contains a residue of all the losses we have experienced: our personality on some level expresses the history of our losses, and particularly the history of our painful efforts to replace the irreplaceable. This is why I've always thought that those who have lost a lot tend to have more complex characters than those who have not; they have learned to live without breaking even though they have had every reason to break.

6

THE AGE OF ANXIETY

Replacing what feels irreplaceable can be heartbreaking. But if there is a bad feeling that seems to capture the essence of our era, it's anxiety, which appears to saturate the very air we breathe. It lurks in corners, hovers over daily life, colonizes our minds, infiltrates our bodies, and insists on being heard during times, such as vacations, when we're most determined to banish it.

This is why I like my idyllic Cape Cod town a lot better in February than in July: during the summer season, it's filled with stressed-out people from New York and New Jersey who sit by the ocean screaming into their cell phones. If that's what their "vacation" looks like, I can only imagine what their days at the office are like. Regrettably, I'm no better when I'm under a deadline or in the middle of a grading period. One doesn't need to gather statistics to know that people in contemporary America are under a lot of pressure: although those in other historical periods have unquestionably experienced anxiety, it seems clear that our fast-paced and achievement-oriented era aggravates it.

It's of course possible that we have merely started to name what has always been a reality, that what has changed is not the level of anxiety but the tendency to diagnose it as a pathology or at the very least to talk about it as a problem. It's possible that people used to interpret anxiety as an inevitable part of the human condition—as the way life sometimes just "is"—rather than as an ailment to be treated. It's even possible that, like depression,[1] anxiety has to some extent been "invented" as a disease by drug companies that make a profit from anti-anxiety medications.

Undoubtedly the fact that anxiety is now discussed extensively in medical contexts, and that pharmaceutical treatments for it are now relatively easy to obtain, has contributed to our heightened awareness of its prevalence, as has a media culture that has latched onto it as a topic of constant commentary. Still, it does also feel like there's something about our era that escalates anxiety. It seems to be the price—the pound of flesh—that many of us pay for the creed of pragmatism that asks for good performance, high productivity, constant self-improvement, and relentless cheerfulness.

Even our efforts to stay healthy can generate anxiety. Our society is emphatic about the idea that we can keep illnesses at bay through a scrupulous management of our bodies: avoiding risk factors such as smoking and drinking, exercising regularly, and eating a balanced diet are supposed allow us to lead long and healthy lives. Obviously this is to some degree true. But it's also a biopolitical strategy for augmenting our productivity and for casting judgment on those who fail to adhere to the right regimen; it's a means of moralizing about pleasure, of telling us which kinds of pleasures are acceptable and which are not.[2]

What's more, focusing on the maintenance of our bodies means that they need constant monitoring, assessment, and surveillance. Daily life has become an exercise in risk management, with the consequence that we can get terribly anxious about all the things that might go wrong: absurdly, the very thing that's supposed to keep us healthy—risk management—is making us uncomfortable and anxious.

While some are killing themselves slowly by eating large quantities of toxic fast food, others are obsessively watching their every meal, making sure that everything is certifiably organic, that nothing impure enters their bodies, and that there's plenty of kale, quinoa, halibut, blueberries, or whatever has been hyped up as the latest superfood in their diet. It's not just that slips in diet can cause agitation in those who fixate on a wholesome diet; it's also that a lot of labor goes into tracking down the right foods for such a diet (and in being able to pay for them). Likewise with many other aspects of healthy living, such as gym visits and meditation classes. I'm not saying that such activities are wrong per se—or that we should stop pursuing healthy lifestyles—but merely that it might be useful to acknowledge the costs of this pursuit, particularly the psychological burdens of constant self-monitoring.

In addition, advances in medical diagnostics mean that we're constantly being screened for future illnesses, so that even when we're perfectly healthy, we're living in an atmosphere of doom where we're waiting for the other shoe to drop. A perfect example of this dilemma are false positives on mammograms, which create so much anxiety for some women that one has to ask whether the benefits of an early diagnosis can outweigh the extensive damage done. Yes, some lives are saved. But countless others are rendered wretched.

The assumption seems to be that a wretched life is invariably better than falling ill due to a lack of early diagnosis. But I'm not sure that this logic works for all of us. Some of us might prefer to take the risk of not knowing. As historian of science Charles Rosenberg observes, the increase in diagnostic capacities means that "we have provided altered narratives for millions of individuals who might otherwise have lived out their lives in ignorance of a nemesis lurking in their bodies."[3] Although I don't want to suggest that screening for potential illnesses is useless, I think that it's unfortunate that many of us fail to feel fully alive because we're constantly worried about being prematurely dead. Some might go as far as to assert that insofar as our anxiety about possible illnesses keeps us from being able to live spontaneously, we're already in some ways dead.

TWO LEVELS OF ANXIETY

At the beginning of this book, I noted the distinction between bad feelings that are intrinsic to the human condition and others that are socially generated. This distinction is perhaps most obvious in the case of anxiety, for there are clearly two different levels of anxiety: the first is existential and unavoidable, whereas the second arises from stressful circumstances and is therefore potentially avoidable. The first level is conceptually related to the kind of lack (nothingness, emptiness, hollowness) that Lacan sees as foundational to human subjectivity; the second level results from more circumstantial forms of lack, such as poverty, or from taxing conditions such as overwork or worrying about getting sick. What can make talking about anxiety particularly tricky is that while it would be difficult to find value in the second of these levels, the Western intellectual tradition has fairly consistently aligned the first—the existential level—with the kind of self-reflexivity that I valorized in the previous chapter.

For instance, Heidegger famously linked our capacity for self-interrogation to our anxiety in the face of our mortality (here not understood as a worry about illness but as a cognizance of the inevitability of death), characterizing human life as a prolonged "being-toward-death" that is self-aware and inquisitive only because it's forced to grapple with the fleeting character of life. Along related lines, Sartre developed existentialism as a philosophy of angst: of standing at the edge of the abyss, of wrestling with the uncertainties of existence. For Sartre, freedom, autonomy, and self-determination were inseparable from anxiety because with the ability to make choices (freedom) comes the recognition that we're responsible for the choices we make and the attendant fear of making the wrong choices (anxiety). Conversely, it's only to the extent that we feel anxious that we recognize ourselves as free in the first place.

What unites these otherwise disparate approaches (Lacanian, Heideggerian, Sartrean) is that they respect life's constitutive vulnerabilities, starting from the assumption that human existence can never be entirely rounded or secure, entirely free of disquiet or anxiety. As I've explained in the Lacanian context, our sense that something is missing from our lives means that we can never feel completely whole, healed, or fulfilled. We have seen that this isn't necessarily a bad thing, that our lack spurs us to reach out into the world in quest of objects (including people) and activities that might appease the emptiness—which we can think of as one genre of anxiety—that might otherwise overwhelm us. From this perspective, even though it would be nice to live without (existential) anxiety, if this became possible, we might also be forced to live without many of the things that we most value.

Consider the fact that many artists, inventors, creators, and intellectuals routinely fall short of the ideal of harmony. It's not for nothing that Freud saw a link between psychic pain and imaginative labor. The sublimation of pain, including anxiety, is one of the most surefire routes to producing books, poems, songs, painting, sculptures, and other products of the imagination. This is why my response to my doctor's concern that my blood pressure is too high is to wonder how it could possibly be otherwise. It's also why I suspect that I sometimes semi-intentionally court a broken heart: no matter how distressing the experience, deep down I know that ultimately it will yield a crop of words on a page.

For me at least, books come into being as a residue of pain that has been transmuted into creative activity. At the same time, this activity cannot take place without a confrontation with lack, even with what I, following Lacan, have been calling castration. The quest for self-mastery, for balance and perfection, thwarts such activity, as is evident in the case of those who suffer from a writing block (as I used to). This was a hard lesson to learn: words will only flow once castration—inadequacy—is acknowledged. They will always flow imperfectly. But at least they will flow.

Whenever I think about psychic suffering, I recall my restless schizophrenic uncle Paavo. Undeniably on many levels he led a terribly pain-filled life. He was trapped in his disease. He hated the fact that even though he knew why he was ill, he couldn't heal himself; he understood his disease but couldn't get rid of it. But when I compare the spark in his eyes to the stony look in the eyes of weary commuters in cities such as Boston, Toronto, and New York, I suspect that his life may also have been quite rewarding.

He may have talked nonsense at times, for instance repeatedly accusing my mother of poisoning the sugar cubes that he sucked compulsively while pacing back and forth in the kitchen. But he also wrote amazing poetry. He played chess with absolute concentration. He had the encyclopedia memorized. He out-argued the Jehovah's Witnesses (the only religious people I ever met in Finland) who sometimes found their way to our isolated village (I think they mostly came because they wanted to debate my uncle). He could have an interesting conversation on countless topics, with the result that people traveled for hours just to talk with him. He's the one who told me about Freud (and other thinkers, such as Nietzsche, who later became so important to me) in our book-deprived household. *You can go to university and study Freud*, he would say with a conspiratorial gleam in his eyes. Toward the end of his life, the drugs had killed that gleam. But for almost as long as I knew him, he was the person who, among those around me, seemed most alive.

My uncle is probably the main reason I've always been drawn to thinkers who don't judge mental imbalance to be a total loss, who see value in what others deem pathological. Freud is foremost among such thinkers. He relativized pathology by illustrating that all of us are to some degree pathological (neurotic). Among other things, he showed that the dreams of so-called normal people have the same scrambled structure as the psychic processes of those who have been diagnosed as mentally ill, so that there's more than a hint of "insanity" in all of us.

Lacan, for his part, taught me to accept the impossibility of self-completion, of lasting equilibrium and satisfaction; he taught me that, on the level of the basic structure of subjectivity, life isn't meant to be neatly packaged. The self-help shelf may be full of titles designed to make it all work, but ultimately it never will as seamlessly as these books promise; it will always to some extent be messy and unmanageable (and therefore haunted by anxiety). Nietzsche convinced me that suffering and creativity are frequently two sides of the same coin. Proust and Barthes installed in me a respect for the disquiets of desire.

Julia Kristeva showed me the imagination buried within melancholia. The list goes on.

Notably, more or less the only major European thinkers who, to the consternation of some of my graduate students, have left me completely cold are Deleuze and Guattari, who valorized schizophrenia as a politically subversive pulverization of subjectivity.[4] What I saw my uncle wanting more than anything was the very antithesis of such pulverization: he wanted an examined life, a life conscious of its outlines, however incoherent and anxiety-saturated these outlines might have been. In a way, he taught me to aim for a space between the calm contemplation that we sometimes—because of ancient Greek philosophy— associate with the examined life and complete disarray.

This may be why I've never liked the idealization of self-shattering that characterizes important strands of contemporary theory, why the critique of this idealization is a thread that runs through much of my academic writing.[5] Inasmuch as this theory constantly—perhaps even compulsively—looks for alternatives to Enlightenment models of fully rational, coherent, and autonomous subjectivity, it devises one model after another of radical self-dissolution. The problem with such models is not just that they are completely unlivable but also that they close off all possibility of rest, thought, and insight; they close off what Arendt called the life of the mind.[6] For example, the self-disintegration that Deleuze and Guattari advocated suggests a life without any psychic or affective guideposts—what Lacan called "quilting points"[7]—whereas even my schizophrenic uncle had such guideposts, including the authors (Freud, Nietzsche, Proust, and Plato) he referenced tirelessly while pacing up and down the kitchen, driving my mother crazy while (though I didn't know this then) offering me an invaluable set of intellectual leads to follow.

The pulverization of subjectivity doesn't hold much appeal for me. At the same time, I recognize that we're probably on the wrong track when we pursue lives that are completely happy, loves that are completely successful, relationships that are completely functioning, and so on. If schizophrenia is not an ideal to aspire to, nor is, perhaps, unwavering sanity. This is why I'm wary of our pragmatic culture's attempts to convince us that bad feelings such as anxiety have a practical solution: drugs, spas, yoga, meditation, therapy, making money, among a host of other potential cures. It's not that I'm opposed to people trying to feel less anxious; I just suspect that we might feel less anxious if we were not so focused on attaining composure in the first place.

I suspect that our society values composure primarily because it helps us perform, produce, improve ourselves, and stay cheerful. It's then all the more ironic that our efforts to do these things can themselves produce so much anxiety. This is the dilemma I mentioned in the opening pages of this book: the very culture that reassures us that it can free us of our bad feelings ends up generating a whole new crop of them; at the same time as our society broadcasts the virtues of balance, our hectic lifestyles produce a surplus of imbalance. It's not just that oppressive social circumstances, such as racism, generate anxiety and other bad feelings "in excess" of the foundational anxieties of human life; it's also that even the relatively privileged find themselves under so much pressure that they experience heightened levels of anxiety (and depression). This is how we slide from the realm of unavoidable anxiety to the realm of anxiety that is in principle avoidable but that we don't manage to avoid.

PHALLIC DETUMESCENCE

In his text on anxiety, Lacan for the most part explores the theme as an unavoidable component of human life. But insofar as he focuses on anxiety as an affect that arises in relation to other people (whom I will call *the other* with the understanding that the term can refer to just one person or a multitude of others,[8] depending on the context), he also gives us valuable clues for understanding why our age is so easy to designate as an age of anxiety. On the one hand, because there can be no human subject without the other—because none of us has been formed independently of others, including those who (however badly) took care of us when we were too young to survive on our own—Lacan's analysis addresses foundational (unavoidable) anxiety. On the other hand, because the surplus (avoidable) anxiety that many of us carry around also most often develops in response to others, his account helps explicate why people in today's (Western) societies seem particularly prone to anxiety.

At the risk of oversimplifying things, I would say that Lacan proposes that there are three ways that the other can generate anxiety. First, the other can deepen my sense of lack and inadequacy (threaten to wound me); second, the other can come too close (threaten to suffocate me); and third, the other can confuse me with its incomprehensible needs, demands, and desires (overagitate me because I can't read its messages well enough to know what's expected of me). These three modes of coming in contact with the other can overlap so that, for instance, the same other who comes too close can also confuse me or the same other who threatens to wound me can also be too close.

If we return to the fact that what Lacan called lack he also called castration, I can recast these three anxiety-inducing faces of the other as follows (loosely modifying the vocabulary that

Lacan himself uses): the other who reveals my inadequacy, who threatens to deepen my lack, is the castrator; the other who comes too close, who threatens to suffocate me, is the praying mantis (the insect that decapitates and devours her mate during or immediately after sex); and the other who is incomprehensible, maddeningly unreadable, and disconcertingly ambiguous is the enigmatic signifier.[9] I'll quickly run through these three scenarios in the hope that they will reveal something useful about the causes of anxiety in the contemporary era.

When explaining the first of these scenarios—the scenario of the other as castrator—Lacan humorously refers to the straight man's sexual performance anxiety. It's not just that the disappearance of his penis into a woman during sex causes a man to (unconsciously) worry that he might never get it back (which is how we get the trope of *vagina dentata*). It's also that he's aware that his partner's capacity for sexual pleasure potentially exceeds his own—by a lot. After all, women are multiorgasmic, which means that even if they in reality are perfectly satisfied with one orgasm, in the worried fantasy life of straight men their capacity for pleasure can seem limitless and therefore anxiety inducing.

Women's pleasure doesn't come to an end with an orgasm, as it (temporarily at least) does for a man, but can be prolonged until she gets too exhausted. This is not how things stand for the man: orgasm not only ends his pleasure; perhaps even more alarmingly, it leads to the loss of erection—that is, it leads to metaphorical castration (and the inability to continue the act).

Lacan talks about phallic "detumescence," or phallic "evanescence," explaining how the penis inevitably falters at the very moment of delivery.[10] Faced with a woman's seemingly boundless potential for pleasure, the penis makes a valiant effort but invariably gives up before reaching its goal. I feel like

I need to quote Lacan here so that you don't think that the feminist in me is making this up: "The . . . organ can be said to yield, each and every time, prematurely. When the time comes at which it could be the sacrificial object, so to speak, well, let's say that, in the ordinary case, it has ducked out a long while before. It's no more than a scrap, it is no longer there for the partner save as a keepsake, a souvenir of tenderness. This is what the castration complex is all about."[11]

Rather than being the majestic organ of mastery that our society portrays it to be, the penis in heterosexual intercourse yields prematurely, ducks out before fully accomplishing its task, deflating into a mere keepsake, "a souvenir of tenderness" that isn't of much use for a woman, which is why male orgasm is just another name for castration. At another moment in the text, Lacan draws an explicit link between male orgasm and anxiety by offering a vivid portrait of a student who ejaculates at the moment of having to turn in a term paper: "What gets scooped up? His work, the thing that was essentially expected of him. Something is wrenched from him. It's time to gather up the papers, and right then and there, he ejaculates. He ejaculates at the height of his anxiety."[12]

Anxiety, then, has to do with the fear of losing mastery, of falling short of expectations, of being found wanting, of not measuring up. Recall that even though women don't have a penis, they can also aspire to phallic power, as I do when I clutch my portable phallus while lecturing. Against this backdrop, it's clear that Lacan uses the straight man's sexual performance anxiety as a metaphor for the kind of anxiety that all of us, regardless of gender, experience when we feel that we might not be up to the task, that the paper or the book we have written isn't good enough, that we're going about things in the wrong way, that we'll never figure out how to tackle the challenge we're facing, or that something about us is just fundamentally amiss.

If I drop my portable phallus—stumble on my words or say something stupid—at the beginning of my three-hour lecture, when I'm not yet sure about how well the whole thing is going to go, I feel much more anxious than if I happen to have the same mishap toward the end of a lecture that I feel I've delivered reasonably well. Anxiety, in this sense, is a synonym for the worry that I'll lose control of the situation. Indeed, it may not be a coincidence that Lacan chooses the straight man's sexual anxiety as his example, for it's the straight man who, in our society, is supposed to be the subject who is in control, who masters both himself and his environment. By targeting this subject specifically, Lacan illustrates that none of us is immune to anxiety; all of us, even the seemingly most confident among us, are in some ways deficient, dislocated, disjointed, mutilated, and so on.

FOMENTING ALMIGHTINESS

Importantly, Lacan argues that if the phallus is "called upon to function as an instrument of might"—if heteropatriarchy privileges the phallus as a signifier of power in the ways that I've outlined—whenever it falters, its possessor is tempted "to foment almightiness."[13] I trust that we're all familiar with men who attempt to appease their anxiety about losing mastery by lashing out at others, by fomenting almightiness. From this perspective, one could argue that heteropatriarchy is merely an elaborate defense mechanism against the threat that women are perceived to pose to men. If some men need to constantly broadcast their accomplishments—if they need to remind us of their almightiness—it's because on a basic level they're feeling insecure; like the man having sex with a woman whose capacity for pleasure seems so immense that he begins to fear that he'll never be able to fully satisfy her, the average heteropatriarchal guy may feel the need to overcompensate for his inadequacies by building impressive edifices of power. What Lacan reveals is that this power is always illusory.

I've already noted that the fact that this power is illusory doesn't mean that it doesn't have real effects: like racism, heteropatriarchy has concrete psychological, emotional, and physical effects. My point—the point that I made already in the introduction—is merely that ultimately it's not founded on anything real, that ultimately men who seem to have power are as lacking, as castrated, as the rest of us. It's just that they foment, have historically fomented, almightiness to obscure this fact.

This should clarify why I've emphasized that some straight men appear particularly bothered by transgenderism: trans guys explicitly reveal the precariousness of phallic power. If those who weren't born with a penis can strap one on, and if the manufactured penis is in some ways superior to the "original" in the sense that it can keep going longer, that it doesn't experience detumescence at the moment of orgasm, then the possessors of the original are *explicitly* in trouble. This is why some of them go after the transgendered with a gun (their own unbreakable phallus). What's in question is not just the most fundamental premise of heteropatriarchy, namely that men have something that women "lack" and that this gives them the right to lord it over women; what's also in question is the sexual performance of those who were born with a penis.

I've stressed that one of the many things that was pioneering about Freud's thinking was that he recognized the symbolic significance of the penis to how our heteropatriarchal social order is organized. Lacan stayed faithful to this insight, which is why the phallus is so central to his thinking. But more than Freud, Lacan was invested in foregrounding the various ways in which phallic power falters; in a sense, he revealed that the phallus only has power insofar as we grant this power to it, that if we stopped dancing around the totem pole of the phallus, its power would dissipate. Among other things, he noted that once a woman realizes that her lover makes love like every other man and "lies uncocked,"[14] she also realizes that her role (within heteropatriarchy) is to prop up his ego, to allow him to pretend that he has the kind of power that he in reality doesn't. The logical conclusion is that the minute she refuses this role, his power starts to crumble.

Some interpreters have accused Lacan of defending the heteropatriarchal order he investigates. But I think that this is a misreading, for Lacan doesn't glorify the phallus but rather illustrates the various ways in which its glory is purely imaginary. As a matter of fact, Lacan explicitly states that if the phallus is central to his theory of subjectivity, it's not because of its magnificence but because of its status as "a fallen object." "Subjectivity," he claims, "is focalized in the falling-away of the phallus. . . . Detumescence in copulation deserves to hold our attention as a way of highlighting one of the dimensions of castration."[15]

That is, if Lacan frequently talks about the phallus, and if his text on anxiety is filled with jokes about the breakdown of the penis, it's because what interests him is detumescence, castration, and lack: subjectivity as "the falling-away of the phallus," as the utter failure of all of our postures of power.[16] This makes it all the more noteworthy that heteropatriarchy, and its homage to the penis as a signifier of stability, has been so difficult to eradicate, even if we have managed over time to alter its parameters. Undoubtedly this is in part because many of us need symbols of authority no matter how fantasmatic these may be.

Be this as it may, Lacan's commentary on the straight man's sexual performance anxiety allows us to recognize that what causes anxiety in today's society is that many of us find ourselves in the same predicament as this man in relation to his lover: we're afraid of failing, of falling into detumescence, in the face of overwhelming demands. As I've shown, the ethos of high productivity, good performance, constant self-improvement, and relentless cheerfulness presses upon us from all sides, making it hard to keep up. Western subjects are taught to strive (and strive and strive). We're taught to proceed as fast and vigorously as we can (and then get up and do it again). We're taught to accomplish things (and to constantly exceed our previous accomplishments). We hope that at the end of the line, there will be some kind of a reward (happiness or some other such thing). But the problem is that like the straight guy in relation to his partner's (fantasized) inexhaustible reservoir of enjoyment, we're constantly out of breath because we're asked to perform beyond our capacities; we're constantly on the verge of castration, of "the falling-away of the phallus."

What's even worse is that the better we do, the higher the expectations get. Imagine you're the straight guy: you've managed to deliver the goods but now—at least in your fantasy life—the woman is going to be positively insatiable; she's going to say, "You have done great but you can do better—*let me show you how.*" In other words, your editor liked your book and now she wants an even better one; your students liked your lecture and now they want an even better one; your professor liked your dissertation chapter and now she wants an even better one.

And there's no mercy. If the straight guy is having sex with a woman who loves him, she's going to have some mercy; at some point, she's going to say, "It's okay, darling, you can go to sleep now." In contrast, those who demand constant performance from us aren't ever going to say, "We know you're tired—get some rest." Instead, they bombard us with steady commentary on how we could do things better: your professor gives you two hundred and forty comments on a dissertation chapter (as I routinely do with my students); your students' written evaluations of your teaching abilities appear in your inbox when you least expect them; your editor sends you peer reviews on your latest manuscript; and the internet overflows with nasty reviews and other assessments of your poor performance.

You read this stuff and your castration is brutal, immediate, and seemingly eternal. Even if the comments you get are mostly positive, you focus on the few negative ones: the one student out of fifty who hated your course; the one point in a peer review that tells you that your book could be better. In addition, thanks to the internet, the commentary now infiltrates your living room. I find that even though I refuse to have online access at home, the castrating other often sits on the couch next to me (because it's not like I can turn off the memory of what I read an hour ago), watching whichever mindless show it is that I'm watching in a desperate effort to take my mind off all the ways in which I could improve myself. This is when I start my Lacanian mantra: you're always already castrated; subjectivity equals castration; learn to live with your lack; embrace the negativity that's in you; mastery is a fantasy, and so on.

The other option is to open a bottle of wine.

THE PRAYING MANTIS

What I've sketched is the first of the three anxiety-inducing faces of the other. The second is the other as praying mantis. Lacan proposes that this is an other who threatens to deprive us of even our lack by suffocating us with its overproximity. If situations that threaten to deepen our lack—to castrate us—are terrifying, so are situations that threaten to completely deprive of us this lack, situations where, as Lacan puts it, "there's no possibility of any lack."[17] These latter are menacing because, as I hope to have shown, our lack is what makes us human, makes us creatures of desire (rather than of pure instinct). It gives rise to consciousness, the capacity for self-reflexivity, the ability to creatively grapple with alienation and inadequacy, and other distinctively human characteristics, which is why we don't want to lose it even as we also don't want it to become a gaping wound.

Lacan maps out the scenario of losing our lack—which I, upon his cue, am calling the praying mantis scenario[18]—in relation to the socially mediated character of basic bodily functions such as eating, seeing, and going to the bathroom. Note that these are activities through which infants first interact with their caretakers (who at that stage of life are omnipotent). Lacan's point is that these formative interactions leave a lasting imprint on our psyches, with the consequence that when we later in life find ourselves in situations that somehow, however vaguely, remind us of them—situations where we may, for example, experience a similar helplessness in relation to others—we're likely to feel anxious.

Let's admit that diaper changing and potty training are situations where the other is frighteningly close. For instance, in potty training, the other (the adult) often stands right next to you, implying that you'd better get down to business right away. On the one hand, this is a scenario of castration in the sense that the other takes the products of your labor and flushes them down the toilet; like the student handing in a term paper, you lose a piece of yourself to the other. On the other hand, the other is overly proximate, scrutinizing your efforts, sometimes even uttering encouragements in the same way that dog owners do with their dogs when they patiently (and sometimes impatiently) wait with plastic bags in their hands.

Judging from the expressions of some of these dogs, I get the sense that in this scenario the other is just a little too close even for the average dog. Likewise perhaps for the average child, even if they can't articulate it, which is why Lacan concludes that even though we tend to assume that children are afraid of being abandoned, what's far more threatening than the possibility that the other—mother, father, whoever—might leave you is that the other might continue wiping your behind, might even keep lifting you onto its lap.[19] I think it's easy enough to imagine scenes from adult life that might revive this type of apprehension.

Consider also eating: breastfeeding (or bottle feeding) is perhaps the most fundamental level on which the other intervenes. Again, Lacan—who was always interested in the psychic and social implications of what might commonly be read as purely biological phenomena—emphasizes that what matters in this encounter with the other is not the breast or the bottle or even the milk but rather the message—"I need you to eat"— that comes with the milk. The act of thrusting the breast or bottle at you contains a need, demand, or desire that you eat; it tells you something about the needs of the other even as it seeks to fulfill yours (appease your hunger). In this sense, the breast or the bottle is a signifier, an early signifier that the infant is asked to decipher before it has the capacity to do so—that is, an enigmatic signifier.

I'll return to a more general discussion of enigmatic signifiers below. But first let's note that this is also a scenario where the other is potentially too close, making requests that are hard to dodge. I think of this every time I visit my parents, for the following scene inevitably ensues: my father cooks an elaborate meal, which I'm happy to eat, but not necessarily when he needs me to eat it, which is always in the middle of the day, when I'm not used to having a big meal. I politely tell him that I'll eat his dish in the evening, at dinner time. He snaps at me, saying "I need you to eat it now."

It's unclear why he needs me to eat it at 2 P.M. This need has to do with him rather than with me. It's as if my inability to be hungry when he wants me to be somehow betrays him. It's as if he's trying to control this part of me because he hasn't been able to control the rest of me. Or maybe he's trying to show love and my refusal to accept it wounds him. I'm sure he doesn't know any better than I do why there's this need in him. Sometimes I do eat the dish right then and there, just to avoid a scene. And then I have to take a nap.

In this scenario, the other isn't threatening to deprive me of anything (except maybe my self-determination) but is instead forcing stuff down my throat. He's too close, too insistent. This is arguably also the case in many less intimate situations, as when a stranger presses himself against me on the subway during rush hour. Ditto for the guy who utters all kinds of vulgarities about my various body parts (some of which are purely in his imagination because in reality they're largely missing) while passing me on the street. Along related lines, a black student on a conference panel recently mentioned that whenever she's in a white neighborhood, she stares down at her iPhone, pretending to read Google Maps. This deters the white people who would otherwise walk up to her to ask if she's lost.

These examples reveal that if none of us can avoid the other in public places, social power differentials mean that some people are more vulnerable in such encounters than others. It's easy enough to jump from Lacan's commentary on anxiety to an analysis of anxiety as the defining affect of late-capitalist, sexist, racist, and homophobic Western society. In other words, we can connect Lacan's commentary to the argument I've made about the ways in which some bad feelings, such as anxiety, come to be unevenly distributed in our society. Although Lacan certainly implies that anxiety is an inescapable element of human life, there's nothing to prevent us from hypothesizing that even though we're all subjected to the unpredictable whims of others, these whims can take a myriad of different forms that impact different people differently. In the examples I've given, gender and race make a difference.

This is not insignificant. There have been times in my life when street harassment made me so anxious that I didn't want to leave my apartment (which is undoubtedly why I keep circling back to this topic). For me, the gaze and commentary of strangers in public places has been a major source of bad feelings. Likewise, two queer friends of mine who also happen to be overweight admit that they're routinely too anxious to leave their house because they fear the assessing eyes—or worse—of others. They also talk about how the simple act of choosing what to wear in the morning brings on enormous anxiety: how does one present oneself as a professional when one is bigger than social norms dictate (and in one case is also genderqueer)? How is one to dress as a senior administrator when others are confused about your gender and defensive about the fact that they're confused?

At one point in his account of anxiety, Lacan talks about an infant being held up to a mirror,[20] specifying that what's important is not just the infant's fascination with its image but also the fact that the infant's relationship to this image is mediated by the adult standing behind it. Lacan mentions that the infant usually turns its head toward the adult, toward the witness, as if asking for approval of its image. Lacan specifies that the mirror image becomes anguishing when it can't be successfully offered to the other, when there's a possibility that the other will find it deficient or even monstrous. This is arguably the predicament of many adults who have been wounded by context-specific forces such as homophobia.

It should already be clear that when it comes to anxiety, it's hard to win: either there's too much lack or too little of it. Either we're afraid that the other will render us even more lacking than we already feel (this is the castration scenario) or we're afraid that the other will suffocate us, will steal our lack so that now we lack even our lack (this is the praying mantis scenario, although admittedly in the final analysis it's also a castration scenario in the sense that being reduced to gooey pulp, as the partner of the copulating praying mantis is, epitomizes castration). It may well be that as human subjects, as subjects of lack and desire, we're inevitably suspended between the castrating other and the devouring praying mantis. By this I don't mean that other people are invariably threatening or intentionally menacing. Rather, my point is that a degree of anxiety may be built into most of our relationships inasmuch as they always on some level replicate (repeat) our earliest relationships, relationships where we were utterly powerless in relation to those around us.

Lacan further jokes that perhaps the most anxiety-inducing "other" is God, particularly an all-powerful God who takes it upon himself to give us instructions on how to enjoy ourselves, as the God of Ecclesiastes apparently does (not having ever read the Bible, I take Lacan's word on this). It's one thing for God to lay down the law. But when this same God starts to meddle with our pleasure, things get too confusing, with the result that enjoyment can no longer be dissociated from anxiety. This is why Lacan remarks that those who believe that the Bible will calm us down clearly have "never even taken a peep at it."[21]

Lacanian commentators such as Slavoj Žižek have translated this idea of a God who tells us to enjoy into the notion that our society, generally speaking, is governed by an "injunction to enjoy," by a collective expectation that we find various ways of enjoying ourselves, preferably through one of consumer culture's latest commodities.[22] This is one way to understand the ethos of self-actualization (and positive thinking) I've discussed: we're asked to realize our potential through our enjoyments.

However, because the enticements of enjoyment crowd upon us from all directions, because our options seem endless, because it's hard to know which enjoyment we should pursue, it can all feel a little overwhelming, like browsing the music selections on iTunes. Not only is it hard to know which enjoyment to try first; it's also impossible to know whether the enjoyment we experience really is the most enjoyable enjoyment available (there could always be a better set of songs than the one we have selected). This is the predicament of a child at an ice cream parlor who is unable to enjoy her enormous chocolate fudge sundae because the child at the next table is eating an even more elaborate concoction. Moreover, because we understand that the profusion of the various "enjoyments" on offer in our culture—from drugs, alcohol, cigarettes, and french fries to pints of Ben & Jerry's—can harm us, we can become hugely anxious about our satisfactions.

THE ENIGMA OF THE OTHER

However, there's perhaps nothing as anxiety-producing as trying to relate to others, particularly on the intimate level. This is because, as I've indicated throughout this chapter, it can be hard to know what the other wants from us: the other's messages can remain deeply and disconcertingly enigmatic.[23] To some degree, such an opacity of communication, like anxiety itself, is an intrinsic component of human life: we can never be entirely sure that we know what others mean, nor can others be sure that they have an accurate sense of what they themselves mean. This is because communications are always infused by unconscious densities of meaning that none of us can fully grasp.

These unconscious densities often remain nonverbal: invisible currents of affect between people that are palpably present but not necessarily nameable. We may be acutely aware of how affects float in the atmosphere, drift about, suddenly crystallize, or get diffused, without being able to articulate their precise meanings: affects are often on the surface, tangible, but the signifiers (words) that would convey their message remain buried.

The enigmatic messages that we receive from others can overagitate us even in the best of circumstances in the sense that when we can't fully process what others—parents, teachers, coworkers, lovers, friends, or even the cashier at the local market who comes across as a little too chatty—want from us, we can become anxious and disoriented. Entering into relationships of any kind with others demands that we risk ourselves by exposing ourselves to their unpredictability. This means that we're often trying to metabolize affects whose meaning eludes us.

In addition, as I've already illustrated, anxiety in relation to the other's enigmatic messages is installed very early on, with that breast or bottle thrust at the child, which, recall, comes with a need. Inasmuch as children don't have the cognitive capacity to understand why things happen the way they do, why the adults who surround them want them to do certain things in a certain way or at a certain time, our status as subjects capable of receiving messages originates in a place of interpersonal opacity and the kind of frustration and misunderstanding that can accompany such opacity.

Interpersonal opacity is therefore yet another existential given. But like the other existential givens I've discussed—lack and anxiety—it can mutate into more circumstantial forms, forms that are in principle avoidable but that certain individuals, due to social power differentials, are unable to avoid. In other words, if there are deposits of lack and anxiety that exceed the normal (existential) level, interpersonal opacity—which can further escalate both lack and anxiety—can also exceed the normal (existential) level; it can even solidify into fairly predictable cultural patterns.

Recall, for instance, that in chapter 3 I argued that straight women are trained to negotiate with men's desire, that the burden of emotional intelligence falls on them in the sense that they're taught to believe that it's their duty to make intimate relationships work by remaining patient, understanding, and so on. Translating this into the vocabulary I've established in this chapter, one can say that they're trained to decipher men's enigmatic messages. More specifically, they're trained to interpret a loss that has already taken place—say, the lack of a phone call—as a matter of male ambivalence, as a temporary obstacle that can be overcome by extra effort.

It can be tempting to equate ambivalence with the idea that we can reason with this ambivalence—or with the person who appears ambivalent—so as to induce desire to flow in the direction that we want it to flow. But we can't. This is precisely why one of the most damaging aspects of our romantic culture—and particularly of our self-help industry—is its attempt to convince women that men are "naturally" (but not irreversibly) ambivalent, that their ambivalence can be overcome, that if women just try hard enough, take all the right steps, and resort to all manner of scheming, eventually they can convince a man to want them.

This leads some women to waste immense amounts of effort on interpersonal endeavors that are doomed from the get-go; it leads them to trade away too much of their peace of mind for the promise of "something"—it's usually not clear exactly what—that never in the end materializes. Either another person wants you or he doesn't. In most cases, it really is that simple. I'm not sure why we need hundreds of books that tell us otherwise.

This predicament of entering into a pointless process of negotiating with another person's ambivalent desire is not always gendered. Indeed, there's a particular genre of ambivalence that seems to trick straight men just as often as straight women: ambivalence that appears to arise from a history of being injured. It's easy to remain overly patient when we believe that the other person's hesitation is due to past traumatization. When we know that our partner, or potential partner, comes from a wounding family history, or has endured wounding romantic failures, it's easy for us to have empathy for his or her skittishness.

I've seen many young men convince themselves that if the woman they're dating treats them badly or blows them off, it's because she has been damaged by her family or prior relationships; for such men, their lover's indifference or coldness is merely a (somewhat endearing) façade for her underlying vulnerability. These men feel compelled to rescue a fragile woman by proving to her that they will stay loyal to her no matter what, that they won't disappoint or hurt her in the way that others have done in the past. Usually what happens is that the men themselves get terribly disappointed and hurt, barely able to limp out of the relationship.

This is a tricky situation because it's entirely possible that a generous interpretation of the emotional ambivalence of those who have been damaged is actually accurate: it's possible that others send mixed signals because the pain they have endured in the past causes them to hesitate. The question is thus less whether the ambivalences of their desire are justified than whether those on the receiving end of these ambivalences should put up with them indefinitely.

As I've argued, the irrationality of desire means that it can't be made to do what we want it to do. This means that people who feel ambivalent usually cannot change their feelings even if they want to; in this fundamental sense, they are not to blame for their uncertainty. But this doesn't alter the fact that trying to tolerate this uncertainty—trying, for example, to be a caring guy who never complains about his lover's aloofness—can over time take a huge toll. In this sense, it doesn't ultimately make much of a difference why we keep getting hurt in a given relationship. There are almost always good reasons for relational tangles. Sometimes there are excellent ones. But beyond a certain point, it doesn't really matter what the reason for our pain is; beyond a certain point, what matters is that we're in more pain than we should be.

THE VIOLENCE OF AMBIGUITY

There are even people who deliberately exploit the ambiguities of relationality in games of power. Coming to recognize the violence of such games has been especially hard for me because, as a scholar in the critical humanities, I've been trained to appreciate all things murky, indefinite, and impenetrable. For instance, because I routinely teach theoretical texts, including those by Lacan, that are more or less incomprehensible to my students (and sometimes to me as well), a significant part of my pedagogy is to teach them to accept their (anxiety-inducing) non-mastery, their intellectual castration.

I routinely explain to my students that many postwar European thinkers saw their unintelligible writing style as part and parcel of their critique of Enlightenment rationalism, which, as I noted in the previous chapter, was frequently coupled with the marginalization of those deemed incapable of it: irrational, overly emotional women and similarly irrational, overly emotional colonized populations. Against the backdrop of such political and epistemological political violence, many postwar thinkers thought of their opaque prose style as a revolutionary act. And in many ways it was: it changed the contours of humanistic scholarship. Even those who scorn it have been touched by it in the sense that they have to think twice about resorting to ideals such as objective truth or clear-cut meaning.

The matter is further complicated by the fact that during recent decades much theorizing about ethics in my field has argued that asking for emotional clarity from others is an ethical failure, whereas patience in the face of interpersonal opacity is an unquestionable ethical virtue; the emphasis in posthumanist ethics has been on the nobility of revering the unreadability of others. I hope that you can see how this is the logical result of rejecting Enlightenment rationalism: if rationality leads to violence, then whatever is the antithesis of rationality—in this case, ambiguity, nontransparency, indecipherability, and unintelligibility—seems to counter violence. This explains in part at least why so many prominent thinkers, such as Theodor Adorno, Emmanuel Levinas, Simone de Beauvoir, Jacques Derrida, and Judith Butler have valorized the ideal of tolerating ambiguity.

Adorno viewed lucidity as a cardinal sin: a capitulation to the demands of mass culture.[24] Levinas theorized the other as a site of inviolable density, suggesting that this other deserves our unconditional respect, deference, and protection regardless of how it behaves.[25] And de Beauvoir saw "the ethics of ambiguity" as an important component of an existentialist attitude that doesn't flee from the anxiety-producing irresolution—lack of closure—that characterizes human life but rather embraces this irresolution as a precondition of freedom.[26]

Closer to our own time, Derrida raised indecisiveness to an art form and aporias (unresolvable contradictions) to a moral good. In his later work, he developed the idea that we should give (and forgive) unconditionally, claiming that a gift is only a genuine gift when we don't expect to receive anything in return and that forgiveness is only genuine forgiveness when it doesn't have any strings (such as the expectation of remorse) attached to it. He even proposed that true forgiveness "forgives the unforgivable" (even though admittedly he had reservations about whether this ideal is ever possible to put into practice).[27] Butler, for her part, explicitly aligns ethics with respect for interpersonal opacity.[28]

This is a formidable edifice of thought to confront, particularly as I myself have also written extensively about the virtues of patience in the context of interpersonal opacity. Yet in recent years I've had to come to terms with the realization that opacity is a complicated interpersonal stance—that, among other things, it can be deployed aggressively. I've come to see that the idea that there's something intrinsically unethical about the need for interpersonal lucidity—that my request that the other give me a straightforward answer is always questionable—can be a little too convenient for those who want to take advantage of the emotional generosity of others.

This may in fact be one of the main twenty-first-century dilemmas of relationality: it feels like the ethics of ambiguity has become the status quo of relating in the sense that many of us are asked to tolerate immensely high levels of relational opacity. One result of this is that we can end up spending hours (and hours and hours) listening to the narcissistic monologues of those who don't want to categorize things—who, for instance, repeatedly launch relationships that are vaguely beyond friendship but not quite in the realm of romance—and who relish the fact that we don't ask them to make any choices (as I've noted several times, not having to make choices, not having to decide, because one feels entitled to everything, seems like one of the defining components of contemporary culture).

When the scenario of endless listening started to happen to me, I had to admit to myself that I was humbly enacting the age-old female role of staying nice even when I was feeling dreadful; I kept smiling even when I felt like screaming. In the end, the old-fashioned feminist in me defeated the opacity-loving, Derrida-teaching, vaguely Foucauldian post-Levinasian scholar so as to utter, to the startled consternation of the man speaking, a vehement *stop—no more!* (Incidentally, this may be one of the most Lacanian things I've ever done, though an explanation of this—of the so-called Lacanian act—is beyond the purview of this book.[29])

I decided that I no longer wanted to feed culturally sanctioned masculine arrogance in the name of an ethics of ambiguity. Equally importantly, I decided that the demand for interpersonal transparency and accountability can be a way of protecting a self that finds ambiguity intolerable. I realized that the default ethical stance that posits that dwelling in ambiguity is more virtuous than asking for clarity makes it impossible to make a case for emotional urgency even though there may be entirely legitimate (or at least understandable) reasons for this urgency. Simply put, those who have been traumatized may find ambiguity retraumatizing; they may need clear-cut answers because they experience unreadability as unbearably overagitating.

Even in the course of "normal" (non-traumatizing) everyday life, the unreadability of others can generate an excess of stimulation that is in the long run enervating. Imagine, then, what the ambiguities of relationality can do to those whose minds and bodies have, perhaps from an early age, been overstimulated to the degree that they cannot rest even when there's no obvious danger on the horizon. Such people remain constantly vigilant in relation to messages originating from the outside world because they register such messages as a potential threat to their basic safety. For such people, the attempt to tolerate the enigmas of relationality, to linger in ambiguity, can generate a deluge of anxiety. For partly personal reasons, I've concluded that the needs of such people are not always secondary to the needs of those who prefer—or are only capable of—interpersonal murkiness.

I experience interpersonal murkiness in the same ominous way as I used to experience the approaching footsteps of my father. This is why I refuse to linger. I don't have the luxury of sticking around people who can't give me a straight answer. It's easy to eroticize emotional ambivalence for the simple reason that desire is fanned by mystery. This is why the interplay of retreat and pursuit is such a common dynamic in the dance of desire. But I've learned that the other's opacity doesn't necessarily make him more fascinating. Much of the time, it makes him draining.

This is why I would rather lose a person than endure prolonged emotional impasses. I've learned to accept my urgency— my sense that I need closure *now* so that I can move on *now*—as a residue of a past that made me constitutionally overagitated. According to progressive (often vaguely Levinasian) ethics, severing interpersonal ties is more or less unacceptable. Yet it's my ability to do so (some would call this dissociation) that has allowed me to survive and (eventually) to fashion a life that feels not just livable but even worth living.

All kinds of traumas can hide in the confines of anxiety, which is one reason anxiety can be so hard to interpret. We often know we're anxious but we don't know why. I recently had dinner with a psychiatrist-psychoanalyst, Trinka, and her husband, Roy. Because I was in the middle of writing this book, and because its personal components were so strongly on the surface of my days, I told them parts of the story. I said to Trinka that I was vaguely worried about the fact that I remember very little of my life before the age of fifteen. As is the way of great analysts, she came up with the one sentence that brought instant insight: "Well, maybe it was just truly miserable."

It was. It's not that there was one element of life in that house by the mysterious lake that was so traumatizing that it caused amnesia—I wasn't sexually abused, for instance—but just a whole bunch of hard stuff that it has been easier to repress than to process. Being repeatedly trapped under a blanket until I thought I would die was probably the most obviously anxiety-producing part of it, but overall it feels like it was the whole damn scene (the poverty, the hopelessness, the harsh words, the anxiety and depression of others) that was damaging.

Roy added to this insight when he asked whether the long commute to school made things more difficult. As I paused to think about this, I realized in a flash why my body holds so much anxiety: it's not just that I cowered from my father but also that I, quite simply, cowered from the cold: the intense cold of winter mornings while waiting for the taxi (why I had to wait outside by the mailbox rather than in the kitchen is an enigma, given that I was the only child being picked up from the village); the piercing cold of the night on the way to the outhouse (for understandable reasons it was at some distance from the house); the still cold of my bedroom in the early evening when I got home from school (when the last trace of warmth was gone from the wood-burning stove). I spent a substantial part of the first twenty years of my life tensing up my body just because I was freezing. I also tensed up every time I had to leave my room after dark (which during winter was after 3 P.M.) because I was afraid of the ghost of the unhappy woman who killed her child with a broomstick. A childish fear, to be sure, but I know I had it even as a teenager.

The body holds the memory of such things. Even becoming conscious of this, actively trying to let go, doesn't change anything. I can tell myself a thousand times that the world is now a more welcoming place, that it's not out to hurt me, but this won't unlock my shoulders. I've even noticed that one of the things that most escalates my back pain is correcting students' grammar. Undoubtedly this has something to do with the history of studying the grammar of five languages on the bus while fighting nausea. Indeed, when I stand up from grading a pile of papers, nausea is what I feel: I want to vomit out all the bad grammar.

What I've tried to show in this chapter is that sometimes our anxieties run deep, all the way down to the kinds of formative experiences that we can't always even remember. Add to these the impact of social inequalities and the challenges of everyday life in our performance-oriented society, and it may well be that when it comes to anxiety, the best most of us can do is strive, fail, and muddle along. Cruelly optimistic like the straight guy in relation to a woman's fantasized capacity for pleasure, we take up our task again and again (and again) only to find that detumescence sneaks in before we reach our goal. And then we lie down exhausted. That is, we muddle along. Some of us become Lacanians because he teaches us to live with the idea that beyond a certain point, the point of avoidable anxieties, there's no cure. There's a perverse solace in that. There's also solace in Lacan's assertion—which I paraphrase wildly out of context—that those who have an assured future have no future at all.[30]

CONCLUSION

At the beginning of the last chapter, I argued that a degree of anxiety is inevitable in human life, that our intellectual tradition has often linked it to the responsibilities of freedom, and that being slightly out of joint, off balance, or just plain wacky can be aligned with creativity and existential intensity. It would be possible to stage similar arguments about the potential benefits of many of the other bad feelings I've discussed in this book. Penis envy can lead to feminist anger, which can over time force a society to become more egalitarian. And sadness can lead to insight, potentially deepening our character. As I noted in chapter 5, Freud already stressed that those prone to melancholia possess an unusual lucidity of perception. Intuitively, many of us understand that there may be something good about feeling bad: we know how to spin bad feelings in such a way that we can imagine something good coming out of them.

Undeniably sometimes suffering is just suffering: pointless pain, useless misery, senseless anguish. But in this book I've suggested that feeling bad can be a way to sidestep the creed of pragmatism that governs our society. If nothing else, bad feelings tend to slow down the pace of our days, making us think twice about what we're doing; they force us to push the pause button on our lives. Sadness is an obvious example of such self-reflexivity: depressed people tend to turn inward and ponder the choices they have made, the direction their lives have taken, and the meaning of it all. Feeling anxious, disappointed, or disillusioned can have the same impact in the sense that these feelings cause us to examine the basic parameters of our lives, perhaps even prompting us to ask whether the life we're living is actually the life we want to live.

When we find ourselves incapable of participating in the usual flow of life, we may gain a keener perspective on the choices we have made. The four pillars of cultural ideology I've interrogated—good performance, high productivity, constant self-improvement, and relentless cheerfulness—have one thing in common: they keep us moving. "Being busy" is the status quo of life in today's utilitarian society; slacking off is frowned upon. Bad feelings, in contrast, force us to slack off. They interrupt the cruel optimism that causes us to keep trying even when we have been repeatedly disappointed. This may sometimes be a good thing in the sense that when we stop running on the hamster wheel of our daily lives, alternative ways of going about the process may become visible; we may be able to discern the outlines of a different kind of life that might become possible if we gave it a chance. When we're feeling bad, we're almost automatically looking for ways to break patterns of living that are causing our dissatisfaction.

Honoring bad feelings also counters the common assumption that those susceptible to bad feelings—and particularly those who have been traumatized—aren't as skilled at the art of living as those who know how to approach things more lightly. According to this mentality, trauma weakens our basic affective aptitude so that we're more likely to be retraumatized. I may have bolstered this view in the last chapter when I revealed that the pain of the past makes it impossible for me to tolerate relational opacity. But even here, much depends on one's perspective. When I look at women who are willing to waste their time on the hopeless process of negotiating with the desire of reluctant men (or women), I conclude that my approach is perhaps the less destructive one.

More generally speaking, the idea that trauma invariably weakens us is a shortsighted assessment that overlooks the agility that can result from difficult experiences. Trauma doesn't inevitably make us more fragile—and therefore unable to meet life's challenges—but, quite the opposite, may enhance our ability to meet fresh suffering. The cheerful among us may get the wind knocked out of them when adversity strikes. In contrast, those who are used to feeling bad are likely to respond with more nimbleness.

Sometimes trying life experiences break us. But other times they make us more multidimensional. Arguably, they shape our personalities more profoundly than happiness does, over time adding depth and nuance to our being. I don't think that it's a coincidence that, as I've noted, people who have suffered a great deal often seem more interesting than those who have not. In addition, an intimate acquaintance with bad feelings may allow us to better relate to the suffering of others. If you're the kind of person who is sometimes sad for no apparent reason, you're more likely to empathize with another person who is similarly prone to bouts of depression.

This isn't to deny that it can be hard to respond to the pain of others when you're yourself in pain. For instance, severely depressed people may have trouble listening to others because their own bad feelings consume their entire experience. Similarly, extreme anxiety makes it difficult to pay attention to anyone else. And we all know that angry people have trouble relating to others. Yet a familiarity with bad feelings may allow us to meet the bad feelings of others with a greater degree of comprehension. Even when their experiences aren't exactly the same as ours, even when it's impossible to draw a clear analogy between their suffering and ours, we can approach them with compassion; we can make ourselves present in ways that those who have been blessed by unruffled lives may find difficult to do.

Is it then the case that there might, broadly speaking, be something good about feeling bad? Despite what I've just said, I don't want to idealize bad feelings as a political or personal strategy. I don't want to imply that it's (existentially, ethically, or otherwise) good to feel bad. Even though I've stressed that bad feelings can function as an antidote to our culture's creed of pragmatism, I don't want to suggest that we should actively court them. If they happen, that's one thing; but I don't want to valorize them as a solution to the impasses of contemporary life.

The matter is in fact complicated because arguing for the "productivity" of bad feelings comes uncomfortably close to the very pragmatic ethos that our society asks us to adopt—an ethos that takes a utilitarian approach even to suffering, confidently promoting the idea that in the same way that effort will be rewarded, hardship will eventually yield a profit of some kind. As I've argued, the ideology of the American dream presupposes that the prosperity it promises be preceded by setbacks and failures. This means that promoting bad feelings could easily play right into the very mentality that I've spent this entire book criticizing.

HOW SHOULD A LIFE BE?

How should a life be? This has always been my question (though Sheila Heti, in *How Should a Person Be?*, gave it a more elegant spin).[1] The answer I've advanced in writing (prior to this book) is the Nietzschean one: life should be a process of becoming. But becoming what? Does it not matter what one becomes as long as one keeps becoming? Or is there something that one should become, some sort of a subjective resting place that one would then spend the rest of one's life honing (so that one would still be in a process of becoming but in a smaller, more controlled way)?

Also—and I blame Adam Phillips for the fact that I now often think of this—I wonder about what I'm missing out on by living the life that I'm living rather than some other life.[2] It seems true that we lead double lives: on the one hand, there's the life we're living, and on the other, there's the one we wish we were living. Is this feeling that we could be living another kind of life a sign that we're still alive? Or is it a form of cruel optimism, an indication that we're squandering what we have in favor of fantasies of what we *could* have? It's hard to tell. It's hard to decide if our fantasies of a more satisfying life are an unnecessary frustration or a precondition of becoming (in the sense that these fantasies drive us on, keep us moving). I know that my personal fantasies of a different life were what helped me actually get that life. So is cruel optimism sometimes not so cruel after all?

I've noted that post-Foucauldian critiques of neoliberal ideology and biopolitical conditioning sometimes make it sound like we're living in the most tyrannical era of Western history. One of the unfortunate side effects of the Foucauldian perspective can be to suggest that people have never been as regulated as they are in contemporary America. I don't believe that this is the case. And, as I've mentioned, I don't believe that our current society is more oppressive than the society of slavery and segregation was, even if it's true that the legacies of that society haven't been surmounted, even if it's true that racism remains rampant in present-day culture.[3] In addition, I want to leave some space for the possibility that our fantasies of a better future, of a better life, are not invariably a bad thing, even as I agree with Berlant that cruel optimism can impede our flourishing.

I'm acutely aware of how easy it is to use the American dream to fault those who can't get out of the mud, as so many of the American poor and racialized individuals can't; it's insidious to blame individuals for not being able to break out of a system that's rigged to ensure their defeat. But, as I've admitted, I'm also not entirely able to discard my personal mythology of rising from the ashes.

So I hold onto this mythology tentatively, with a degree of self-reproach, in the understanding that its rewards aren't available to everyone. And even when these rewards are accessible, they aren't reliable: good things rarely last and the Lacanian in me tells me that feeling lacking (castrated) is inevitable for those of us who don't want to (or can't) resort to fantasies of omnipotence. Indeed, a further problem with the Foucauldian approach is that it downplays this basic Lacanian insight. I certainly agree—and hope to have illustrated in this book— that our cultural environment and social inequalities can exacerbate the baseline malaise of human existence. But I wouldn't go as far as to argue that this malaise arises entirely from biopolitical manipulation, for this would imply that there's a way out, that a different society would completely dissolve our bad feelings. This seems unlikely.

If anything, it seems worth raising the possibility that when social critics present dissatisfaction primarily as a consequence of biopolitical manipulation—rather than admitting that at least some of it is an unavoidable part of the human condition—their discourse begins to converge with the pragmatic tenor of our society that tells us that every problem has a practical solution. After all, when people believe that bad feelings come with the territory of being human, they might not consider such feelings as a disease in need of a remedy. It's precisely when we begin to think that bad feelings are a pathology that invariably has an external cause—in this case, our social environment—that they become a problem that needs to be overcome. Some bad feelings certainly can be overcome. But others cannot. The Lacanian in me tells me that I need to accept this.

There are those who argue that there's no contradiction in vehemently condemning the very system that one participates in. I've never been comfortable with this line of reasoning, particularly in cases where being part of the system means that one automatically reaps its benefits. Accepting the benefits of the very system that one attacks—or attacking the system whose benefits one accepts—seems greedy, (once again) indicative of a conviction that one doesn't have to choose, that one should be able to have one's cake and eat it too. I'm not saying that we shouldn't criticize aggressive foreign policy or domestic inequalities. I'm not even saying that we shouldn't criticize neoliberalism and biopolitics. After all, this is exactly what I've done in this book. But I do hesitate in the face of the ways in which our lives so often fall short of our critical ideals.

A couple of years ago, I attended a lecture by a prominent scholar who staged a vigorous critique of neoliberal capitalism. After the event, one of my students told me that she had overheard the speaker complain, right before starting his lecture, that the university had not put him up in a nice enough hotel. This anecdote sums up the paradoxes of criticism when the very thing that we criticize is also the thing we enjoy.

The system we criticize gives us enough benefits to neutralize our resistance (beyond talking and writing about it). It renders biopolitical control pleasurable to us in the same way that heteropatriarchy has found a way to render self-objectification pleasurable to (some) straight women. In this sense, all of us (critics of neoliberalism and biopolitics)—and not just this speaker—are complicit in the very system we denounce. It buys us off by offering us a variety of items from washing machines to shoes, watches, computers, and video games in compensation for our obedient and diligent participation. These rewards aren't always illusory: they do in fact make our lives easier, cushier, smoother, and yes, more enjoyable. When I throw my laundry into the washing machine, I often think back to what it was like to wash everything by hand, particularly in the winter when water needed to be heated on the stove.

Neoliberal culture is so hard to resist because it's convenient. It's particularly convenient for those with money. But it's also to some extent convenient for those without money, for some of the basic comforts of consumer society—running water, flushing toilets, central heating, television channels, and fast food—are available to most people in our society except the least privileged. It's precisely because the comforts of consumer capitalism are tangible that they are politically placating. As long as I can take a daily shower, my television works, and I can order cheap pizza, I might be fairly content to stay in my apartment, no matter how modest, rather than agitate for social change.

Cultural critics have long recognized that the genius of Western capitalism is that it offers its subjects—including those who work long hours to survive—some rewards for their suffering. As

I mentioned at the beginning of this book, foremost among these is an extensive entertainment system that streams escapist fantasies into the living rooms of those whose real lives feel challenging. Turning on the television at the end of the day to some extent makes up for the monotony or difficulty of your work at the same time as it revitalizes you so that you'll be ready to work again the next day. This is one way in which our economy is able to extract a huge amount of labor from us, the poor, the affluent, and those in between alike; it offers us a handy way to renew our energies so that we don't burn out too quickly.

On one level, this is obviously a matter of disciplining pleasure in the Foucauldian sense: it's a matter of teaching us to enjoy in socially condoned, commercially lucrative ways. At the same time, it's hard to deny that our enjoyment feels "real," and that if it was taken away, we might complain bitterly, as people do when power outages shut down their flat screens. In so many ways, it's easier to push the on button instead of the pause button: it's easier to drown our bad feelings in mass entertainment and other offerings of consumer culture than it is to actively assess the contours of our lives.

The highbrow critical impulse—in part inherited from Adorno—is to condemn such complacency. But I'm not so sure I can reproach this impulse to turn things off, to just forget, if even just for an evening (more on this shortly). It feels to me that most of us need some way of periodically tuning out and that escapist fantasies are perhaps among the most benign ways of doing so.

There are those, such as Žižek, who claim that only a full-blown rejection of the present social order (a revolution) can change things.[4] Others, such as Julia Kristeva, advocate a more intimate revolt of the mind, a life of self-interrogation and constant questioning.[5] I'm drawn to both ideas, depending on

whom I'm reading. But it interests me that in recent years, some
critics, such as Maggie Nelson, have started to rethink what
radical politics might look like, proposing that small-scale changes
in how people choose to live might at times be just as rebellious—
not to mention more realistic—than the call for a revolution
(which, as Nelson correctly suggests, sometimes sounds suspi-
ciously masculinist).[6]

Nelson arguably ends up in a fairly traditional place in reval-
orizing, albeit in a queer and trans context, the "goodness" of
the nuclear family, given that the triad of mother, father, and
child retains a privileged position in her text. At the same time,
it feels like it's difficult to avoid the specter of conservatism
even in the most earnest attempts to rethink the state of the
world along more egalitarian lines. If revolutionary rhetoric
sounds annoyingly masculinist, my own argument about the
intractability of some bad feelings might elicit the charge of
defeatism from those looking for a more revolutionary approach.
Along related lines, even though Kristeva's idea that constantly
revising the way we think can gradually revise the world is true,
I know—in part from having observed the lives of my parents—
that this ideal often eludes those who have to work so hard that
they don't have any mental space left for the luxury of repeatedly reassessing their existence.

Plus it's not like doing so would necessarily improve their
lives in any concrete way; it might even make them feel worse
about all the things they're missing out on. In this sense, asking
people who work at physically demanding or mentally numbing
jobs to lead a life of critical contemplation is too much to ask
(though a society where everyone could lead a life of critical
contemplation is certainly appealing). So perhaps one place to
start—the place to begin a quiet revolution without asking for

any more sacrifices from those who have already sacrificed so much—is to simplify things, to get rid of the excess that clutters our lives.

Here I return to a theme I've already explored (I return to it because it speaks to me personally): getting rid of clutter. Consumer culture controls us not because it constrains us but because it proliferates pleasures; it gets us hooked into a system where it's relatively easy for us to run from one pleasure to the next even as we simultaneously also work very hard. Perhaps the only thing that it hasn't calculated on is the possibility that when our lives are too saturated by enjoyment, we might no longer enjoy anything; it's conceivable that when there's too much to choose from, nothing fully satisfies.

Todd McGowan proposes that when objects and services multiply, as they do in consumer culture, it may in fact become harder to sustain the cruelly optimistic illusion that we'll one day be fulfilled; once we have already tried multiple routes to satisfaction, we may start to lose faith in the idea that it's ever attainable.[7] McGowan sees in this loss of faith a way to defeat the appeal of consumer culture altogether: he hypothesizes that if we realized that the objects and services on offer won't satisfy us, we might begin to reject them. And indeed, if everyone decided to pare down, to lead a simplified life, our consumer culture would lose much of its power.

I think of this whenever I, while visiting my parents, open my mother's closet in search of a towel: I'm struck by how very few clothes she possesses. My mother, who always dreamt of becoming a clothing designer, and who always manages to look lovely, only has about five hangers in her closet and a couple of very narrow shelves for the rest of her clothes. This practice of paring things down is one of the many useful things I've inherited from her, which explains why a friend who used my Cape apartment for a few weeks while I was elsewhere emailed *where's all your stuff?*

I don't know how a person should be. But I do know that I appreciate people who do not hoard things—materials, objects, commodities—as a way to flee from their lack-in-being. The attempt to heal the emptiness of existence by buying stuff is a flimsy strategy at best, as is clear from the prevalence of depression in our society. And it's what has led our world to the brink of an environmental disaster. This is why accepting lack as an irremediable component of human life, and perhaps even accepting the fact that some bad feelings are inevitable, is not just existentially but also politically significant.

PARING DOWN BY FORGETTING

My appreciation for the practice of paring things down may also explain why forgetting (mostly the bad but sometimes even the good) has played such a huge part in my life: it's a way to unclutter the mind. This is why I've always been drawn to Nietzsche's claim that the best way to overcome what is difficult is simply just to forget about it. This claim may sound counterintuitive because it goes against the grain of our therapeutic culture, including the Freudian perspective that I otherwise value, which tells us that the only way to process trauma is to remember it so as to gradually work through its legacies. And that Nietzsche himself fell into madness at the end of his life makes it hard to view him as a source of sound psychological advice.

But I think that Nietzsche was onto something important when he asserted that there can be no happiness, no cheerfulness, no action in the present moment, without a degree of forgetfulness.[8] Forgetting, for Nietzsche, acts like a bouncer at the door who imposes order on our psychic and affective life so that we can rest and consequently, ideally, forge forms of life that feel vitalizing; it makes the present—the present as a space of creative and meaningful activity—possible for us.

Nietzsche proposes that when we're crowded by too many memories, we're like insomniacs who are too agitated to sleep but too enervated—too exhausted by our own agitation—to accomplish anything useful; we are frenetic in a futile way.[9] In this situation, a surplus of memory overanimates us at the same time as it paralyzes and mortifies us. When there is too much memory—particularly when there are too many painful memories—there is no space for mental clarity; our activities become too scattered, too diffuse, to crystallize into an artifact of any kind.

Nietzsche specifies that those who can't forget about their hardships are like dyspeptics who "cannot 'have done' with anything," whereas those capable of forgetting have excellent stomachs.[10] With a rhetorical flourish characteristic of him, Nietzsche claims that if the soul of the person who can't forget "squints," those who are able to forget shake off "with a *single* shrug many vermin that eat deep into others."[11]

Nietzsche's valorization of the ability to shrug off wounding experiences sometimes makes him sound like the worst of Wild West capitalists: suffering is a sign of weakness; victims are pathetic; stop whining; if you fall, pick yourself up by your bootstraps and keep marching. Moreover, it would be possible to argue that his vision of creativity—of the kind of activity that *gets things done*—is merely an early articulation of the very neoliberal dogma of high productivity and efficiency I've criticized. However, Nietzsche's ideal of overcoming the agitation of insomnia so as to be able to act seems quite different from the mentality of the neoliberal busybody who is intent on breaking the latest performance record.

Nor would it be reasonable to equate Nietzsche's advocacy of happiness and cheerfulness with the creed of positive thinking that governs contemporary society, for Nietzsche never loses track of the manner in which happiness and cheerfulness presuppose a familiarity with unhappiness and seriousness; lightness and gravity, the ability to skid across the surface of life and the willingness to peer into its abysses are, for Nietzsche, always two sides of the same coin.

Alenka Zupančič correctly argues that Nietzsche's ideal of forgetting what has caused suffering isn't a matter of denying suffering but rather of not letting this suffering define one's being. It's a way for the traumatized person to reject the mantle of the victim, to refuse to be defined by his or her injury.[12] Forgetting, as it were, allows the traumatized person to dissociate her suffering from her basic self-understanding; it renders trauma external to her, something that may have happened *to* her but that is not synonymous *with* her, with who she is.

This way of looking at the matter reveals that what initially seems like an irreconcilable difference between Freud and Nietzsche, between therapeutic practice and the practice of forgetting, is perhaps not so irreconcilable after all, for the externalization of injury is arguably also the aim of therapeutic practice: the talking cure gradually weaves a cloak of words between the patient and her trauma so as to create some distance between them—so as to make the trauma less immediately felt, less identical with the patient's sense of self.

The obvious difference between Freud and Nietzsche is that in the Freudian paradigm the externalization of trauma can only be achieved through the ability of the talking cure to gradually release the painful affects that have become congealed in traumatic fixations, whereas the Nietzschean paradigm is based on a stoic refusal to speak one's pain. In the Freudian model, words burn with affect even as they allow the patient to gain distance from her trauma, whereas what Nietzsche advocates is a kind of "decision," a determination to shut out the traumatic experience, a refusal to allow it to dominate one's consciousness. I suspect that such a "decision" is often powerless against acute forms of traumatization. Yet I've also come to see that in some instances it may allow those who have been injured to live "to the side of" or "next to" their injury rather than in the middle of it.

Discussions of trauma tend to imply that one is either "within" it—unable to forget, acting out, repeating patterns, having flashbacks, or paralyzed by it—or "beyond" it, in a place where the trauma has been worked through, overcome, or integrated into the flow of life. Most clinicians and trauma theorists of course recognize that working through trauma is an ongoing and open-ended process, one that is never definitively "done." Still, the dominant either/or paradigm tends to obscure the fact that many trauma survivors ultimately end up living neither "within" their trauma nor "beyond" it but rather somewhere in its vicinity.

On some level, this is what I hear in Nietzsche's statements regarding forgetting. His message seems to be that, given that you cannot banish trauma, that you cannot transcend it, perhaps the best you can do is to learn to live in such a way that you exist next to it rather than in its disorienting vortex. If you can't fix the past—as none of us can—then perhaps the best thing to do is to get as far away from it as possible. This is why I don't think that Nietzsche's commentary on forgetting is simply a matter of celebrating the stoicism of strong wills. Rather, he's outlining one of the preconditions of creativity: the process of clearing the slate so that fresh shoots of life can take root.

Nietzsche believes that creativity demands a limit of some kind, a degree of constraint, "a defined horizon."[13] He thinks that only those who are able to draw a perceptual horizon within which they can function without being crushed by an excess of stimulation will thrive. Forgetting is one way to establish such a horizon, to forge a void that opens a space for new things to come into being—that, in short, makes creativity possible. Simply put, when we're pulled in too many directions at once, when we're filled with too many recollections, too attuned to the grievances of the past, we can't relax enough to create anything. Forgetting, in contrast, clears out some of the clutter of our lives, making room for new preoccupations. This is why Nietzsche insists that forgetting is a prerequisite of living in the present.

The refusal to linger in interpersonal ambiguity that I talked about at the end of the last chapter is also a form of forgetting. Such ambiguity crowds the mind, just as an excess of memory does. It weighs you down psychically and emotionally. It keeps you from living in the present—that is, it keeps you from living—just as effectively as painful memories do. And it revives these memories in ways that consume even more of your resources. My resources feel too scarce to be squandered in this manner. This is why I cut interpersonal ties whose opacity encumbers me, trying to focus instead on what is rewarding because it's honest and candid.

Moreover, I know, as Nietzsche also argues, that if forgetting opens space for new passions, becoming passionate about something new in turn extinguishes painful memories, as happens, for instance, when the arrival of a new lover makes it possible for us to stop mourning the one we have lost. Likewise, nothing allows me to sever ambiguous emotional entanglements better than the coming-into-being of a new preoccupation (maybe a person, maybe a project) whose luminescence outshines—and therefore banishes—the ambiguous; it pushes aside what is irrelevant. In this sense, if I sidestep murkiness in order to make room for lucidity, I also cultivate lucidity in order to render murkiness superfluous.

THE DUDLEY HOUSE BATHROOM

Lucidity, uncluttering, paring down, getting rid of murkiness: it's only now that I write these words that I see that they're all versions of the minimalism that has become my personal credo. No wonder that I haven't managed to be a dutiful poststructuralist scholar, for aporias, enigmas, opacities, ambiguities, and syntax that seeks to strangle the reader—the godly ideals of poststructuralism—are clearly not designed for me. I like a straightforward presentation of ideas (even complex ones) just as much as I like straightforward relationships and apartments stripped of surplus.

Okay, so, admittedly I *love* Lacan. But that's because his impenetrability is so over the top that one has no choice but to give up: there's no possibility of mastery and that's refreshing. And there are so many good jokes, including penis jokes, along the way. I guess I'll qualify my statement by saying that impenetrability is enticing when the ideas it shrouds are genuinely powerful; it's less so when it's calculated to artificially prop up puny ones.

Uncluttered countertops, clean surfaces, simple sentences. I do, however, have the ocean right outside my window, which is an extravagant luxury. My rent is cheap but my view definitely isn't: a house a couple of doors down recently sold for more than a million dollars, so I guess I literally have a million-dollar view.

Nowadays, as I write, the ocean is my constant companion. I love watching the sun creep up the buildings across the harbor early in the morning. On sun-drenched days—of which there are many—the sun makes the water sparkle like a billion diamonds. On foggy days—my favorite—the landscape softens into an impressionist painting. During sunsets, the sky turns from a fierce red into a golden yellow. During clear nights—like tonight (it's 3:45 A.M.)—the (full) moon hangs over the harbor in a manner that combines the sublime with the friendly. Whenever I look up from my laptop, the moon and its incandescent reflection on the water are what I see. There's nothing wanting from this scene of writing.

A friend who visited a couple of years ago said, "I can't stand it here, it's too beautiful." I felt obliged to punch him in the arm and say, "Don't be crazy." But I know what he meant. The beauty of my setting makes me think about death all the time for the simple reason that I know that something this good can't last. I've never been more aware of my own mortality than during recent years of living in this place whose exquisiteness overwhelms me every day. It makes me recognize, somehow very concretely, what I've repeated throughout this book, namely that the possibility of loss hovers over every gain, that the prospect of deprivation nibbles at the edges of every satisfaction, that there truly is no fullness without emptiness, no happiness without sadness, no harmony without anxiety.

While the moon silently inches across the black sky, I have to admit—as so many have before me—that life has slipped past me like a thief slips out of the bedroom of a woman whose necklace he has stolen. It used to be that when I looked in the mirror, it was all ahead of me, it was all just beginning. But then one day it all seemed behind me. I looked in the mirror of the Harvard Dudley House bathroom, realizing that the mirror, like the rest of the bathroom, looked exactly as it had twenty-eight years ago when I first applied lipstick in front of it. It was I who had changed: the bone structure was the same, as was the hair, but the face that looked back felt alien, disturbingly wilted (beyond being fixable with lipstick).

Svetlana Boym, who was a member of my dissertation committee, and who defended my insane decision to try to reinvent the soul at the height of poststructuralism (my first public rebellion),[14] recently died. She wrote a famous book: *Death in Quotation Marks*.[15] And then she died: no more quotation marks. The demise of postmodern irony. Barbara Johnson, also on my dissertation committee, died years ago. The demise of so much that remains inarticulable (because that's how BJ was: the ultimate enigmatic signifier, a true Derridean, the target of a thousand crushes, and someone I loved but also disappointed by not becoming a deconstructionist).[16]

These formidable women were not much older than I am now when they died. Standing in the Dudley House bathroom, I thought of them and I thought about the recent words of a colleague of mine: "The academy will kill you, especially if you're a woman." I know that the academy is not a Congolese cobalt mine. Still, I thought that it was uncanny that everything about the bathroom looked the same but that these two powerful women, both of whom probably used that bathroom, were gone.

I often feel intensely resentful toward inanimate objects—rocks, books, tables—because I know that they won't die with me. When I look at the huge rock next to the wheat field (the one that my aunt ran across) that I used to climb as a child, I think that it's unfair that it gets to live while my parents, who have worked so much harder, suffered so much more than this rock, do not. Even the house I grew up in is decaying more slowly than they are. Standing in the Dudley House bathroom, I thought about Freud's essay on transience, where he claims that we appreciate life all the more because we know that it's fleeting.[17] Because I know that this is true, melancholia is never far off. It gently tugs at me; it clings to the moon outside my window. (It's now 4:15 A.M., which means that in an hour I'll lose the moon, but not before it turns the color of carrots.)

THE SCENE OF WRITING

For some, melancholia is a politically poignant affect, a way of staying faithful to what we're asked to relinquish;[18] for others, it's a breeding ground for political passivity and inaction, a space of self-absorption and disconnectedness from others, a problematic clinging onto lost objects and ideals, which are imagined to be more precious than anything new that could be found or invented;[19] yet for others, it's the foundation of creativity and imaginative activity.[20] I suspect that melancholia can be all of these things, depending on the context and the moment. And I know that, for me, life is largely a process of repeatedly negating melancholia without expecting to definitively defeat it. Or more precisely, writing—which, for me, in many ways has become a synonym for living—is this process.

On the one hand, writing is difficult to undertake when one is too full of memory, which is why melancholics—those imprisoned in the cocoon of their loss—often find it hard to enter the scene of writing. On the other, writing pushes melancholia aside or at least makes it feel less overpowering; writing consumes one's attention to such an extent that it excludes the recollection of what has been painful. At least this is how I experience it: when I write, the past recedes from my consciousness—unless I'm explicitly talking about it, as I've done at points in this book—so that I'm momentarily freed from its influence. Even though I don't always literally "forget" about what has happened, I become so deeply immersed in my task that whatever did happen falls to the wayside. Writing is my oblivion, which is why it allows me to grasp what Nietzsche means about new passions pushing old griefs into the margins of one's life.

Writing can thus be a means of using up energy that would otherwise be bound up in overagitating (or saddening) memories of the past. This is one reason that my relationship to our society's performance principle is complicated, for I've chosen obsessive productivity over the greater evil of dwelling in, and therefore being constantly defeated by, the past. I could defend myself by arguing, as Herbert Marcuse already did, that creative forms of labor function differently from the performance principle, that high productivity in domains like writing is not oppressive in the same way as high productivity in other domains.[21] But I'm not sure this distinction holds. It certainly doesn't convince those who tell me—usually because they pity me—that I should slow down, that I've written too many books. Those who say this usually haven't read my books, so my assumption is that they're not saying that I should slow down because my books suck (though that may also be true); rather, it's the sheer volume of books that bothers them, no doubt because it seems pathological.

They're right of course: the surplus of writing is a pathology, a coping mechanism. Yet this "pathology" is the best I can do. This is why I experience warnings about working too hard as an attempt to discipline me, to render me less "excessive." In a way, although the performance principle tells us that we need to stay productive, other social ideals—such as the notion that we're supposed to lead balanced lives—suggest that excessive productivity is as big a problem as not producing. Both of these creeds can be oppressive: extracting performance from people who are already exhausted is tyrannical; but so is the demand that we curtail our "excessive" passions in the name of a sensible life.

The night after I finished the first draft of this book I had a terrible nightmare. I was visiting my parents. It was 2 A.M. (as it was in real life). Though I was in the habit of waking up at that hour to write, the scene of writing that I concocted in my dream was otherwise entirely unrealistic: I had perched my laptop on the counter of my parents' kitchen, between the sink and the microwave. My mother was having insomnia and she kept interrupting me every few minutes. I tried to tell her to go back to sleep so that I could write but she wouldn't leave me alone, wanting instead to use the microwave. At some point, my brother (yes, I have one—five years younger) arrived and insisted on washing his shirt in the sink. Both of them pestered me to move until I was filled with despair: *they were trying to keep me from writing*. Finally, my father walked in the door—he seemed to be coming home from work, as always—and asked me what was wrong. As I burst out crying, he cupped my face in his dirty hands and drew me close for an embrace.

None of this would have happened in real life: my father would never embrace me; my mother would never pester me; and my brother has probably never hand washed a shirt in his life. But the interesting part of the dream, for me, was the terror I felt at not being able to write. I could just as well have been chased by Earth-conquering aliens or bugs the size of houses.

Still, I can't say that this was the only time my father—this father with a lacerating tongue—saved my life. The first time was when he intuitively pulled the brakes of his tractor when I fell next to its wheel from the hay cart he was pulling (he didn't see or hear me fall but somehow he knew that something was wrong). The second time was when he raced me to the hospital after I had been bitten by a poisonous snake (*kyykäärme*—yet another uncanny word), the kind that can kill a child under the best of circumstances, but I'm also allergic to its venom, so things weren't looking good. To this day, I don't know why my father happened to be home that day (it was a sunny day in the summer, the kind of day that usually had him pulling an eighteen-hour workday), but I do know that he drove faster than any ambulance could have because he knew the tight curves of the country road better than anyone.

He also saved me (not my life, but me) when he sent me two thousand dollars one summer so that I could break the cycle of working so much that I couldn't finish my dissertation; I knew he didn't have that money, that he had to take out yet another loan to give it to me. Interestingly, already then it was a question of writing: after being stuck for nine years (not counting the first MA, the totally useless one in sociology), I wrote the damn thing in six weeks (it wasn't very good). So I'm not sure what it means that he saved my life—my writing—in my dream. I suspect that it has something to do with the fact that, once upon a time, he exemplified the person who was castrated—growing a deadly tumor between his legs—without dying. A bit of Oedipus here, certainly. But also the beginning of what was to become a scene of writing, the scene of surviving my own inadequacy.

It's 5 A.M. The moon has turned the color of carrots. The sky is a kaleidoscope of blue, purple, and pumpkin pie. Soon the first rays of the sun will kiss the buildings across the harbor, making them look vaguely like the gilded castle of Versailles. They will set the water on fire while slowly pushing the moon over the sharp edge of the horizon.

Yesterday I talked to my parents on the phone. The email from my brother said to call because of a mattress. It turned out that my father wanted to know what kind of a mattress I want for the new bed he has bought in anticipation of my visit in August. An American or a Scandinavian? *The American are softer so one of those.* "Alright, then, American it is."

Last summer's visit was the first time in fifty years that my father managed to go for ten days without uttering a reproach of any kind. At the end of the visit, I shook his hand and told him that it had been a nice ten days. "He's really trying," my mother said while driving me to the train station. "I know," I said. It turns out that since that visit he has completely renovated that room next to the attic, the one he never used to enter. I have no idea what it looks like now, only that this is where the bed with the American mattress is going to be.

It strikes me now, thinking back, that as cold as that room often was, it was nicely decorated even when I hid there sobbing. I hated the green wallpaper but I always understood why my mother—a redhead who loves green—had chosen it. And the furniture was state of the art for a teenage girl. I have no recollection of when they furnished it. But they furnished it with care: a care that should have been visible in the clean oak surfaces but that remained invisible to me.

My father said on the phone that an oak bed is what he had bought this time too. "Those are hard to find these days," he added. This time I do see the care. And when I see the room in August, I'll make sure to say that it's beautiful even if the wallpaper is green. But I'm betting it will be blue because now my mother knows me, as I also know her. I just don't know my father.

So in two months' time, while sitting by the mysterious lake and (graciously) eating a dish he has prepared, I'll ask him about the brother who drowned in it; about the other brother who died in the war; about the brother who survived the war but never left the village; about the sister who died of tuberculosis; about my grandfather (whom I never knew); about my grandmother (whom I barely remember); about the funeral of my schizophrenic uncle Paavo, my childhood inspiration, who died during the seven years when I didn't visit, call, or write; about the death of his other sister (the one who ran across the wheat field) during the same years; about what it was like, a few years ago, to find his hermit brother dead on the hill next to the sauna; about what it was like in that village seventy years ago; about what it felt like to see the Iron Curtain go up in his backyard, to no longer be able to pick the berries on what used to be his parents' land; and about where he slept as a boy.

What I won't ask him is what it's like to have reached an age when one knows for sure that there can't be much of life left. Does one just ignore that reality? Forget it from one minute to the next? I've never dared to ask anyone. But I will ask him how he has managed to survive the life that was handed to him, how he has managed to get to the point where, on the phone, chattering about the redone room and the oak bed, he met my laughter about the American mattress with a good-humored chuckle. How does a man who has led the kind of life that he has led have any laughter left in him?

PS: The room was blue.

ACKNOWLEDGMENTS

Many components of this book originated in my 2015 seminars at Harvard's Program for Studies of Women, Gender, and Sexuality: the galvanizing students who attended these seminars, as well as the equally incredible ones who attended my 2016–2017 Harvard seminars, are what every professor dreams of. My argument about anxiety in chapter 6 developed in my University of Toronto 2016 graduate seminar on the same topic: I thank the motivated students who spent the semester talking about bad feelings with me. A special thanks to Sheila Heti, my talented friend, for her thoughtful contributions to that course and for inviting me to give a talk on anxiety at her monthly Tambourine Hall event in Toronto.

This somewhat comic talk grew into a plenary address at a Lacanian conference (LACK) at Colorado College. I'm grateful to Jennifer Friedlander, Henry Krips, Todd McGowan, and Hilary Neroni—the cofounders of LACK—for inviting me to deliver this address. The audience at that conference was the best I've ever had, completely demolishing the stereotype of arrogant Lacanians. I'm particularly thankful to Todd McGowan for having been such a loyal intellectual ally in recent years.

It's impossible to sufficiently thank my editor, Wendy Lochner, for her ongoing support of my work; her passion for, and defense of, theoretical thinking; her willingness to indulge writing that crosses genres; and her uncanny ability to respond to emails in less than thirty seconds. Kathryn Jorge at Columbia University Press has done everything in her power to accommodate my obsessiveness about readable sentences, even indulging my request for the most talented copyeditor I have ever worked with: Heather Jones. Like many authors, I find the copyediting stage stressful, but Heather manages to make it a pleasure. Her suggestions are invariably astute and thoughtful. I am deeply grateful for her meticulous yet nonintrusive labor.

A heartfelt thanks also to Gail Newman for her generous reading of the manuscript. I also appreciate the equally generous feedback I received from her students at Williams College. Likewise, I thank Emma Childs at Harvard for organizing a Dudley House event where I got a chance to share some sections of the manuscript.

My magnificent research assistant Philip Sayers continues to give me the precious gift of freeing me of dozens of practical aggravations so that I have more time to write: I'm tempted to delay his dissertation defense just so that I can continue to employ him. A sincere thanks to Michael Cobb, Alexandra Gillespie, and Holger Syme at the University of Toronto for always having my back. I would not have survived the last decade without your support. Working with my Harvard colleagues—Michael Bronski, Ana Iona, Alice Jardine, Caroline Light, Afsaneh Najmabadi, Amy Parker, Sarah Richardson, Linda Schlossberg, and Phyllis Thompson—continues to feel like attending a really great dinner party.

Thanks to Sara Salih for many tasty meals and lively conversations. Julia Cooper, Heather Jessup, and Margeaux Feldman, graduate-students-turned-friends, are the definition of delight. Spencer Mackoff continues to be a rare treat. And Kathryn Kuitenbrouwer totally gets my insanity (perhaps because she's insane in much the same way). Jess Gauchel and Steph Gauchel: to you I owe what there is of sanity; I can't thank you enough for our little circle of friendship. Finally, I thank my parents for having let me go. I'm grateful for what you gave me, which I know was more than you had, more than you could afford.

NOTES

INTRODUCTION

1. Sigmund Freud, "Three Essays on the Theory of Sexuality " (1905), in *The Standard Edition of the Complete Psychological Works of Sigmund Freud*, ed. James Strachey (London: Hogarth Press, 1956–1974), 194–195. See also the following texts by Freud, all published in the *Standard Edition*: "The Dissolution of the Oedipus Complex" (1924); "Some Psychical Consequences of the Anatomical Difference between the Sexes" (1925); and *New Introductory Lectures on Psychoanalysis* (1933).

2. I make this argument about penis envy in my undergraduate film theory primer *Feminist Film Theory and "Pretty Woman"* (New York: Bloomsbury Press, 2016).

3. Jacques Lacan, "The Signification of the Phallus," in *Écrits: The First Complete Edition in English*, trans. Bruce Fink (New York: Norton, 2007). See also *The Seminar of Jacques Lacan, Book XX: On Feminine Sexuality, the Limits of Love and Knowledge*, trans. Bruce Fink (New York: Norton, 1999).

4. Academic readers may appreciate knowing that in response to W. R. D. Fairbairn's claim that penis envy is not natural in women, Lacan writes: "Who told him it was natural? Of course it's symbolic. It is in so far as the woman is in a symbolic order with an androcentric perspective that the penis takes on this value" (*The Seminar of Jacques Lacan, Book II: The Ego in Freud's Theory and in the Technique of Psychoanalysis*, trans. Sylvana Tomaselli [New York: Norton, 1991], 272).

5. Jean-Paul Sartre, *Being and Nothingness: A Phenomenological Essay on Ontology*, trans. Hazel E. Barnes (New York: Washington Square Press, 1992). Lacan talks about lack in many of his seminars and across his collection of essays, *Écrits*, referenced in note #3.

6. See Friedrich Nietzsche, *The Genealogy of Morals*, trans. Walter Kaufmann (New York: Vintage, 1989).

7. The most famous formulation of this argument can be found in Max Horkheimer and Theodor Adorno, *Dialectic of Enlightenment*, trans. Edmund Jephcott (Stanford: Stanford University Press, 2007). This book was originally published in 1944, so the idea is not new.

8. The classic source on neoliberalism is Michel Foucault's *The Birth of Biopolitics: Lectures at the Collège de France, 1978–1979*, trans. Graham Burchell (New York: Palgrave Macmillan, 2008). I'll be deploying Foucault's ideas throughout this book. For more recent incisive analyses, see Lisa Duggan, *The Twilight of Equality? Neoliberalism, Cultural Politics, and the Attack on Democracy* (Boston: Beacon Press, 2003) and Wendy Brown, *Edgework: Critical Essays on Knowledge and Politics* (Princeton, NJ: Princeton University Press, 2005).

9. Affect theory is a relatively recent theoretical approach associated with critics such as Sara Ahmed, Lauren Berlant, Ann Cvetkovich, and Sianne Ngai, all of whom are referenced in this book and who have generally speaking had a tremendous impact on its arguments. Like psychoanalytic theory, affect theory is interested in human emotions (affects—thus the label "affect theory"), including their visceral, bodily manifestations. And like psychoanalysis, it studies trauma: the various ways in which human beings get damaged by their environment. However, it tends to politicize trauma more explicitly than psychoanalysis by focusing on the type of traumatization that results from social inequalities such as poverty, sexism, racism, and homophobia. That said, contemporary psychoanalysis is often also interested in such traumatization, so that the distinction between psychoanalysis and affect theory isn't always precise. Many critics, myself included, find both approaches helpful.

10. Paul Preciado, *Testo Junkie: Sex, Drugs, and Biopolitics in the Pharmacopornographic Era*, trans. Bruce Benderson (New York: The Feminist Press, 2013); Maggie Nelson, *The Argonauts* (New York: Graywolf

Press, 2015); Diane Enns, *Love in the Dark: Philosophy by Another Name* (New York: Columbia University Press, 2016).

11. Preciado, *Testo Junkie*, 347.

12. See Micah McCrary, "Riding the Blinds," *Los Angeles Review of Books* (April 26, 2015).

13. Nelson, *The Argonauts*, 60.

14. Roland Barthes, "The Death of the Author," *Image, Music, Text*, trans. Stephen Heath (New York: Fontana Press, 1977); Michel Foucault, "What Is an Author?," *Language, Counter-memory, Practice: Selected Essays and Interviews*, trans. Donald F. Bouchard (Ithaca, NY: Cornell University Press, 1977); Philip Sayers, "Communication: Maggie Nelson and the Literary Text as Letter" (unpublished dissertation chapter, University of Toronto, 2016).

15. See, for instance, Roland Barthes's *A Lover's Discourse: Fragments*, trans. Richard Howard (New York: Hill & Wang, 1977); *Roland Barthes by Roland Barthes*, trans. Richard Howard (New York: Farrar, Straus, & Giroux, 1977); and *Mourning Diary*, trans. Richard Howard (New York: Hill & Wang, 2012).

16. On this theme, see Nancy Miller, *Getting Personal: Feminist Occasions and Other Autobiographical Acts* (New York: Routledge, 1991).

17. Luce Irigaray, *To Be Two*, trans. Monique M. Rhodes and Marco F. Cocito-Monoc (New York: Routledge, 2001), 9–10.

18. David Eng talks about the distinction between affective history and factual history in *The Feeling of Kinship: Queer Liberalism and the Racialization of Intimacy* (Durham, NC: Duke University Press, 2010).

19. Here are some key thinkers: Sara Ahmed, Kimberly Juanita Brown, Anne Cheng, Ta-Nehisi Coates, Angela Davis, Nadia Ellis, David Eng, Paul Gilroy, Saidiya Hartman, bell hooks, Fred Moten, José Muñoz, Sianne Ngai, Jasbir Puar, Claudia Rankine, Darieck Scott, Jared Sexton, Hortense Spillers, and Frank Wilderson. This is an incomplete list at best.

20. Lauren Berlant, *Cruel Optimism* (Durham, NC: Duke University Press, 2011).

21. Some readers may appreciate knowing the contents of the syllabus (listed in the order in which the class discussed the texts): Teresa Brennan, *The Transmission of Affect* (New York: Columbia University

Press, 2004); Kathleen Stewart, *Ordinary Affects* (Durham, NC: Duke University Press, 2007); Sianne Ngai, *Ugly Feelings* (Cambridge, MA: Harvard University Press, 2007); Anne Anlin Cheng, *The Melancholy of Race: Psychoanalysis, Assimilation, and Hidden Grief* (Oxford: Oxford University Press, 2001); Heather Love, *Feeling Backward: Loss and the Politics of Queer History* (Cambridge, MA: Harvard University Press, 2009); Sara Ahmed, *The Promise of Happiness* (Durham, NC: Duke University Press, 2010); Lauren Berlant, *Cruel Optimism* (Durham, NC: Duke University Press, 2011); Jack Halberstam, *The Queer Art of Failure* (Durham, NC: Duke University Press, 2011); Ann Cvetkovich, *Depression: A Public Feeling* (Durham, NC: Duke University Press, 2012); Ta-Nehisi Coates, *Between the World and Me* (New York: Spiegel & Grau, 2015); and Jessica Valenti, *Sex Object: A Memoir* (New York: Dey Street Books, 2017).

22. *The Seminar of Jacques Lacan, Book VII: The Ethics of Psychoanalysis*, trans. Dennis Porter (New York: Norton, 1992), 299–300.

23. Judith Butler has argued along related lines in much of her work on ethics. Allow me to simply name one text: *Giving an Account of Oneself* (New York: Fordham University Press, 2005).

24. See Mari Ruti, *The Summons of Love* (New York: Columbia University Press, 2011) and *The Call of Character: Living a Life Worth Living* (New York: Columbia University Press, 2013).

25. Some of the earliest Anglo-American theory to draw on French theory was feminist film theory. Key thinkers in the field include Joan Copjec, Teresa de Lauretis, Mary Ann Doane, Ann Kaplan, Laura Mulvey, and Kaja Silverman. To these names, I want add other feminist theorists, such as Judith Butler, Jane Gallop, Alice Jardine, and Naomi Schor. Again, this is a partial list.

26. Mari Ruti, *The Case for Falling in Love: Why We Can't Master the Madness of Love—and Why That's the Best Part* (Naperville, IL: Sourcebooks Casablanca, 2011).

27. This book draws most heavily on my most recent academic books: *The Age of Scientific Sexism: How Evolutionary Psychology Promotes Gender Profiling and Fans the Battle of the Sexes* (New York: Bloomsbury Press, 2015); *Feminist Film Theory and "Pretty Woman"* (New York: Bloomsbury Press, 2016); and *The Ethics of Opting Out: Queer Theory's Defiant*

Subjects (New York: Columbia University Press, 2017). Whenever pertinent, a note guides the reader to the relevant text(s).

28. See, in particular, *The Summons of Love.*

29. On this, see Mari Ruti, *The Singularity of Being: Lacan and the Immortal Within* (New York: Fordham University Press, 2012) and *Between Levinas and Lacan: Self, Other, Ethics* (New York: Bloomsbury Press, 2015). However, because these are my most strictly academic books, you should not waste your time unless you have a scholarly interest in the topic.

30. On this topic, see *Between Levinas and Lacan.*

I. THE CREED OF PRAGMATISM

1. Michel Foucault, *The Birth of Biopolitics: Lectures at the Collège de France, 1978–1979*, trans. Graham Burchell (New York: Palgrave Macmillan, 2008), 63.

2. Todd McGowan, *Capitalism and Desire: The Psychic Cost of Free Market*s (New York: Columbia University Press, 2016).

3. This section on positive thinking rearticulates arguments that can be found in Mari Ruti, *The Ethics of Opting Out: Queer Theory's Defiant Subjects* (New York: Columbia University Press, 2017).

4. Barbara Ehrenreich, *Bright-Sided: How Positive Thinking Is Undermining America* (New York: Picar, 2009), 8.

5. Sara Ahmed, *The Promise of Happiness* (Durham, NC: Duke University Press, 2010), 91.

6. Friedrich Nietzsche, *The Gay Science*, trans. Walter Kaufmann (New York: Vintage, 1974), 223.

7. Eve Sedgwick, *A Dialogue on Love* (Boston: Beacon Press, 2000), 142.

8. Margaret Crastnopol, *Micro-trauma: A Psychoanalytic Understanding of Cumulative Psychic Injury* (New York: Routledge, 2015), 22–23.

9. Ibid., 192.

10. This is perhaps even more strongly the argument of Ann Cvetkovich in *Depression: A Public Feeling* (Durham, NC: Duke University Press, 2012).

11. Lauren Berlant, *Cruel Optimism* (Durham, NC: Duke University Press, 2011),

12. Ibid., 114.

13. Ibid., 116–117.

14. Brock Hessel, "Queers, Plain Crackpots, and Fallen Women" (unpublished term paper, University of Toronto, 2016).

2. THE RATIONALIZATION OF INTIMACY

1. I discuss some of the arguments of this chapter in a more academic fashion in *The Age of Scientific Sexism: How Evolutionary Psychology Promotes Gender Profiling and Fans the Battle of the Sexes* (New York: Bloomsbury Press, 2015) and *The Ethics of Opting Out: Queer Theory's Defiant Subjects* (New York: Columbia University Press, 2017).

2. See Michel Foucault, *The Birth of Biopolitics: Lectures at the Collège de France, 1978–1979*, trans. Graham Burchell (New York: Palgrave Macmillan, 2008), 245.

3. See chapter 8 of McGowan's *Capitalism and Desire: The Psychic Cost of Free Markets* (New York: Columbia University Press, 2018).

4. This is particularly true of much of queer theory. A classic in the field is Michael Warner's *The Trouble with Normal: Sex, Politics, and the Ethics of Queer Life* (New York: Free Press, 1999). For a more recent discussion, see Tim Dean's *Unlimited Intimacy: Reflections on the Subculture of Barebacking* (Chicago: University of Chicago Press, 2009).

5. McGowan, *Capitalism and Desire*, 171.

6. See Alain Badiou, *Ethics: An Essay on the Understanding of Evil*, trans. Peter Hallward (London: Verso, 2001) and Mari Ruti, *The Summons of Love* (New York: Columbia University Press, 2011). Badiou also has a more recent book on the topic: *In Praise of Love*, trans. Peter Bush (New York: New Press, 2012).

7. This idea can be traced at least back to Nietzsche. From the twentieth century, I want to name two landmark texts: Louis Althusser, "Ideology and Ideological State Apparatuses," *Lenin and Philosophy*, trans. Ben Brewster (New York: Monthly Review Press, 1971) and Roland Barthes, *Mythologies*, trans. Annette Lavers (New York: Hill and Wang, 1972).

8. Hilary Neroni, *Feminist Film Theory and "Cléo from 5 to 9"* (New York: Bloomsbury Press, 2016).

9. This line is from "Blank Space," which can be found on Taylor Swift's 2014 album *1989*.

10. Foucault makes this argument in *The History of Sexuality*, vol. 1, trans. Robert Hurley (New York: Vintage, 1980). See also Judith Butler's hugely influential *Gender Trouble: Feminism and the Subversion of Identity* (New York: Routledge, 1990).

11. Let me name three texts (but there are many more): Butler's contributions to Judith Butler, Ernesto Laclau, and Slavoj Žižek, *Contingency, Hegemony, Universality* (London: Verso, 2000); Heather Love, *Feeling Backward: Loss and the Politics of Queer History* (Cambridge, MA: Harvard University Press, 2007); Jack Halberstam, *The Queer Art of Failure* (Durham, NC: Duke University Press, 2011).

12. Kath Weston, *Families We Choose: Lesbians, Gays, Kinship* (New York: Columbia University Press, 1997).

13. See Laura Kipnis, *Against Love: A Polemic* (New York: Vintage, 2003), 18.

14. Michael Cobb, *Single: Arguments for the Uncoupled* (New York: New York University Press, 2012), 4–5.

15. See Kate Bolick, *Spinster: Making a Life of One's Own* (New York: Crown Publishers, 2015).

16. I tell this anecdote in a chapter I co-authored with Adrian Cocking: "When Love Is Not All We Want: Queers, Singles, and the Therapeutic Cult of Relationality," in *Critical Psychotherapy, Psychoanalysis, and Counselling: Implications for Practice*, ed. Del Loewenthal (London: Routledge, 2015).

3. THE OBSESSIONS OF GENDER

1. Many feminists have called attention to this issue. See, for instance, Jasbir Puar, *Terrorist Assemblages: Homonationalism in Queer Times* (Durham, NC: Duke University Press, 2007) and Lila Abu-Lughod, *Do Muslim Women Need Saving?* (Cambridge, MA: Harvard University Press, 2013).

2. Jack Halberstam analyzes the problem in *Female Masculinity* (Durham, NC: Duke University Press, 1998).

3. I reproduce this list from the opening pages of *The Age of Scientific Sexism: How Evolutionary Psychology Promotes Gender Profiling and Fans*

the Battle of the Sexes (New York: Bloomsbury Press, 2015). Generally speaking, *The Age of Scientific Sexism* contains a fuller treatment of some of the ideas discussed in this chapter.

4. Susan Dominus, "Is an Open Marriage a Happier Marriage? What the Experiences of Nonmonogamous Couples Can Tell Us about Jealousy, Love, Desire and Trust," *New York Times Magazine*, May 11, 2017.

5. Ta-Nehisi Coates, *Between the World and Me* (New York: Spiegel & Grau, 2015). See also the work of Cornell West.

6. John Gray, *Men Are from Mars, Women Are from Venus: The Classic Guide to Understanding the Opposite Sex* (New York: HarperCollins, 1992).

7. Toni Morrison highlights this predicament in *The Bluest Eye* (New York: Knopf, 1993).

8. Hanna Rosin, *The End of Men: And the Rise of Women* (New York: Riverhead Books, 2013).

4. THE REINVENTION OF HETEROPATRIARCHY

1. The first half of this chapter recontextualizes arguments from my undergraduate film theory primer *Feminist Film Theory and "Pretty Woman"* (New York: Bloomsbury Press, 2016).

2. See Michelle Lazar, "The Right to Be Beautiful: Postfeminist Identity and Consumer Beauty Advertising," in *New Femininities: Postfeminism, Neoliberalism, and Subjectivity*, ed. Rosalind Gill and Christina Scharff (London: Palgrave Macmillan, 2013). Gill and Scharff's collection also contains other relevant essays.

3. Laura Mulvey, "Visual Pleasure and Narrative Cinema," in *Feminist Film Theory: A Reader*, ed. Sue Thornham (New York: New York University Press, 1999). Mulvey's essay was originally published in *Screen* 16, no. 3 (1975): 6–18.

4. For an excellent analysis of this phenomenon, see Susan Douglas, *The Rise of Enlightened Sexism: How Pop Culture Took Us from Girl Power to Girls Gone Wild* (New York: St. Martin's Griffin, 2010).

5. Joan Riviere, "Womanliness as a Masquerade," in *Psychoanalysis and Female Sexuality*, ed. Hendrik Ruitenbeek (New Haven, CT: College and University Press, 1966). Riviere's essay was originally published in *International Journal of Psychoanalysis* 10 (1929): 3–13.

6. See Margeaux Feldman's blog: https://floralmanifesto.com.

7. For an insightful account of this theme, see Ann Kaplan, "Is the Gaze Male?," in *Feminism and Film*, ed. Ann Kaplan (Oxford: Oxford University Press, 2000).

8. Elaine Scarry makes this argument in *On Beauty and Being Just* (Princeton: Princeton University Press, 2001). For a related Lacanian account, see Joan Copjec, *Read My Desire: Lacan Against the Historicists* (New York: Verso, 2015).

9. Simone de Beauvoir, *The Second Sex*, trans. Constance Borde and Sheila Malovany-Chevallier (New York: Alfred A. Knopf, 2010). This text was originally published in 1949.

10. Douglas, *The Rise of Enlightened Sexism*, 10.

11. Ibid.

12. Ibid., 13.

13. Ariel Levy, *Female Chauvinist Pigs: Women and the Rise of Raunch Culture* (New York: Free Press, 2006), 92.

14. I'm grateful to Kathryn Klingle for this articulation.

15. I thank my student Indiana Seresin for helping me think through this issue.

16. See Catherine MacKinnon, *Only Words* (Cambridge, MA: Harvard University Press, 1993).

17. "Pro-sex" feminism coincided with the rise of queer theory and claims some prominent queer theorists—such as Gayle Rubin, Janet Halley, and (to some extent) Judith Butler—as its proponents.

18. Paul Preciado, *Testo Junkie: Sex, Drugs, and Biopolitics in the Pharmacopornographic Era*, trans. Bruce Benderson (New York: The Feminist Press, 2013), 49.

19. Ibid., 274; 289.

5. THE SPECIFICITY OF DESIRE

1. See, for instance, Hannah Arendt, *The Human Condition* (Chicago: University of Chicago Press, 1958) and Jean-Paul Sartre, *Existentialism Is a Humanism*, trans. Carol Macomber (New Haven, CT: Yale University Press, 2007).

2. This struggle began with my dissertation, which became my first book: *Reinventing the Soul: Posthumanist Theory and Psychic Life* (New York: Other Press, 2006).

3. Early critics include Homi Bhabha, Hélène Cixous, Jacques Derrida, Luce Irigaray, and Gayatri Spivak, among many others.

4. I'm referring to scholars within animal studies and object-oriented ontology.

5. See Michel Foucault, *The Care of the Self: Volume Three of the History of Sexuality*, Robert Hurley (New York: Pantheon, 1986).

6. See, for instance, "The Subversion of the Subject and the Dialectic of Desire in the Freudian Unconscious," *Écrits: The First Complete Edition in English*, trans. Bruce Fink (New York: Norton, 2007).

7. See Sigmund Freud, *Civilization and Its Discontents*, trans. James Strachey (New York: Norton, 1989).

8. Sigmund Freud, "Mourning and Melancholia," *The Standard Edition of the Complete Psychological Works of Sigmund Freud, Volume XIV*, trans. James Strachey (London: Hogarth Press, 1957): 239–260. This essay was originally published in 1917.

9. Freud, "Mourning and Melancholia," 246.

10. Plato, *The Symposium* (New York: Penguin, 2003).

11. See the final chapter of *The Seminar of Jacques Lacan, Book XI: The Four Fundamental Concepts of Psychoanalysis*, trans. Alan Sheridan (New York: Norton, 1981).

12. I talk about this theme in *The Summons of Love* (New York: Columbia University Press, 2011).

13. David Henry Hwang, *M. Butterfly* (New York: Plume, 1988).

14. For a fuller analysis of this process, see Mari Ruti, *Feminist Film Theory and "Pretty Woman"* (New York: Bloomsbury Press, 2016).

15. Todd McGowan, *Capitalism and Desire: The Psychic Cost of Free Markets* (New York: Columbia University Press, 2016), 180.

16. I've appropriated—with modifications—Barthes's argument from *A Lover's Discourse: Fragments*, trans. Richard Howard (New York: Hill &Wang, 1977).

17. See, for instance, Judith Butler, *The Psychic Life of Power: Theories in Subjection* (Stanford: Stanford University Press, 1997).

18. See Mari Ruti, *The Singularity of Being: Lacan and the Immortal Within* (New York: Fordham University Press, 2012).

19. I examine this theme both in *The Singularity of Being* and in *The Ethics of Opting Out: Defiance and Affect in Queer Theory* (New York: Columbia University Press, 2016).

20. My student Julia Cooper makes this argument in her dissertation *Melancholy Utopia: Loss and Fantasy in Contemporary American Literature and Film* (unpublished dissertation, University of Toronto, 2016).

6. THE AGE OF ANXIETY

1. See Gary Greenberg, *Manufacturing Depression: The Secret History of a Modern Disease* (New York: Simon & Schuster, 2010).
2. I make this argument in *The Call of Character: Living a Life Worth Living* (New York: Columbia University Press, 2013).
3. Charles E. Rosenberg, *Our Present Complaint: American Medicine, Then and Now* (Baltimore: Johns Hopkins University Press, 2007), 67.
4. Gilles Deleuze and Felix Guattari, *Anti-Oedipus: Capitalism and Schizophrenia*, trans. Robert Hurley (New York: Penguin, 2009).
5. An exception to this trend is my analysis of the so-called Lacanian act in *Between Levinas and Lacan: Self, Other, Ethics* (New York: Bloomsbury Press, 2015) and *The Ethics of Opting Out: Queer Theory's Defiant Subjects* (New York: Columbia University Press, 2017).
6. Hannah Arendt, *The Life of the Mind* (New York: Harcourt, 1978). The ideal of self-pulverization can be found in the work of some queer theorists, such as Leo Bersani, Lee Edelman, and Lynne Huffer. Slavoj Žižek also sometimes leans in that direction.
7. See *The Seminar of Jacques Lacan, Book III: The Psychoses*, trans. Russell Grigg (New York: Norton, 1993).
8. Those familiar with Lacanian theory will know that Lacan often capitalizes this word, in which case it's synonymous with the collective social order into which we are inserted at birth (what he also calls *the symbolic order*). The distinction between the collective Other and the interpersonal other can be blurry and resides beyond the scope of this book.
9. The discussion of the enigmatic signifier can be found in *The Seminar of Jacques Lacan, Book XI: The Four Fundamental Concepts of Psychoanalysis*, trans. Alan Sheridan (New York: Norton, 1981). The analysis of castration and the reference to the praying mantis can be found in *The Seminar of Jacques Lacan: Book X: Anxiety*, trans. A. R. Price (New York: Polity Press, 2014). The latter seminar is the inspiration for this chapter and all subsequent references to Lacan are from it.

10. See Lacan, *The Seminar of Jacques Lacan: Book X: Anxiety*, 167–169; 263–264.

11. Ibid., 264.

12. Ibid., 169.

13. Ibid., 269.

14. Ibid., 264.

15. Ibid., 168.

16. I challenge anyone to read Lacan's text on anxiety and (still) accuse him of defending heteropatriarchy.

17. Lacan, *The Seminar of Jacques Lacan: Book X: Anxiety*, 53.

18. Ibid., 22.

19. Ibid., 53–54.

20. Ibid., 120. Lacan is here elaborating on his concept of "the mirror stage."

21. Ibid., 80.

22. See Žižek's contribution to Slavoj Žižek, Eric L. Santner, and Kenneth Reinhard, *The Neighbor: Three Inquiries in Political Theology* (Chicago: University of Chicago Press, 2005). Alenka Zupančič also offers an incisive commentary on the topic in *The Shortest Shadow: Nietzsche's Philosophy of the Two* (Cambridge, MA: MIT Press, 2003).

23. Even though Lacan discussed the theme of enigmatic signifiers, it's Jean Laplanche who gave it its fullest formulation. See, for example, Laplanche's *Essays on Otherness*, ed. John Fletcher (New York: Routledge, 1999).

24. My favorite text by Adorno is *Minima Moralia: Reflections from Damaged Life*, trans. E. F. N. Jephcott (New York: Verso, 2006).

25. The best introduction to Levinas's work is his collection of essays *Entre Nous: Thinking-of-the-Other*, trans. Michael B. Smith and Barbara Harshav (New York: Columbia University Press, 1998).

26. Simone de Beauvoir, *The Ethics of Ambiguity* (New York: Citadel Press, 1948).

27. See Jacques Derrida, *The Gift of Death*, trans. David Wills (Chicago: University of Chicago Press, 1995) and *On Cosmopolitanism and Forgiveness*, trans. Mark Dooley and Michael Hughes (New York: Routledge, 2001).

28. Judith Butler, *Giving an Account of Oneself* (New York: Fordham University Press, 2005).

29. Again, I discuss this concept at length in *Between Levinas and Lacan* and *The Ethics of Opting Out*.
30. Lacan, *The Seminar of Jacques Lacan: Book X: Anxiety*, 130.

CONCLUSION

1. Sheila Heti, *How Should a Person Be?* (New York: Picador, 2012).
2. Adam Phillips, *Missing Out: In Praise of the Unlived Life* (New York: Picador, 2013).
3. Afropessimists such as Jared Sexton and Frank Wilderson might disagree with me on this.
4. Slavoj Žižek often argues along these lines. However, perhaps the strongest articulation of this stance can be found in Lee Edelman, *No Future: Queer Theory and the Death Drive* (Durham, NC: Duke University Press, 2004).
5. Julia Kristeva advocates this perspective in some of her later work, especially *Intimate Revolt: The Powers and Limits of Psychoanalysis*, trans. Jeanine Herman (New York: Columbia University Press, 2002).
6. Maggie Nelson, *The Argonauts* (New York: Gray Wolf Press, 2015), 27.
7. Todd McGowan, *Desire and Capitalism: The Psychic Cost of Free Markets* (New York: Columbia University Press, 2016).
8. Friedrich Nietzsche, *Between Good and Evil*, trans. Walter Kaufmann (New York: Vintage, 1989), 58.
9. Friedrich Nietzsche, *Unfashionable Observations*, trans. Richard T. Gray (Stanford, CA: Stanford University Press, 1995), 89.
10. Friedrich Nietzsche, *The Genealogy of Morals*, trans. Walter Kaufmann (New York: Vintage, 1989), 58.
11. Ibid., 38.
12. Alenka Zupančič, *The Shortest Shadow: Nietzsche's Philosophy of the Two* (Cambridge, MA: MIT Press, 2003), 57.
13. Friedrich Nietzsche, *The Gay Science*, trans. Walter Kaufmann (New York: Vintage, 1974), 58.
14. As I mentioned in note 2 of chapter 5, this became my first book: *Reinventing the Soul: Posthumanist Theory and Psychic Life* (New York: Other Press, 2006).
15. Svetlana Boym, *Death in Quotation Marks: Cultural Myths of the Modern Poet* (Cambridge, MA: Harvard University Press, 1991).

16. Some of Barbara Johnson's most influential essays have been collected in *The Barbara Johnson Reader: The Surprise of Otherness* (Durham, NC: Duke University Press, 2014). She was also the author of many influential books on literary criticism and theory, as well as the translator of Jacque Derrida's *Dissemination* (Chicago: University of Chicago Press, 1983).

17. This short essay can be found here: http://www.freuds-requiem.com /transience.html.

18. See, for instance, David Eng, *The Feeling of Kinship: Queer Liberalism and the Racialization of Intimacy* (Durham, NC: Duke University Press, 2010).

19. See, for instance, Wendy Brown's critique of left melancholia in *Edgework: Critical Essays on Knowledge and Politics* (Princeton, NJ: Princeton University Press, 2005).

20. See, for instance, Julia Kristeva, *Black Sun: Depression and Melancholia*, trans. Leon Roudiez (New York: Columbia University Press, 1989).

21. Herbert Marcuse, *Eros and Civilization: A Philosophical Inquiry into Freud* (Boston: Beacon Press, 1974).

INDEX

and fear of being engulfed,
184–189; God and, 188–189;
Lacanian subject, 137; and men's
anxieties about being
inadequate, 179–181; and
ontological lack-in-being,
xxi–xxii, xl, 3–5, 148–151, 154–155
(*see also* lack-in-being); and
penis envy, xiii, xxxix, 231n4;
and phallic authority, xx–xxi,
177–181; and "quilting points,"
174; and self-determination,
157–158
lack, context-specific, xxxv, xl, 37,
146, 170, 232n9. *See also* familial
hardship; homophobia; poverty;
racism; sexism
lack-in-being, xxi–xxii; and
anxiety, 170–171; and desire,
xxii, 3–6; distinction between
ontological and context-specific
modalities of lack, xl; and
falling in love, 155; as
inescapable part of the human
condition, xl, 3–5; Lacan's
theory described, 148–151; and
melancholia, 144; and the quest
for satisfaction, 3–6
Levinas, Emmanuel, 195
Levy, Ariel, 116
LGBTQ+ community: and bad
feelings, xiii, 187, 188; and
bigotry in the U.S., 68–71;
and changing norms, 50;
homophobia, xvii, 68–69, 188,
232n9; and marginalization of
singles, 57–58; transgender

bathroom controversy, xviii,
67–70
love: Badiou on, 153; Barthes on,
154; and cruel optimism, 59, 66;
and disillusionment, xl; and
emotional ambivalence, 86–87;
and evolutionary psychology,
140, 142; falling in love, 152–155;
and gender stereotyping,
97–100; labor-intensive
intimacy, 58–61, 66, 79, 96; and
Lacan's theory of lack and
desire, 152, 154–155; life-altering
potential of, 40, 153; McGowan
on, 153; and melancholia,
143–147, 155, 165–166; and
rationalization of intimacy,
33–61; and specificity of desire,
xlviii, 139–143, 155, 164–165;
tyrannies of, 62–66. *See also*
desire; marriage; relationships,
intimate
Love in the Dark (Enns), xxxi

MacKinnon, Catherine, 120–121
makeup, 43–44, 101–102, 105, 107
Marcuse, Herbert, 221
marriage: attachment to harmful
relationships, 58–61, 65; and
biopolitical conditioning, 65; and
consumer culture, 6; and
cruel optimism, 35, 59; and
devaluation of other avenues
of fulfillment, 63–64; and
devaluation of singles, 54,
57–58, 60–61; and fantasy of
complementarity of the sexes,